MW01174298

Lisa

Nov. /97

HARRAP'S

Spanish

BUSINESS MANAGEMENT TERMS

Julian Amey
Executive Director BBC English

James Coveney
*Emeritus Professor of Modern Languages
University of Bath*

HARRAP

First published in Great Britain 1994
by Chambers Harrap Publishers Ltd
43–45 Annandale Street, Edinburgh EH7 4AZ

© Chambers Harrap Publishers Ltd 1994

ISBN 0 245 60359 X (UK)
ISBN 0 671 89990 2 (USA)

Typeset by Kevin O'Connor Typesetting
Printed in Great Britain by Clays Ltd, St Ives plc

Introduction

The rapid growth of the management sciences has resulted in the coining of many terms to describe new techniques and concepts, terms which are not easily found in current English-Spanish and Spanish-English dictionaries. A comprehensive glossary of business management terms is therefore urgently needed both by business practitioners and by students of business administration.

Our glossary is an attempt to fill this gap. The terms included have been drawn from the main areas of business management interest: business policy and corporate planning, finance, information technology, marketing, operational research, personnel management, and production.

We have tried to keep a proper balance by not overemphasizing any one area. Moreover, since the scope of the subject is very wide, we have selected only those terms in most frequent use.

We wish to thank Ms Asunción Rodríguez Sobrino, graduate in English Philology of the Universidad Complutense and graduate in professional translation of the Madrid Escuela de Traductores e Intérpretes, for her invaluable advice on the Spanish terms. Finally, we wish to express our gratitude to the McKinsey Foundation for Management Research for making possible the publication some years ago of a smaller work which has provided the basis for our glossary — its updated and considerably enlarged successor.

Julian Amey
James Coveney

Introducción

El rápido crecimiento de las ciencias de la gestión ha dado como
resultado la introducción de muchos nuevos términos para describir
conceptos y técnicas modernos que no figuran en los diccionarios
bilingües usados corrientemente.

Nuestro léxico tiene como objetivo llenar este vacío. Los términos que se
incluyen han sido extraídos de los sectores más importantes de la gestión:
política empresarial y planificación de la empresa, finanzas, informática,
márketing, investigación operativa, administración de personal, y
producción.

Para evitar descompensaciones hemos evitado destacar un sector especial
más que otro. Al seleccionar los términos decidimos dar prioridad a los
conceptos de uso más frecuente, en vez de dársela a los términos muy
especializados.

Agradecemos especialmente la revisión de la traducción al español que
fue llevada a cabo por Asunción Rodríguez Sobrino, Licenciada en
Filología Inglesa por la Universidad Complutense de Madrid y traductora
profesional titulada por la Escuela de Traductores e Intérpretes de
Madrid.

Finalmente, queremos manifestar nuestro agradecimiento a la McKinsey
Foundation for Management Research que hace varios años ayudó en la
publicación de un léxico menor, que ha sido la base de este léxico — su
sucesor mayor y actualizado.

Julian Amey
James Coveney

ENGLISH-SPANISH

A

abandonment: product ...	abandono *(m)* del producto
above par	sobre par/por encima del valor nominal
absenteeism	absentismo *(m)*
absorption	absorción *(f)*
absorption cost	absorción *(f)* de costes
acceptance: brand ...	aceptación *(f)* de una marca
acceptance: consumer ...	aceptación *(f)* por parte del consumidor
access (to)	acceder
access: multi-...	entrada *(f)* múltiple
access: random-...	entrada *(f)* aleatoria
accountability	responsabilidad *(f)*
accountant: chief ...	jefe *(m)* de contabilidad
accounting	contabilidad *(f)*
accounting department	departamento *(m)* de contabilidad
accounting model	modelo *(m)* de contabilidad
accounting period	período *(m)* de contabilidad
accounting ratio	"ratio" *(m)* contable
accounting: cost ...	contabilidad *(f)* de costes
accounting: creative ...	contabilidad *(f)* flexible
accounting: electronic ... system	sistema *(m)* electrónico de contabilidad
accounting: management ...	contabilidad *(f)* gerencial
accounting: profit centre ...	contabilidad *(f)* de centro de beneficio
accounting: responsibility ...	responsabilidad *(f)* contable
accounts department	departamento *(m)* de contabilidad
accounts: consolidated ...	estados *(mpl)* financieros consolidados
accounts: group ...	estados *(mpl)* financieros del grupo
acquisition	adquisición *(f)*
acquisition profile	perfil *(m)* de adquisición
acquisition: data ...	adquisición *(f)* de datos
acquisitions: mergers and ... (M & A)	fusiones y adquisiciones *(fpl)*
across-the-board increase	aumento *(m)* lineal de salarios
action plan	plan *(m)* de acción

action: industrial ...	acción (f) industrial
action: unofficial ...	acción (f) no sindicada
actionable	accionable
	procesable
activate (to)	activar
activity chart	esquema (m) de actividades
activity sampling	muestreo (m) de actividades
activity: support ...	actividades (fpl) de apoyo
actualization: self-...	autorealización (f)
adaptive control	control (m) adaptivo
add-on equipment	equipo (m) auxiliar
added: value ...	valor (m) añadido
added: value ... tax (VAT)	impuesto (m) sobre el valor agregado
administration-production ratio	índice (m) administración-producción
administration: financial ...	gestión (f) financiera
	administración (f) financiera
administrative control procedure	proceso (m) de control administrativo
administrative expenses	gastos (mpl) de administración
administrative overheads	gastos (mpl) generales de administración
administrative theory	teoría (f) de la administración
ADP (automatic data processing)	proceso (m) automático de datos (ADP)
advancement	adelantamiento (m)
	ascenso (m)
advancement: executive ...	ascenso (m) ejecutivo
	ascenso (m) de ejecutivos
advantage: competitive ...	ventaja (f) competitiva
advertising agent	agente (m) de publicidad
advertising appropriation	asignación (f) para publicidad
advertising budget	presupuesto (m) de publicidad
advertising campaign	campaña (f) de publicidad
advertising drive	empuje (m) publicitario
advertising effectiveness	eficacia (f) de publicidad
advertising manager	jefe (m) de publicidad
advertising media	medios (mpl) de publicidad
advertising message	tema (m) publicitario
advertising research	investigación (f) publicitaria
advertising theme	tema (m) publicitario
advertising: corporate ...	publicidad (f) empresarial

advertising: point-of-sale ... (POS)	publicidad *(f)* en local de venta
advertising: product ...	publicidad *(f)* de productos
advertising: subliminal ...	publicidad *(f)* subliminal
advisory services	asesores *(mpl)*
	consultores *(mpl)*
affiliate company	empresa *(f)* filial
after-sales service	servicio *(m)* postventa
agenda: hidden ...	orden *(m)* del día confidencial
agenda: to be on the ...	estar en el orden del día
agent: advertising ...	agente *(m)* de publicidad
agent: forwarding ...	agente *(m)* de despacho
agent: sole ...	agente *(m)* en exclusiva
agreement (written ...)	acuerdo *(m)* escrito
agreement: collective bargaining ...	convenio *(m)* colectivo negociado
agreement: gentleman's ...	acuerdo *(m)* entre caballeros
	pacto *(m)* entre caballeros
agreement: productivity ...	convenio *(m)* de productividad
algorithm	algoritmo *(m)*
alliance: strategic ...	alianza *(f)* estratégica
allocate (to)	asignar
	adjudicar
	atribuir
	dotar
allocation of costs	asignación *(f)* de costes
allocation of responsibilities	asignación *(f)* de responsabilidades
allocation: resource ...	asignación *(f)* de recursos
allotment: budget ...	asignación *(f)* presupuestaria
	dotación *(f)* presupuestaria
allowance: capital ...	desgravación *(f)* sobre bienes de capital
allowance: depreciation ...	reserva *(f)* para amortización
amalgamate (to)	integrar
	concentrar
	fusionar
amalgamation	unión *(f)*
	fusión*(f)*
analog computer	ordenador *(m)* analógico
analog(ue) representation	representación *(f)* analógica
analysis: breakeven ...	análisis *(m)* del punto de equilibrio
analysis: competitor ...	estudio *(m)* de la competencia
analysis: contribution ...	análisis *(m)* de aportaciones

analysis: cost ...	análisis *(m)* de costes
analysis: cost-benefit ... (CBA)	análisis *(m)* coste-beneficio
analysis: cost-volume-profit ...	análisis *(m)* de coste volumen y beneficio
analysis: critical path ... (CPA)	análisis *(m)* del camino crítico
analysis: decision ...	análisis *(m)* de decisiones
analysis: depth ...	análisis *(m)* a fondo
analysis: environmental ...	análisis *(m)* del medioambiente
analysis: financial ...	análisis *(m)* financiero
analysis: functional ...	análisis *(m)* funcional
analysis: input-output ...	análisis *(m)* de entradas y salidas
analysis: investment ...	análisis *(m)* de inversiones
analysis: job ...	análisis *(m)* de puestos de trabajo
analysis: marginal ...	análisis *(m)* marginal
analysis: media ...	análisis *(m)* de los medios de comunicación
analysis: morphological ...	análisis *(m)* morfológico
analysis: multiple regression ... (MRA)	análisis *(m)* de regresión múltiple
analysis: needs ...	análisis *(m)* de necesidades
analysis: network ...	análisis *(m)* de la red
analysis operations	análisis *(m)* de operación
analysis part-... training	análisis *(m)* de formación por étapas
analysis: problem ...	análisis *(m)* del problema
analysis: product ...	análisis *(m)* del producto
analysis: profit-factor ...	análisis *(m)* de factores de beneficio
analysis: profitability ...	análisis *(m)* de la rentabilidad
analysis: project ...	estudio *(m)* de proyectos
analysis: quantitative ...	análisis *(m)* cuantitativo
analysis: regression ...	análisis *(m)* de regresión
analysis: risk ...	análisis *(m)* de riesgos
analysis: sales ...	análisis *(m)* de ventas
analysis: sensitivity ...	análisis *(m)* de sensibilidad
analysis: sequential ...	análisis *(m)* secuencial
analysis: skills ...	análisis *(m)* de pericias
analysis: social ...	análisis *(m)* social
analysis: systems ...	análisis *(m)* de sistemas
analysis: training needs ...	análisis *(m)* de las necesidades de formación
analysis: transactional ... (TA)	análisis *(m)* transaccional
analysis: value ... (VA)	análisis *(m)* del valor
analysis: variance ...	análisis *(m)* de las varianzas
analytic accounting	contabilidad *(f)* analítica

analytical training	formación (f) analítica
ancillary operations	servicios (mpl) auxiliares
answerback code	indicativo (m)
answerphone	contestador telefónico
anticipatory response	respuesta (f) anticipada
appeal: sales ...	atracción (f) comercial
	garra (f) comercial
applications: software ...	aplicaciones (fpl) de software
apportion (to)	imputar
	repartir
apportionment	distribución (f)
apportionment: cost ...	distribución (f) de costes
appraisal	evaluación (f)
appraisal: capital expenditure ...	evaluación (f) de gastos de capital
appraisal: financial ...	evaluación (f) financiera
appraisal: investment ...	evaluación (f) de inversiones
appraisal: market ...	evaluación (f) del mercado
appraisal: performance	evaluación (f) del rendimiento
appraisal: resource	evaluación (f) de recursos
appraisal: self-...	autoevaluación (f)
appraisal: staff ...	evaluación (f) de personal
appraise (to)	evaluar
	valorar
	tasar
	informar
appreciate (to)	revalorizar
appreciation: capital ...	revalorización (f) del capital
	plusvalía (f) del capital
approach: functional ...	enfoque (m) funcional
approach: systems ...	enfoque (m) sistemático
approach: top management ...	enfoque (m) según la alta dirección
appropriate (to)	asignar
	dotar
appropriation: advertising ...	asignación (f) para publicidad
appropriation: budget ...	asignación (f) de presupuestos
appropriation: marketing ...	asignación (f) para márketing
aptitude test	prueba (f) de aptitud
arbitrage	arbitraje (m)
arbitrageur	arbitrador (m)
arbitration	arbitraje (m)
area manager	director (m) de área
area network: wide ... (WAN)	red (f) de área extendida

area: growth ...	sector *(m)* de crecimiento
area: problem ...	área *(f)* de problemas
area: product ...	sector *(m)* de productos
area: sales ...	zona *(f)* de ventas
area: trading ...	zona *(f)* comercial
arm's length	(al) alcance de la mano
artificial intelligence	inteligencia *(f)* artificial
assembly line	línea *(f)* de montaje
assess (to)	tasar
	valorar
	calcular
assessment	evaluación *(f)*
	apreciación *(f)*
assessment centre	centro *(m)* de tasación
assessment: demand ...	evaluación *(f)* de la demanda
assessment: problem ...	evaluación *(f)* del problema
assessment: project ...	evaluación *(f)* de proyectos
assessment: quality ...	valoración *(f)* de la calidad
assessment: risk ...	apreciación *(f)* de riesgos
asset liability management	gestión *(f)* del circulante
asset management	gestión *(f)* del activo
asset portfolio	cartera *(f)* del activo
asset-stripping	liquidación *(f)* de activos
asset turnover	rotación *(f)* del activo
asset value	valor *(m)* del activo
	valor *(m)* contable
assets	activo *(m)*
assets: capital ...	activo *(m)* de capital
	activo *(m)* fijo
assets: current ...	activo *(m)* circulante
	activo *(m)* realizable
assets: earnings on ...	rendimiento *(m)* del activo
assets: fixed ...	activo *(m)* fijo
assets: hidden ...	activo *(m)* oculto
	diferencia *(f)* entre valor contable y de mercado
assets: intangible ...	activo *(m)* inmaterial
assets: liquid ...	activo *(m)* disponible
	activo *(m)* líquido
assets: net ...	activo *(m)* neto
assets: net current ...	activo *(m)* circulante neto
assets: quick ...	activo *(m)* disponible a corto plazo
	fondos *(mpl)*

assets: return on ...	rendimiento *(m)* del activo
assets: revaluation of ...	revalorización *(f)* del activo
assets: tangible ...	activo *(m)* material
assets: wasting ...	activo *(m)* amortizable
assignment of expenditure	asignación *(f)* de gastos
assignment: job ...	asignación *(f)* de tareas
assistant director	director *(m)* adjunto
assistant manager	director *(m)* adjunto
assistant to manager	adjunto *(m)* al director
assistant: line ...	auxiliar *(m)* de línea
assistant: staff ...	auxiliar *(m)* consultivo
associate company	empresa *(f)* afiliada
association: trade ...	asociación *(f)* de comerciantes
assurance: quality ...	garantía *(f)*
	aseguramiento *(f)* de la calidad
at par	a la par
attitude survey	encuesta *(f)* de opiniones
	encuesta *(f)* de actitudes
attitude: user ...	actitud *(f)* de los usuarios
audiovisual aids	ayudas *(fpl)* audiovisuales
audit	auditoría *(f)*
audit (to)	revisar cuentas *(fpl)*
	verificar cuentas *(fpl)*
audit: efficiency ...	control *(m)* de rendimiento
audit: internal ...	auditoría *(f)* interna
audit: management ...	valoración *(f)* de gestión
audit: manpower ...	revisión *(f)* de la mano de obra
audit: operations ...	evaluación *(f)* de operaciones
audit: staff ...	control *(m)* de personal
auditing: balance sheet ...	verificación *(f)* del balance
auditor	auditor *(m)*
	censor *(m)* de cuentas
authority structure	estructura *(f)* de autoridad
authority: contraction of ...	limitación *(f)* de autoridad
authority: line ...	autoridad *(f)* de línea
authorized capital	capital *(m)* social autorizado
automate (to)	automatizar
automatic data processing (ADP)	proceso *(m)* automático de datos
automation	automatización *(f)*
automation: office ...	automatización *(f)* de la oficina
	ofimática *(f)*

average	promedio *(m)*
	término *(m)* medio
average cost	coste *(m)* medio
average revenue	ingresos *(mpl)* medios
average yield	rendimiento *(m)* medio
average: weighted ...	media *(f)* ponderada
awareness level	nivel *(m)* de percepción
awareness: brand ...	conocimiento *(m)* de la marca
awareness: cost ...	conciencia *(f)* del coste
awareness: market ...	percepción *(f)* del mercado

B

back burner: put on the ... ... (to)	poner en cuarentena (f)
back-up facility	instalación (f) de seguridad
backlog	pila (f) de trabajo atrasado
bad-debt losses	deudas (f) incobrables
bad debts	créditos (m) incobrables
	deudores (mpl) morosos
balance sheet	balance (m) de situación
balance sheet auditing	verificación (f) del balance
balanced portfolio	cartera (f) de compensación
ball game: different ...	esa es otra guerra (coloquial)
ballpark figure	cifra (f) orientativa
bank rate	tipo (m) bancario
bank: commercial ...	banco (m) comercial
bank: computer ...	banco (m) de datos del ordenador
bank: data ...	banco (m) de datos
bank: investment ...	banco (m) de inversiones
bank: merchant ...	banco (m) de negocios
bar chart	gráfico (m) de barras
bargaining: collective ...	negociación (f) colectiva
bargaining: collective ... agreement	convenio (m) colectivo negociado
bargaining: plant ...	negociación (f) a nivel de fábrica
bargaining: productivity ...	negociación (f) de productividad
barrier: non-tariff ... (NTB)	barrera (f) no arancelaria
barrier: tariff ...	barrera (f) arancelaria
barter trade	comercio (m) de trueque
base rate	tipo (m) base
	tasa (f) base
base year	año (m) base
base: data ...	base (f) de datos
batch control	control (m) del lote
batch processing	elaboración (f) por lotes
batch production	producción (f) por lotes
batch: economic ... quantity	tamaño (m) del lote económico
bear	especulación (f) (a la baja)
	bajista (m)
bear market	mercado (m) bursátil a la baja
	mercado (m) minoritario
behaviour: buying ...	conducta (f) en la compra

behaviour: consumer ...	conducta *(f)* del consumidor
behaviour: organizational	conducta *(f)* del hombre en una organización
behavioural science	ciencia *(f)* de la conducta
below par	bajo par
benchmark	nivel *(m)* de referencia
benefit: cost-... analysis (CBA)	análisis *(m)* coste-beneficio
benefits: fringe ...	ventajas *(fpl)* supletorias
	ingresos *(mpl)* accesorios
best-case scenario	en el mejor de los casos
bid: leveraged ...	licitación *(f)* por apalancamiento
bid: pre-emptive ...	licitación *(f)* prioritaria
	licitación *(f)* preferente
bid: takeover ... (TOB)	oferta *(f)* pública de compra
blackleg	esquirol *(m)*
blue-chip stock	valor *(m)* de primera clase
	acción *(f)* de primera clase
blueprint	anteproyecto *(m)*
blue-sky research	investigación *(f)* de base
board control	control *(m)* del consejo de administración
board meeting	reunión *(f)* del consejo de administración
board of directors	consejo *(m)* de administración
board: executive ...	consejo *(m)* de administración
boardroom	sala *(f)* de consejos
body language	lenguaje *(m)* corporal
bond: junk ...	bonos *(m)* basura
bonus	prima *(f)*
bonus scheme	sistema *(m)* de primas
bonus: group ...	prima *(f)* colectiva
bonus: premium ...	prima *(f)* por rendimiento
book value	valor *(m)* según balance
	valor *(m)* en libros
boom	boom *(m)*
	alza *(f)*
	auge *(m)*
booster training	reeducación *(f)* profesional
	readaptación *(f)* profesional
borrowing facility	línea *(f)* de crédito
bottleneck	cuello *(m)* de botella
bottom line	línea *(f)* final
bottom out (to)	tocar fondo

bottom-up	del fondo para arriba
brains trust	consultorio *(m)* de expertos
brainstorming	análisis *(m)* intensivo de grupo
branch office	sucursal *(f)*
	delegación *(f)*
brand	marca *(f)*
brand acceptance	aceptación *(f)* de marca
brand awareness	conocimiento *(m)* de la marca
brand image	imagen *(m)* de la marca
brand loyalty	lealtad *(f)* a la marca
brand manager	jefe *(m)* de marca
brand name	nombre *(m)* de marca
brand portfolio	cartera *(f)* comercial
	fondo *(m)* de comercio
brand positioning	posicionamiento *(m)* comercial
brand recognition	identificación *(f)* de la marca
brand strategy	estrategia *(f)* de la marca
breakdown of operations	descomposición *(f)* de las tareas
break-even (to)	alcanzar el punto de equilibrio
break-even analysis	análisis *(f)* de equilibrio
break-even point	punto *(m)* de equilibrio
	umbral de rentabilidad
break-even quantity	cantidad *(f)* necesaria para alcanzar el punto de equilibrio
breakthrough	logro *(m)* tecnológico
	avance *(m)* importante
break-up value	valor *(m)* en liquidación
	valor *(m)* de recuperación
brief (to)	resumir
	recopilar
briefing	informe *(m)*
	reunión *(f)* para dar órdenes
broker	comisionista *(m)*
	corredor *(m)*
broker: software ...	comisionista *(m)* de sistemas
brokerage	corretajes *(mpl)*
brokerage fees	honorarios *(mpl)* de corretaje
brown goods	electrodomésticos *(mpl)* (que no forman parte de la línea blanca)
budget	presupuesto *(m)*
budget (to)	presupuestar
budget allotment	dotación *(f)* presupuestaria
budget appropriation	asignación *(f)* del presupuesto

budget constraint	restricción *(f)* del presupuesto
budget forecast	previsión *(f)* presupuestaria
budget forecasting	previsión *(f)* presupuestaria
budget standard	estándares *(mpl)* de presupuesto
budget: advertising ...	presupuesto *(m)* de publicidad
budget: capital ...	presupuesto *(m)* de gastos de capital
budget: cash ...	presupuesto *(m)* de caja
budget: flexible ...	presupuesto *(m)* flexible
budget: investment ...	presupuesto *(m)* de inversiones
budget: marketing ...	presupuesto *(m)* de márketing
budget: sales ...	presupuesto *(m)* de ventas
budget: zero-base ...	presupuesto *(m)* de punto cero
budgetary control	control *(m)* presupuestario
budgetary variance	varianza *(f)* presupuestaria
budgeting	contabilidad *(f)* presupuestaria
budgeting control	control *(m)* presupuestario
budgeting: capital ...	control *(m)* presupuestario de gastos de capital
budgeting: cash ...	control *(m)* presupuestario de caja
budgeting: output ...	control *(m)* de producción
budgeting: performance ...	control *(m)* de rendimiento
budgeting: planning-programming ... system (PPBS)	sistema *(f)* de programación y planificación de presupuestos
budgeting: programme ...	sistema *(m)* de presupuestos programados
buffer stock	stock *(m)* regulador
bug	error *(m)*
building: team ...	formación *(m)* del equipo de trabajo
built-in	incorporado
	interno
built-in obsolescence	obsolencia *(f)* interna
bull	alcista *(m)*
bull market	mercado *(m)* alcista
bulletin board	tablón *(m)* de anuncios
bundling	agrupación *(f)*
bureau: computer services ...	agencia *(f)* de servicios de ordenador
bureau: employment ...	oficina *(f)* de empleo
business corporation	sociedad *(f)* anónima
business cycle	ciclo *(m)* económico
business economist	economista *(m)* empresarial
business forecasting	previsión *(f)* comercial
	pronóstico *(m)* comercial

business game	simulación *(f)* de gestión
business management	gestión *(f)* de negocios
	dirección *(f)* comercial
business outlook	perspectiva *(f)* empresarial
business policy	política *(f)* comercial
business portfolio	cartera *(f)* de negocios
business proposition	propuesta *(f)* de negocios
business relations	relaciones *(fpl)* comerciales
business strategy	estrategia *(f)* de negocios
	estrategia *(f)* comercial
business stream	flujo *(m)* de negocios
	flujo *(m)* empresarial
business system	sistema *(m)* empresarial
business unit: strategic ...	unidad *(f)* empresarial
	unidad *(f)* de actividad estratégica
buy in (to)	proveerse del exterior
buy out (to)	comprar (parte mayoritaria del activo)
buyer: chief-...	jefe *(m)* de compras
buyer: potential ...	comprador *(m)* potencial
buyers' market	mercado *(m)* de oferta
buying behaviour	conducta *(f)* en la compra
buying: impulse ...	compra *(f)* imprevista
buyout	compra *(f)*
buyout: employee ...	compra *(f)* por los empleados
buyout: leveraged ... (LBO)	compra *(f)* por apalancamiento
buyout: management ...	compra *(f)* por los directivos de la empresa
buyout: worker ...	compra *(f)* por los obreros
buzz-word	palabra *(f)* de moda
bypass (to)	rodear
	evitar rodeando
by-product	subproducto *(m)*
	derivado *(m)*
byte	byte *(m)*

C

CAD (computer-aided design)	CAD (diseño *(m)* asistido por ordenador)
CAL (computer-aided learning)	CAL (aprendizaje *(m)* asistido por ordenador)
CAM (computer-aided manufacturing)	CAM (fabricación *(f)* asistida por ordenador)
campaign: advertising ...	campaña *(f)* de publicidad
campaign: productivity ...	campaña *(f)* de productividad
canvass (to)	solicitar
	buscar órdenes
capability	capacidad *(f)*
capacity utilization	utilización *(f)* de la capacidad
capacity: excess ...	capacidad *(f)* excesiva
capacity: full ...	plena *(f)* capacidad
capacity: idle ...	capacidad *(f)* no utilizada
capacity: manufacturing ...	capacidad *(f)* de fabricación
capacity: plant ...	capacidad *(f)* de planta
capacity: spare ...	capacidad *(f)* sobrante
capex (capital expenditure)	evaluación *(f)* de gastos de capital
capital allowance	desgravación *(f)* sobre bienes de capital
capital appreciation	crecimiento *(m)* de capital
capital assets	capital *(m)* disponible
capital budget	presupuesto *(m)* de gastos de capital
capital budgeting	control *(m)* presupuestario de gastos de capital
capital commitment	compromiso *(m)* de inversión
capital employed	capital *(m)* invertido
capital employed: return on ... ... (ROCE)	rendimiento *(m)* del capital invertido
capital expenditure	gastos *(mpl)* en capital
capital expenditure appraisal	evaluación *(f)* de gastos de capital
capital formation	aporte *(m)* de capital
capital gain	ganancia *(f)* de capital
	plusvalía *(f)*
capital goods	bienes *(mpl)* de capital
	bienes *(mpl)* de equipo
capital-intensive	predominio *(m)* de capital
capital loss	pérdida *(f)* de capital
	minusvalía *(f)*

capital-output ratio	"ratio" *(m)* rendimiento-capital
capital project evaluation	evaluación *(f)* de proyectos de capital
capital raising	movilización *(f)* de fondos
capital rationing	racionamiento *(f)* de capital
capital structure	estructura *(f)* del capital
capital: authorized ...	capital *(m)* autorizado
capital: circulating ...	capital *(m)* circulante
	liquidez *(f)*
capital: issued ...	capital *(m)* emitido
capital: loan ...	créditos *(mpl)* bancarios
capital: return on ...	rendimiento *(m)* del capital
capital: risk ...	capital *(m)* de riesgo
capital: share ...	capital *(m)* en acciones
capital: venture ...	capital *(m)* arriesgado
capital: working ...	capital *(m)* circulante
	fondo *(m)* de maniobra
capitalist: venture ...	inversor *(m)* de riesgo
capitalization	capitalización *(f)*
capitalize (to)	capitalizar
care: customer ...	atención *(f)* al cliente
career planning	planificación *(f)* del desarrollo profesional
car phone	teléfono *(m)* de coche
cartel	cartel *(m)*
case study	estudio *(m)* de casos
cash	caja *(f)*
	dinero *(m)* contante
	efectivo *(m)*
cash budget	presupuesto *(m)* de caja
cash budgeting	control *(m)* presupuestario de caja
cash deal	acuerdo *(m)* al contado
cash flow	"cash flow" *(m)*
cash flow: negative	"cash flow" *(m)* negativo
cash forecasting	previsión *(f)* de caja
cash management	gestión *(f)* del activo disponible
cash-poor	falta *(f)* de caja
cash ratio	proporción *(f)* de valores disponibles
cash-rich	rico de caja
cash-strapped	falto de caja
cash: discounted ... flow (DCF)	"cash flow" *(m)* actualizado
cash: incremental ... flow	"cash flow" *(m)* marginal
cash: petty ...	caja *(f)* para gastos menores

CAT (computer-aided teaching)	enseñanza *(f)* asistida por ordenador
CBA (cost-benefit analysis)	análisis *(m)* coste-beneficio
CBT (computer-based training)	formación *(f)* asistida por ordenador
ceiling: wage ...	techo *(m)* salarial
cellphone	teléfono *(m)* portátil
central processing unit (CPU)	unidad *(f)* de proceso central (UPC)
centralization	centralización *(m)*
centralize (to)	centralizar
centre: assessment ...	centro *(m)* de tasación
centre: computer ...	centro *(m)* informático
centre: cost ...	centro *(m)* de coste
centre: profit ...	centro *(m)* de beneficio
centre: profit ... accounting	contabilidad *(f)* por centros de beneficios
centre: responsibility ...	centro *(m)* de responsabilidad
chain of command	cadena *(f)* de mando
chain of distribution	cadena *(f)* de distribución
chain of production	cadena *(f)* de producción
chain production	producción *(f)* en cadena
chain: value ...	cadena *(f)* de valor
chairman	presidente *(m)*
chairman and managing director	presidente *(m)* y director *(m)* gerente
chairman: vice-...	vicepresidente *(m)*
challenge: job ...	incentivo *(m)* del puesto
change management (management of change)	gestión *(f)* de cambio
change: organizational ...	transformación *(f)* de la organización
channel: distribution ...	canales *(mpl)* de distribución
channels of communication	canales *(mpl)* de comunicación
characteristics: job ...	características *(fpl)* del puesto (de trabajo)
chart: activity ...	esquema *(m)* de actividades
chart: bar ...	gráfico *(m)* de barras
chart: flow ...	diagrama *(m)* de circulación
chart: flow process ...	diagrama *(m)* del proceso
chart: management ...	esquema *(m)* de gestión
chart: milestone ...	esquema *(m)* de objetivos
chart: organization ...	organigrama *(m)*
chart: pie ...	gráfico *(m)* circular
chart: Z ...	gráfico *(m)* Z

chief accountant	jefe *(m)* de contabilidad
chief buyer	jefe *(m)* de compras
chief executive	director *(m)* general
Chinese wall	secreto *(m)* profesional
chip	chip *(m)*
chunk a project (to)	poner a prueba un proyecto
	muestrear a gran escala un producto
chunk down (to)	reducir tamaño
CIM (computer-integrated manufacturing)	producción *(f)* integrada por ordenador
circle: quality ...	círculo *(m)* de calidad
circulating capital	capital *(m)* circulante
classification: job ...	clasificación *(f)* de puestos de trabajo
clearing house	cámara *(f)* de compensación
clerical work measurement (CWM)	medición *(f)* del trabajo administrativo
clerical worker	oficinista *(m/f)*
climate: economic ...	clima *(m)* económico
closed loop	ciclo *(m)* cerrado
	lazo *(m)*
closed shop	fábrica *(f)* con obreros sindicados exclusivamente
closing-down costs	coste *(m)* de liquidación
co-determination	cogestión *(f)*
COINS (computerized information system)	sistema *(m)* (automatizado) de información
collaborative	colaborativo
collateral	colateral
collateral security	garantía *(f)* colateral
collective bargaining	negociación *(f)* colectiva
collective bargaining agreement	convenio *(m)* colectivo negociado
collusion	confabulación *(f)*
command: chain of ...	cadena *(f)* de mando
command: line of ...	línea *(f)* de mando
commercial bank	banco *(m)* comercial
commitment: capital ...	compromiso *(m)* de inversión
commitment: staff ...	cometido *(m)* del personal
committee: works ...	comité *(m)* de empresas
commodity	mercancía *(f)*
	artículo *(m)* de comercio
	bien *(m)* de primera necesidad
commodity market	mercado *(m)* de productos básicos
commodity: primary ...	productos *(mpl)* de primera necesidad

common currency	divisas *(fpl)*
common language	lenguaje *(m)* común
Common Market	Mercado *(m)* Común
communication: channels of ...	canales *(mpl)* de comunicación
communication: electronic ...	comunicación *(f)* electrónica
communications network	red *(f)* de comunicaciones
communications theory	teoría *(f)* de comunicación
company goal	objetivo *(m)* de la empresa
company logo	logotipo *(m)* de empresa
company model	modelo *(m)* de la empresa
company objective	objetivos *(mpl)* empresariales
company objectives: overall ...	objetivos *(mpl)* globales de la empresa
company philosophy	filosofía *(f)* de la empresa
company planning	planificación *(f)* empresarial
company policy	política *(f)* de la empresa
company profile	perfil *(m)* de la empresa
company reconstruction	reconstitución *(f)* de la empresa
company strategy	estrategia *(f)* de la empresa
company structure	estructura *(f)* de la empresa
company: affiliate ..	empresa *(f)* filial
company: associate ...	empresa *(f)* afiliada
company: holding ...	sociedad *(f)* "holding"
company: joint-venture ...	sociedad *(f)* en participación conjunta
company: overall ... philosophy	filosofía *(f)* global de la empresa
company: parent ...	empresa *(m)* matriz
company: publicly listed ...	empresa *(f)* cotizada en bolsa
company: quoted ...	empresa *(f)* cotizada en bolsa
company: subsidiary ...	filial *(f)*
	sucursal *(f)*
company: system-managed ...	empresa *(f)* dirigida de forma sistematizada
company: unlisted ...	empresa *(f)* no cotizada en bolsa
comparison: interfirm ...	comparación *(f)* interempresarial
compartmentalize (to)	compartimentar
compatible	compatible
compensation: executive	remuneración *(f)* de los ejecutivos
competence: executive ...	aptitud *(f)* del directivo
competence: job ...	aptitud *(f)* en el trabajo
competency	capacidad *(f)*
competition	competencia *(f)*
competition: fair ...	competencia *(f)* leal
competition: the ...	la competencia *(f)*
	los competidores *(mpl)*

competition: unfair ...	competencia *(f)* desleal
competitive	competitivo *(m)*
competitive advantage	ventaja *(f)* competitiva
competitive edge	ventaja *(f)* sobre la competencia
competitive position	situación *(f)* competitiva
competitive price	precio *(m)* competitivo
competitive stimulus	estímulo *(m)* competitivo
competitive strategy	estrategia *(f)* competitiva
competitive tactics	tácticas *(fpl)* competitivas
competitive tendering	licitación *(f)* pública
competitive thrust	empuje *(m)* competitivo
competitiveness	competitividad *(f)*
competitor analysis	análisis *(m)* de la competencia
complex: production ...	complejo *(m)* de producción
comptroller	verificador *(m)* de cuentas
computer	ordenador *(m)*
	computador *(m)*
computer-aided design (CAD)	CAD (diseño *(m)* asistido por ordenador)
computer-aided learning (CAL)	aprendizaje *(m)* asistido por ordenador (CAL)
computer-aided manufacturing (CAM)	fabricación *(f)* asistida por ordenador (CAM)
computer-aided teaching (CAT)	enseñanza *(f)* asistida por ordenador (CAT)
computer bank	banco *(m)* de datos del ordenador
computer-based training (CBT)	formación *(f)* asistida por ordenador (CBT)
computer centre	centro *(m)* informático
computer consultant	consultor *(m)* informático
computer expert	experto *(m)* informático
computer input	entrada *(f)* al ordenador
computer-integrated manufacturing (CIM)	fabricación *(f)* integrada por ordenador (CIM)
computer language	lenguaje *(m)* de ordenador
computer-literate	con conocimientos *(mpl)* de informática
computer memory	memoria *(f)* de ordenador
computer output	salida *(f)* del ordenador
	producto *(m)* del ordenador
computer program	programa *(f)* informático
computer programmer	programador *(m)* informático
computer programming	programación *(f)*

computer services	servicios *(mpl)* del ordenador
	servicios *(mpl)* informáticos
computer services department	departamento *(f)* de proceso de datos
computer simulation	simulación *(f)* por ordenador
computer storage	almacenamiento *(m)* del ordenador
computer terminal	terminal *(f)* del ordenador
computer virus	virus *(m)* informático
computer: analog ...	ordenador *(m)* analógico
computer: desktop ...	ordenador *(m)* portátil
computer: digital ...	ordenador *(m)* digital
computer: laptop ...	ordenador *(m)* portátil
computer: personal ... (PC)	ordenador *(m)* personal (PC)
computerize (to)	automatizar
computerized information system (COINS)	sistema *(m)* mecanizado de información (COINS)
computerized management	gerencia *(f)* automatizada
concept: value ...	concepto *(m)* del valor
conception: product ...	concepción *(f)* de productos
conciliate (to)	conciliar
conciliation	conciliación *(f)*
conditions *(of a contract)*	términos *(mpl)* (de un contrato)
conditions of employment	condiciones *(fpl)* de empleo
confidentiality	confidencialidad *(f)*
conglomerate	conglomerado *(m)*
	grupo *(m)*
consciousness: cost ...	conciencia *(f)* del coste
consensus	consenso *(m)*
consolidated accounts	estados *(mpl)* financieros consolidados
consolidation	consolidación *(f)*
consortium	consorcio *(f)*
constraint: budget ...	límite *(m)* del presupuesto
consult (to)	consultar
	asesorar
consultant	asesor *(m)*
consultant: computer ...	consultor *(m)* informático
consultant: management ...	consultor *(m)* de dirección
consultation: joint ...	consultación *(f)* conjunta
consultative	consultivo
consumer acceptance	aceptación *(m)* por parte del consumidor
consumer behaviour	conducta *(f)* del consumidor

consumer durables	bienes *(mpl)* de consumo no perecederos
consumer goods	artículos *(mpl)* de consumo
consumer goods: fast-moving ... ... (FMCG)	bienes *(mpl)* de consumo bienes *(mpl)* de venta fácil
consumer orientation	orientación *(f)* al consumidor
consumer price index	índice *(m)* de precios al consumo (IPC)
consumer protection	protección *(f)* al consumidor
consumer research	investigación *(f)* de consumidores
consumer resistance	resistencia *(f)* del consumidor
consumer-responsive	de reacción consumista
consumer satisfaction	satisfacción *(f)* del consumidor
consumerism	consumismo *(m)*
consumers' panel	"panel" *(m)* de consumidores
container	contenedor *(m)*
containerization	utilización *(f)* de contenedores
content: work ...	contenido *(m)* del trabajo
contingencies	gastos *(mpl)* extraordinarios
contingency reserve	reserva *(f)* para imprevistos
contingency theory	teoría *(f)* de las contingencias
continuous-flow production	producción *(f)* contínua
continuous stocktaking	inventario *(m)* continuo de mercancías
contract hire	alquiler *(m)* de larga duración
contract out (to)	subcontratar
contract: management ...	contrato *(m)* de dirección
contract: work by ...	trabajo *(m)* a base de contrato
contracting out	prestación *(f)* de servicios
contraction of authority	disminución *(f)* de autoridad
contribution analysis	análisis *(f)* de aportaciones
control	control *(m)* verificación *(f)*
control information	información *(f)* de control
control: adaptive ...	control *(m)* adaptivo
control: administrative ... procedure	proceso *(m)* de control administrativo
control: batch ...	control *(m)* del lote
control: board ...	control *(m)* del consejo de administración
control: budgetary ...	control *(m)* de presupuestos
control: budgeting ...	control *(m)* presupuestario
control: cost ...	control *(m)* de costes
control: financial ...	control *(m)* financiero

control: inventory ...	control *(m)* del inventario
control: managerial ...	control *(m)* directivo
control: manufacturing ...	control *(m)* de fabricación
control: process ...	control *(m)* del proceso
control: production ...	control *(m)* de producción
control: production planning and ...	planificación *(f)* y control *(m)* de la producción
control: progress ...	control *(m)* de la marcha del trabajo
control: quality ... (QC)	control *(m)* de calidad
control: span of ...	organización *(f)* de mando
control: statistical ...	verificación *(f)* estadística
control: stock ...	control *(m)* de existencias
control: total quality ... (TQC)	control *(m)* total de calidad
controller	interventor *(m)*
controlling interest	inversión *(m)* dominante participación *(f)* de control
convenience goods	artículos *(mpl)* de consumo de frecuente adquisición
coordination	coordinación *(f)*
core product	producto *(m)* clave
corner	monopolio *(m)* acaparamiento *(m)*
corner the market (to)	monopolizar acaparar el mercado
corporate advertising	publicidad *(f)* empresarial
corporate culture	cultura *(f)* empresarial
corporate goal	objetivo *(m)* de la empresa
corporate growth	crecimiento *(m)* de la empresa
corporate image	imagen *(f)* de la empresa
corporate mission	misión *(f)* de la empresa
corporate model	modelo *(m)* de la empresa
corporate objective	objetivo *(m)* de la empresa
corporate planning	planificación *(f)* empresarial
corporate policy	política *(f)* de la empresa
corporate raider	predador *(m)* de acciones de empresas
corporate strategy	estrategia *(f)* empresarial
corporate structure	estructura *(f)* empresarial
corporation tax	impuesto *(m)* de sociedades
corporation: business ...	sociedad *(f)* anónima (SA)
corporatism	corporativismo *(m)*
correlate (to)	correlacionar
correlation	correlación *(f)*
cost accounting	contabilidad *(f)* de costes

cost allocation	asignación *(f)* de costes
cost analysis	análisis *(m)* de costes
cost apportionment	distribución *(f)* de costes
cost awareness	conciencia *(f)* del coste
cost-benefit analysis (CBA)	análisis *(m)* coste-beneficio
cost centre	centro *(m)* de coste
cost consciousness	conciencia *(f)* del coste
cost control	control *(m)* de costes
cost-effective	eficaz en relación con el coste
cost-effectiveness	coste *(m)* de la eficacia
cost-efficient	eficiente *(m)* en relación con el coste
cost factor	elemento *(m)* de coste
cost of living	coste *(m)* de la vida
cost of production	coste *(m)* de producción
cost-push inflation	inflación *(f)* de costes
cost reduction	reducción *(f)* de costes
cost-sensitive	sensible a los costes
cost standard	estándares *(mpl)* de costes
cost structure	estructura *(f)* de costes
cost variance	varianza *(f)* de costes
cost-volume-profit analysis	análisis *(m)* de coste volumen y beneficio
cost: absorption ...	absorción *(f)* de costes
cost: full-... method	método *(m)* de costes completos
costing	evaluación *(f)* de costes
costing: direct ...	método *(m)* de costes directos
costing: functional ...	método *(m)* de costes por función
costing: marginal ...	contabilidad *(f)* marginal método *(m)* de costes
costing: product ...	evaluación *(f)* del coste del producto
costing: standard ...	método *(m)* de costes estándar
costs: allocation of ...	asignación *(f)* de costes
costs: average ...	coste *(m)* medio
costs: closing-down ...	coste *(m)* de liquidación
costs: direct ...	coste *(m)* directo
costs: distribution ...	costes *(mpl)* de distribución
costs: estimating systems ...	evaluación *(f)* de costes de sistemas
costs: fixed ...	costes *(mpl)* fijos
costs: indirect	coste *(m)* indirecto
costs: managed ...	costes *(mpl)* controlados
costs: marginal ...	coste *(m)* marginal
costs: opportunity ...	coste *(m)* de oportunidad
costs: replacement ...	costes *(mpl)* de sustitución

costs: semi-variable ...	costes *(mpl)* semi-variables
costs: set-up ...	costes *(mpl)* de constitución
costs: standard ...	costes *(mpl)* estándar
costs: start-up ...	coste *(m)* de puesta en marcha
costs: unit labour ...	coste *(m)* unitario de la mano de obra
costs: variable ...	costes *(mpl)* variables
council: works ...	consejo *(m)* de obreros
counselling: employee ...	consejo *(m)* de empleados
countertrade	ventas *(fpl)* al contado
country: less-developed ... (LDC)	país *(m)* menos desarrollado
cover ratio	proporción *(f)* de cobertura
coverage: sales ...	alcance *(m)* del servicio de ventas
CPA (critical path analysis)	análisis *(m)* del camino crítico
CPM (critical path method)	método *(m)* del camino crítico
CPU (central processing unit)	unidad *(f)* de proceso central (CPU)
crash	quiebra *(f)*
crash (to ... a program)	hundir (hundir un programa)
creative accounting	contabilidad *(f)* flexible
creative marketing	márketing *(m)* creativo
creative thinking	espíritu *(m)* creativo
credit control	control *(m)* de crédito
credit management	gestión *(f)* de créditos
credit rating	clasificación *(f)* de solvencia
credit squeeze	restricción *(f)* crediticia
credit: revolving ...	crédito *(m)* renovable
crisis management	gestión *(f)* de crisis
criteria: investment ...	criterios *(mpl)* de inversión
critical mass	masa *(f)* crítica
critical path analysis (CPA)	análisis *(m)* del camino crítico
critical path method (CPM)	método *(m)* del camino crítico
cross-licensing	concesión *(f)* recíproca de licencias
culture	cultura *(f)*
culture: corporate ...	cultura *(f)* empresarial
culture: organization ...	cultura *(f)* de la organización
currency: common ...	divisas *(fpl)*
currency: parallel ...	moneda *(f)* paralela
currency: single ...	moneda *(f)* única
current assets	activo *(m)* circulante
	activo *(m)* realizable
current expenditure	gastos *(mpl)* actuales
current liabilities	pasivo *(m)* circulante
	pasivo *(m)* real

current ratio	índice *(m)* de liquidéz
current: net ... assets	activo *(m)* circulante neto
cursor	cursor *(m)*
curve: learning ...	curva *(f)* de aprendizaje
curve: salary progression ...	curva *(f)* de incremento de salarios
custom and practice	usos *(m)* y costumbres *(f)*
custom-made	hecho a la medida
customer care	atención *(f)* al cliente
customer orientation	orientación *(f)* del consumidor
customer profile	perfil *(m)* del consumidor
customer service	servicio *(m)* al cliente
customer: prospective ...	cliente *(m)* potencial
customized	a medida *(f)* del usuario
cut one's losses (to)	disminuir las pérdidas propias
cut prices (to)	abaratar *(mpl)* precios
cut-back: staff ...	reducción *(f)* de personal
cut-off point	punto *(m)* límite
cutting edge	límite *(m)* de filo
cutting: price ...	abaratamiento *(f)* de precios
CWM (clerical work measurement)	medición *(f)* de trabajo administrativo
cybernetics	cibernética *(f)*
cycle: business ...	ciclo *(m)* económico
cycle: life ... (*of a product*)	ciclo *(m)* de la vida (de un producto)
cycle: trade ...	ciclo *(m)* comercial
cycle: work ...	ciclo *(m)* de trabajo

D

daisy wheel	margarita (f)
damage limitation	limitación (f) de daños
data acquisition	adquisición (f) de datos
data bank	banco (m) de datos
database	base (f) de datos
data flow chart	diagrama (m) de flujo de datos
data gathering	recogida (f) de datos
data processing	proceso (m) de datos
data protection	protección (f) de datos
data retrieval	recuperación (f) de datos
data: automatic ... processing (ADP)	proceso (m) automático de datos (ADP)
data: electronic ... processing (EDP)	proceso (m) electrónico de datos (EDP)
date: due ...	fecha (f) de vencimiento
date: expected ...	fecha (f) prevista
date: latest ...	fecha (f) límite
date: sell-by ...	fecha (f) de caducidad
date: use-by ...	fecha (f) de caducidad
day shift	turno (m) de día
DCF (discounted cash flow)	"cash flow" actualizado
deadline	fecha (f) límite
deal	intermediación (f)
deal: cash ...	intermediación (f) al contado
deal: package ...	oferta (f) combinada
deal: reach a ... (to)	llegar a un acuerdo
dealer	dealer (m)
	intermediador (m)
	corredor (m) de bolsa
dealing: insider ...	trato (m) con información privilegiada
debenture	obligaciones (fpl)
debottleneck (to)	desatascar
debrief (to)	recabar informes
debriefing	informe (m) sobre una operación
debt financing	financiación (f) de la deuda
debt ratio	ratio (m) de endeudamiento
debt-equity ratio	ratio (m) deuda-activo
debtor	deudor (m)
debts: bad ...	créditos (mpl) incobrables
	deudores (mpl) morosos

debug (to)	comprobar sistemas (de ordenador)
decentralization	descentralización *(f)*
decentralize (to)	descentralizar
decentralized management	dirección *(f)* descentralizada
decision analysis	análisis *(m)* de decisiones
decision-making	proceso *(m)* de tomar decisiones
decision model	modelo *(m)* de decisiones
decision process	procedimientos *(mpl)* de decisión
decision theory	teoría *(f)* de decisiones
decision tree	árbol *(m)* de decisiones
deductible: tax ...	deducible de impuestos
defensive strategy	estrategia *(f)* defensiva
deficit financing	financiación *(f)* de déficit
deindustrialization	desindustrialización *(f)*
delegate (to)	delegar
delegation	delegación *(f)* de poderes
delivery time	tiempo *(m)* de entrega
demand assessment	evaluación *(f)* de la demanda
demand forecasting	previsión *(f)* de la demanda
demand-pull inflation	inflación *(f)* por la demanda
demanning	disminución *(f)* del número de empleados
demerger	separación *(f)* comercial
democracy: industrial ...	democracia *(f)* industrial
demotivate (to)	desmotivar
demotivation	desmotivación *(f)*
department: accounting ...	departamento *(m)* de contabilidad
department: engineering and design ...	departamento *(m)* técnico y de proyectos
department: marketing ...	departamento *(m)* de márketing
department: personnel ...	departamento *(m)* de personal
department: planning ...	departamento *(m)* de planificación
department: research ...	departamento *(m)* de investigación
department: sales ...	departamento *(m)* de ventas
departmental head	jefe *(m)* de departamento
departmental management	gerencia *(f)* de departamento
departmental manager	director *(m)* de departamento
departmental plan	plan *(m)* departamental
departmentalization	organización *(f)* por secciones
deploy (to)	organizar desplegar
deployment	despliegue *(m)*
depreciate (to)	depreciar

depreciation allowance	reserva *(f)* para amortización
depth analysis	análisis *(m)* a fondo
depth interview	entrevista *(f)* a fondo
deputy chairman	vicepresidente *(m)*
deputy manager	subdirector *(m)*
deputy managing director	director *(m)* gerente adjunto
deregulate (to)	desregular
deregulation	desregulación *(f)*
description: job ...	descripción *(f)* del puesto de trabajo
design engineering	estudio *(m)* de proyectos
design office	departamento *(m)* de diseño
design: computer-aided ... (CAD)	CAD (diseño *(m)* asistido por ordenador)
design: engineering and ... department ...	departamento *(m)* técnico y de proyectos
design: job ...	objetivo *(m)* del trabajo
design: product ...	diseño *(m)* del producto
design: systems ...	elaboración *(m)* de sistemas
desk research	investigación *(m)* de gabinete
desktop computer	ordenador *(m)* portátil
desktop publish (to)	autoeditar
desktop publishing	autoedición *(f)*
determination: price ...	fijación *(f)* de precios
developer	urbanizador *(m)*
development potential	potencial *(m)* de explotación
development programme	programa *(m)* de desarrollo
development: executive ...	formación *(f)* de ejecutivos
development: human resource ...	desarrollo *(m)* de recursos humanos
development: management ...	formación *(f)* de la dirección
development: new-product ...	desarrollo *(m)* de nuevos productos
development: organizational ...	desarrollo *(m)* de la organización
development: product ...	desarrollo *(m)* de productos
development: research and ... (R & D)	investigación *(f)* y desarrollo *(m)*
deviation: standard ...	desviación *(f)* estándar
diagnostic routine	rutina *(f)* del diagnóstico
diagram: flow ...	diagrama *(m)* de flujos
diagram: scatter ...	diagrama *(m)* de dispersión
different ball game	otro juego *(m)*
differential price	diferencia *(f)* de precios
differential pricing	valoración *(f)* diferencial

differential: earnings ...	escalado *(m)* de ganancias
differential: price ...	escalado *(m)* de precios
differential: wage ...	escalado *(m)* de salarios
differentiate (to)	diferenciar
differentiate: product-... (to)	diferenciar productos
differentiation: product ...	diferenciación *(f)* entre productos
digital	digital
digital computer	ordenador *(m)* digital
digitize (to)	digitalizar
dilution of equity	dilución *(f)* de accionariado
dilution of labour	incorporación *(f)* de mano de obra no capacitada
direct costing	método *(m)* de costes directos
direct costs	coste *(m)* directo
direct expenses	gastos *(mpl)* directos
direct labour	mano *(f)* de obra directa
direct mail	publicidad *(f)* por correspondencia
direct marketing	márketing *(m)* directo
direct selling	venta *(f)* directa
director	director *(m)*
director: assistant ...	director *(m)* adjunto
director: deputy managing ...	director *(m)* gerente adjunto
director: executive ...	director *(m)* ejecutivo
director: financial ...	director *(m)* financiero
director: managing ... (MD)	director *(m)* gerente
director: non-executive ...	vocal *(m)* consejero *(m)*
director: outside ...	director *(m)* suplente
director: production ...	director *(m)* de producción
directorate: interlocking ...	dirección *(f)* entrelazada
directors: board of ...	consejo *(m)* de administración
disburse (to)	desembolsar
disbursement	desembolso *(m)*
discounted cash flow (DCF)	"cash flow" *(m)* actualizado
discretion: time span of ...	tiempo *(m)* máximo discrecional
discriminate (to)	discriminar
discrimination	discriminación *(f)*
discrimination: positive ...	discriminación *(f)* positiva
discrimination: price ...	discriminación *(f)* de precios
diseconomy of scale	deseconomía *(f)* de escala
disincentive	elemento *(m)* demotivante freno *(m)*

disintegration	desintegración *(f)*
disinvestment	desinversión *(f)*
disk	disco *(m)*
disk drive	unidad *(f)* de discos
disk: floppy ...	"floppy" *(m)*
	disco *(m)* flexible
disk: hard ...	disco *(m)* duro
disk: Winchester ...	disco *(m)* winchester
dismissal	despido *(m)*
dismissal: summary ...	despido *(m)* sumario
dismissal: unfair ...	despido *(m)* injusto
dispatching	expedición *(f)* envío *(m)*
display unit	unidad *(f)* de representación
display unit: visual ... ... (VDU)	(VDU) unidad *(f)* de representación visual
disposable income	ingresos *(mpl)* disponibles
disposition: source and ... of funds	origen *(m)* y aplicación *(f)* de recursos
dispute: industrial ...	conflicto *(m)* industrial
dispute: labour ...	conflicto *(m)* laboral
dissolution	disolución *(f)*
distance learning	aprendizaje *(m)* a distancia
distributed profit	beneficios *(mpl)* repartidos
distribution	distribución *(f)*
distribution channel	canal *(m)* de distribución
distribution cost	coste *(m)* de distribución
distribution manager	jefe *(m)* de distribución
distribution network	red *(f)* de distribución
distribution planning	planificación *(f)* de distribución
distribution policy	política *(f)* de distribución
distribution: chain of ...	cadena *(f)* de distribución
distribution: frequency ...	distribución *(f)* de frecuencia
distribution: physical ... management	gestión *(m)* de la distribución física
diversification	diversificación *(f)*
diversification strategy	estrategia *(f)* de diversificación
diversification: product ...	diversificación *(f)* de productos
diversify (to)	diversificar
divestment	reducción *(f)* del activo
	desinversión *(f)*
dividend	dividendos *(mpl)*
dividend policy	política *(f)* de dividendos
division: operating ...	división *(f)* operacional

divisional management	gestión *(f)* por secciones
doomwatcher	profeta *(m)* de fracaso
double taxation relief	desgravación *(f)* de impuestos duplicados
down-market	mercado *(m)* abajo
downstream	más abajo
downswing	viraje *(m)* abajo
down the line	subordinados *(mpl)*
down time	tiempo *(m)* inactivo
	horas *(fpl)* bajas
downturn	bajada *(f)*
drift: wage ...	deriva *(f)* de salarios
drip-feeding	alimentar gota a gota
drive: advertising ...	empuje *(m)* publicitario
drive: disk ...	unidad *(f)* de discos
drive: market ...	empuje *(m)* comercial
drive: productivity ...	campaña *(f)* de productividad
drive: sales ...	empuje *(m)* de ventas
dual sourcing	suministración *(f)* de dos fuentes
due date	fecha *(f)* límite
dummy activity	actividad *(f)* artificial
dumping	"dumping" *(m)*
	rebaja *(f)* desleal de precios
durables	productos *(mpl)* duraderos
durables: consumer ...	productos *(mpl)* duraderos de consumo
dynamic evaluation	evaluación *(f)* dinámica
dynamic management model	modelo *(m)* dinámico de administración
dynamic programming	programación *(f)* dinámica
dynamics: group ...	dinámica *(f)* de grupos
	dinámica *(f)* colectiva
dynamics: industrial ...	dinámica *(f)* industrial
dynamics: market ...	dinámica *(f)* del mercado
dynamics: product ...	dinámica *(f)* de productos
dysfunction	disfunción *(f)*

E

e-mail (electronic mail)	correo *(m)* electrónico
early retirement	jubilación *(f)* prematura
earning power	capacidad *(f)* de beneficios
earnings differential	escalado *(m)* de ganancias
earnings on assets	rendimiento *(m)* del activo
earnings per share (EPS)	beneficio *(m)* por acción
earnings performance	rentabilidad *(f)*
earnings yield	rédito *(m)*
earnings: price-... ratio (P/E)	PER
	tasa *(f)* de capitalización de beneficios (TCB)
EC (European Community)	Comunidad *(f)* Europea (CE)
econometric	econométrico
economic batch quantity	tamaño *(m)* del lote económico
economic climate	ambiente *(m)* económico
economic intelligence	información *(f)* económica
economic life	vida *(f)* económica
economic manufacturing quantity	tamaño *(f)* del lote económico de fabricación
economic mission	misión *(f)* económica
economic order quantity	magnitud *(f)* económica de un pedido
economic research	investigación *(f)* económica
economic trend	tendencia *(f)* económica
economist: business ...	economista *(m)* comercial
economy of scale	economía *(f)* de escala
economy: motion ...	economía *(f)* de movimientos
ecu (European Currency Unit)	ECU (European Currency Unit)
ecu: hard ...	ECU duro
edge: competitive ...	ventaja *(f)* sobre la competencia
edge: cutting ...	límite *(m)* de reducción
edge: leading ...	tecnología *(f)* punta
EDP (electronic data processing)	proceso *(m)* electrónico de datos
effective management	dirección *(f)* eficaz
effective: cost-...	eficaz en relación con el coste
effectiveness	eficacia *(f)*
effectiveness: advertising ...	eficacia *(f)* de publicidad
effectiveness: cost-...	coste *(m)* de la eficacia
effectiveness: managerial ...	eficacia *(f)* directiva
effectiveness: organizational ...	eficacia *(f)* de la organización

efficiency	rendimiento *(m)*
	eficiencia *(f)*
efficiency audit	control *(m)* del rendimiento
efficient	eficiente
efficient: cost-...	eficiente *(m)* en relación con el coste
effort: sales expansion ...	esfuerzo *(m)* para aumentar ventas
EFTPOS (electronic funds transfer at point of sale)	transferencia *(f)* electrónica de fondos al punto de venta
elasticity	elasticidad *(f)*
electronic accounting system	sistema *(m)* electrónico de contabilidad
electronic communication	comunicación *(f)* electrónica
electronic data processing (EDP)	proceso *(m)* electrónico de datos EDP
electronic funds transfer at point-of-sale (EFTPOS)	transferencia *(f)* electrónica de fondos al punto de venta
electronic mail (e-mail)	correo *(m)* electrónico
electronic office	oficina *(f)* electrónica
electronic processing	proceso *(m)* electrónico
empirical	empírico
employed: capital ...	capital *(m)* invertido
employed: return on capital ... (ROCE)	rendimiento *(m)* del capital invertido
employee buyout	compra *(f)* de una empresa por los empleados
employee counselling	consejo *(m)* de empleados
employee relations	relaciones *(fpl)* con el personal
employees: front-line ...	empleados *(mpl)* de primera línea
employment bureau	agencia *(f)* de colocaciones
employment: conditions of ...	condiciones *(fpl)* de empleo
employment: full-time ...	pleno *(m)* empleo
employment: part-time ...	empleo *(m)* a tiempo parcial
EMS (European Monetary System)	Sistema *(m)* Monetario Europeo
EMU (European Monetary Union)	Unión *(f)* Monetaria Europea
engineer: sales ...	ingeniero *(m)* comercial
engineer: software ...	ingeniero *(m)* de software
engineer: systems ...	ingeniero *(m)* de sistemas
engineering	ingeniería *(f)*
engineering and design department	departamento *(m)* técnico y de proyectos
engineering: design ...	estudio *(m)* de proyectos

engineering: human ...	adaptación *(f)* del trabajo al hombre
	ergonómica *(f)*
engineering: industrial ...	ingeniería *(f)* industrial
	organización *(f)* industrial
engineering: methods ...	estudio *(m)* de métodos
engineering: product ...	estudio *(m)* de productos
engineering: production ...	técnica *(f)* de producción
engineering: systems ...	elaboración *(f)* de sistemas
engineering: value ...	análisis *(m)* de costes
	análisis *(m)* de valores
enlargement: job ...	ampliación *(f)* de tareas
enrichment: job ...	valoración *(f)* del puesto
enterprise	empresa *(f)*
enterprise: private ...	iniciativa *(f)* privada
enterprise: public ...	empresa *(f)* pública
	empresa *(f)* del estado
enterprising	emprendedor
entrepreneurial spirit	espíritu *(m)* empresarial
environmental analysis	análisis *(m)* del medio ambiente
environmental forecasting	previsión *(f)* sobre el medioambiente
environmental scan	examen *(m)* del medio ambiente
EPS (earnings per share)	beneficios *(mpl)* por acción
equal employment opportunity	igualdad *(f)* de oportunidad en el empleo
equal opportunity	igualdad *(f)* de oportunidad
equal pay	igualdad *(f)* de salarios
equality	igualdad *(f)*
equipment leasing	arrendamiento *(m)* de medios de producción
equipment: add-on ...	equipo *(m)* auxiliar
equipment: peripheral ...	equipo *(m)* periférico
equipment: process ... layout	producción *(f)* agrupada
equity	acciones *(fpl)* de dividendo no fijo
	derechos *(mpl)* sobre el activo
equity market	mercado *(m)* de acciones
equity: dilution of ...	dilución *(f)* del accionariado
equity: return on ... (ROE)	rendimiento *(m)* de las acciones
ergonometrics	medidas *(fpl)* del trabajo
ergonomics	ergonómica *(f)*
	adaptación *(f)* del trabajo al hombre
ERM (Exchange Rate Mechanism)	mecanismo *(m)* de tasas de cambio
escalation: price ...	escalada *(f)* de precios

espionage: industrial ...	espionaje *(m)* industrial
establishment	establecimiento *(m)*
estimate: sales ...	estimación *(f)* de ventas
estimating systems costs	evaluación *(f)* de costes de sistemas
eurobond	obligación *(f)* europea
eurocurrency	divisa *(f)* europea
eurodollar	eurodólar *(m)*
euromarket	euromercado *(m)*
European Community (EC)	Comunidad *(f)* Europea (CE)
European Currency Unit (ecu)	Unidad *(f)* Monetaria Europea (ECU)
European Monetary System (EMS)	Sistema *(m)* Monetario Europeo (SME)
European Monetary Union (EMU)	Unión *(f)* Monetaria Europea (UME)
evaluate (to)	evaluar
	valorar
evaluation: capital project ...	evaluación *(f)* de proyectos de inversión
evaluation: dynamic ...	evaluación *(f)* dinámica
evaluation: job ...	evaluación *(f)* de puestos de trabajo
	clasificación *(f)* de tareas
evaluation: performance ...	evaluación *(f)* del rendimiento
***ex gratia* payment**	paga *(f)* voluntaria
exception: management by ...	dirección *(f)* por excepción
excess capacity	capacidad *(f)* excesiva
exchange rate	tasa *(f)* de cambio
Exchange Rate Mechanism (ERM)	mecanismo *(m)* de tasas de cambio
exchange rate: forward	tasa *(f)* de cambio en fecha futura
execution: policy ...	ejecución *(f)* de la política
executive	directivo*(m)*
	ejecutivo*(m)*
	director *(m)*
executive advancement	ascenso *(m)* de directivos
executive board	consejo *(m)* de administración
executive compensation	recompensa *(f)* de directivos
executive competence	aptitud *(f)* del directivo
executive development	formación *(f)* de ejecutivos
executive director	director *(m)* ejecutivo
executive manpower strategy	estrategia *(f)* de personal directivo
executive promotion	ascenso *(m)* de directivos
executive remuneration	remuneración *(f)* de directivos

executive search	reclutamiento *(m)* de directivos
executive training	formación *(f)* de ejecutivos
executive: chief ...	director *(m)* general
executive: line ...	directivo *(m)* de línea
expansion strategy	estrategia *(f)* de desarrollo
expansion: sales ... effort	esfuerzo *(m)* para el desarrollo de ventas
expectations: job ...	expectativas *(fpl)* del puesto
expectations: sales ...	expectativas *(fpl)* de venta
expected date	fecha *(f)* prevista
expenditure: capital ... (capex)	gastos *(mpl)* de capital
expenditure: current ...	gastos *(mpl)* actuales
expense account	cuenta *(f)* de gastos
expenses: administrative ...	gastos *(mpl)* administrativos
expenses: direct ...	gastos *(mpl)* directos
expenses: indirect ...	gastos *(mpl)* indirectos
expenses: operating ...	gastos *(mpl)* de operación
expenses: petty ...	gastos *(mpl)* pequeños
expenses: recovery of ...	recuperación *(f)* de gastos
expenses: running ...	gastos *(mpl)* corrientes
expert system	sistema *(m)* experto
expert: computer ...	experto *(m)* en ordenadores
exploration: market ...	investigación *(f)* del mercado
exponential smoothing	aproximación *(f)* exponencial
exponential trend	tendencias *(fpl)* exponenciales
extension services	servicios *(mpl)* logísticos
external relations	relaciones *(fpl)* externas
externalities	externalidades *(fpl)*
externalize (to)	exteriorizar

F

facility: borrowing ...	facilidades *(fpl)* de crédito
facsimile	facsimile *(m)*
factor	factor *(m)*
factor: cost ...	elemento *(m)* de coste
factor: load ...	factor *(m)* de carga
	grado *(m)* de saturación
factor: profit-... analysis	análisis *(m)* de centros de beneficio
factoring	descomposición *(f)* en factores
factors of production	factores *(mpl)* de producción
factory overheads	gastos *(mpl)* generales de fabricación
failure (*of firm*)	quiebra *(f)*
fair competition	competencia *(f)* leal
fair return	rendimiento *(m)* justo
family tree	árbol *(m)* genealógico
fast-moving consumer goods (FMCG)	bienes *(mpl)* de consumo de venta fácil
fast-track	ascenso *(m)* vertiginoso
fax (to)	enviar un fax
fax	fax *(m)*
fax machine	fax (aparato) *(m)*
feasibility study	estudio *(m)* de viabilidad
feasible	factible
featherbedding	lecho *(m)* de pluma
feedback	respuesta *(f)*
fiddle (to)	amanar (los libros)
field research	investigación *(f)* de campo
field testing	prueba *(f)* de campo
figure: ballpark ...	cifra *(f)* aproximada
finance (to)	financiar
financial administration	administración *(f)* financiera
financial analysis	análisis *(m)* financiero
financial appraisal	valoración *(f)* financiera
financial control	control *(m)* financiero
financial director	jefe *(m)* de finanzas
financial futures	futuros *(mpl)* financieros
financial incentive	incentivos *(mpl)* financieros
financial involvement	implicación *(f)* financiera
financial management	dirección *(f)* financiera
financial market	mercado *(m)* financiero
financial planning	planificación *(f)* financiera

financial position	posición *(f)* financiera
financial ratio	ratio *(m)* financiero
financial review	análisis *(m)* financiero
financial standard	norma *(f)* financiera
financial statement	balance *(m)*
financial strategy	estrategia *(f)* financiera
financial year	económico *(m)*
	ejercicio *(m)*
financing	financiación *(f)*
financing: debt ...	financiación *(f)* de la deuda
financing: deficit ...	financiación *(f)* del déficit
financing: self-...	autofinanciación *(f)*
	autofinanciamiento *(m)*
fire (to)	despedir
fire-fighting	apagando fuegos
firing: hiring and ...	contratación *(f)* y despido *(m)*
first-line manager	jefe *(m)* de alto nivel
fiscal drag	traba *(f)* fiscal
fiscal policy	política *(f)* fiscal
fiscal year	año *(m)* fiscal
	ejercicio *(m)* fiscal
fixed assets	activo *(m)* fijo
fixed costs	costes *(mpl)* fijos
fixed expenses	gastos *(mpl)* fijos
flexible budget	presupuesto *(m)* flexible
flexible firm	empresa *(f)* flexible y ágil
flexible working hours	horario *(m)* de trabajo flexible
flexitime	horario *(m)* flexible
floppy disk (floppy)	disco *(m)* flexible
	"floppy" *(m)*
flotation	flotación *(f)*
flow chart	diagrama *(m)* de flujos
flow chart: data	diagrama *(m)* de flujos de datos
flow diagram	diagrama *(m)* de flujos
flow line	nivel *(m)* de producción
flow process chart	diagrama *(m)* de flujos del proceso
flow production	fabricación *(f)* en cadena
flow: cash ...	"cash flow" *(m)*
flow: continuous-... production	producción *(f)* continua
flow: discounted cash ... (DCF)	"cash flow" *(m)* actualizado
flow: funds	movimiento *(m)* de capital
flow: incremental cash ...	"cash flow" *(m)* marginal
flow: information ...	flujo *(m)* de información

FMCG (fast-moving consumer goods)	bienes *(mpl)* de consumo de venta fácil
focus (to)	enfocar
focus	enfoque *(m)*
follow up (to)	hacer el seguimiento
force: sales ...	fuerza *(f)* de venta
force: task ...	grupo *(m)* de intervención
forces: market ...	tendencias *(fpl)* del mercado
forecast	previsión *(f)*
forecast: budget ...	previsión *(f)* presupuestaria
forecast: market ...	previsión *(f)* de mercado
forecast: sales ...	previsión *(f)* de ventas
forecast: technological ...	previsión *(f)* tecnológica
forecasting	previsión *(f)*
forecasting: budget ...	previsión *(f)* de presupuesto
forecasting: business ...	previsión *(f)* de la empresa
forecasting: cash ...	previsión *(f)* de tesorería
forecasting: demand ...	previsión *(f)* de la demanda
forecasting: environmental ...	previsión *(f)* del medio ambiente
forecasting: manpower ...	previsión *(f)* de mano de obra
forecasting: staff ...	previsión *(f)* de personal
foreman	capataz *(m)*
formation: capital ...	formación *(f)* de capital
formulation: policy ...	elaboración *(f)* de una política
formulation: strategy ...	elaboración *(f)* de una estrategia
forward exchange rate	tasa *(f)* de cambio en fecha futura
forward market	mercado *(m)* a futuro
forward planning	planificación *(f)* a largo plazo
forward rate	cambio *(m)* a plazo
forward swap	acciones *(fpl)* canjeables con fecha futura
forwarding	envío *(m)*
forwarding agent	agente *(m)* de despacho
fractionalize (to)	fraccionar
franchise (to)	franquiciar
franchise	franquicia *(f)*
franchising	trabajo *(m)* bajo franquicia *(f)*
freelance (to go)	trabajar por cuenta propia freelance
freeze (to)	bloquear congelar
freeze: wage ...	congelación *(f)* salarial

frequency distribution	distribución *(f)* de frecuencia
friendly: user-...	fácil de utilizar
fringe benefits	ventajas *(fpl)* supletorias
fringe market	mercado *(m)* marginal
front-line employees	empleados *(mpl)* del terreno
full capacity	plena capacidad
full-cost method	método *(m)* de costes completos
full-time employment	pleno empleo *(m)*
full-timer	empleado *(m)* a tiempo total
function	función *(f)*
function key	función *(f)* clave
function: managerial ...	función *(f)* de dirección
functional	funcional
functional analysis	análisis *(m)* funcional
functional approach	enfoque *(m)* funcional
functional costing	metodo *(m)* de costes por función
functional layout	disposición *(f)* funcional
functional management	gestión *(f)* funcional
functional organization	organización *(f)* funcional
functional relations	relaciones *(fpl)* funcionales
functional responsibility	responsabilidad *(f)* funcional
fund: sinking ...	fondo *(m)* de amortización
fund: slush ...	caja B *(f)*
funding	financiación *(f)*
funds flow	movimiento *(m)* de capital
funds: source and disposition of ...	provisión *(f)* de fondos provisión *(f)* de recursos financieros
futures	futuros *(mpl)*
futures market	mercado *(m)* de futuros
futures: financial ...	futuros *(mpl)* financieros

G

gain: capital ...	ganancias *(fpl)* de capital
	plusvalía *(m)*
game theory	teoría *(f)* de juegos
game: business ...	simulación *(f)* de gestión
game: management ...	simulación *(f)* de gestión
gap	intervalo *(m)*
	varianza *(f)*
gap study	análisis *(m)* de las varianzas
gateway	puerta *(f)*
gathering: data ...	recogida *(f)* de datos
GDP (gross domestic product)	PIB (producto interior bruto)
gearing	engranaje *(m)* financiero de la empresa
gearing ratio	índice *(m)* de deuda
	índice *(m)* de efectivo
general management	dirección *(f)* general
general manager	director *(m)* general
generate ideas (to)	estimular ideas
generation: product ...	generación *(f)* de productos
generic	genérico
gentleman's agreement	acuerdo *(m)* de caballeros
gilt	valor *(m)* del Estado
gilt-edged security	valores *(mpl)* garantizados por el Estado
gilt-edged stock	valores *(mpl)* garantizados por el Estado
global image	imagen *(f)* global
global marketing	márketing *(m)* global
globalization	globalización *(f)*
globalize (to)	globalizar
	internacionalizar
GM (gross margin)	margen *(m)* bruto
GNP (gross national product)	PNB (producto *(m)* nacional bruto)
go public (to)	cotizar en la Bolsa
go-getter: be a go-getter (to)	tener espíritu emprendedor
go-getting	tener iniciativa
go-slow	huelga *(f)* de trabajo lento
goal-seeking	identificación *(f)* de objetivos
goal-setting	fijación *(f)* de objetivos
goal: company ...	objetivo *(m)* de la empresa

goal: profit ...	objetivo *(m)* de beneficio
goal: sales ...	objetivo *(m)* de ventas
goals: hierarchy of ...	jerarquía *(f)* de objetivos
going rate	tasa *(f)* en vigor
golden handcuffs	prima *(f)* de permanencia
	salario *(m)* de oro
golden handshake	indemnización *(f)* por despido
golden hello	prima *(f)* de enganche
golden parachute	indemnización *(f)* por despido
golden share	prima *(f)*, acción *(f)* preferencial
goods: brown ...	electrodomésticos *(mpl)* (que no forman parte de la línea blanca)
goods: capital ...	bienes *(mpl)* de capital
	bienes *(mpl)* de equipo
goods: consumer ...	artículos *(mpl)* de consumo
goods: convenience ...	productos *(mpl)* de consumo habitual
goods: durable ...	productos *(mpl)* no perecederos
goods: fast-moving consumer ... (FMG)	productos *(mpl)* de consumo de venta rápida
goods: impulse	productos *(mpl)* de venta por impulso
goods: industrial ...	bienes *(mpl)* industriales
goods: investment ...	bienes *(mpl)* de inversión
goods: non-durable ...	productos *(mpl)* perecederos
goods: white ...	electrodomésticos *(mpl)* (línea blanca)
goodwill	fondo *(m)* de comercio
	valor *(m)* extrínseco
	crédito *(m)*
	valor *(m)* de prestigio de una empresa
grade: salary ...	nivel *(m)* salarial
grapevine	comunicación *(f)* por rumor
graphics	gráficos *(mpl)*
green issues	temas *(mpl)* del medio ambiente
grey market	mercado *(m)* paralelo
grid structure	estructura *(f)* de red
grid: managerial ...	plantilla *(f)* de dirección
grievance	queja *(f)*
grievance procedure	tramitación *(f)* de quejas
gross domestic product (GDP)	producto *(m)* interior bruto (PIB)
gross margin (GM)	margen *(m)* bruto
gross national product (GNP)	PNB (producto *(m)* nacional bruto)
gross profit	beneficio *(m)* bruto
group accounts	estados *(mpl)* financieros del grupo
group bonus	prima *(f)* colectiva

group dynamics	dinámica *(f)* de grupos
group incentive	incentivo *(m)* colectivo
group training	formación *(f)* en grupos
group: product ...	grupo *(m)* de productos
group: T-... training	diagnóstico *(m)* de grupos
growth area	sector *(m)* de crecimiento
growth index	índice *(m)* de crecimiento
growth industry	industria *(f)* en desarrollo
growth potential	potencial *(m)* de crecimiento
growth strategy	estrategia *(f)* de crecimiento
growth: corporate ...	crecimiento *(m)* de la empresa
growth: organic ...	crecimiento *(m)* orgánico
growth: personal ...	formación *(f)* personal
guesstimate	cálculo *(m)* aproximado
guidance: vocational ...	orientación *(f)* profesional
guideline	pauta *(f)*
	línea *(f)* de guía
	directriz *(f)*

H

hacker	pirata *(m)* (informática)
hacking	pirateado *(m)* (informática)
halo effect	efecto *(m)* de halo
handcuffs: golden ...	prima *(f)* de permanencia
	salario *(m)* de oro
handling: information ...	manejo *(m)* de datos
handling: materials ...	movimientos *(mpl)* de materiales
hands-on	manos *(fpl)* a la obra
hands-on training	formación *(f)* práctica
handshake: golden ...	indemnización *(f)* por despido
harassment: sexual ...	acoso *(m)* sexual
hard copy	versión *(f)* impresa de datos
hard disk	disco *(m)* duro
hard ecu	ecu *(m)* duro
hard landing	entrada *(f)* en la depresión (economía)
hard sell	venta *(f)* agresiva
hardware	equipo *(m)* "hardware"
harmonization	armonización *(f)*
harmonize (to)	armonizar
hazard: occupational ...	riesgo *(m)* ocupacional
hazchem (hazardous chemicals)	productos *(mpl)* químicos de alta peligrosidad
head office	central *(f)*
	oficina *(f)* principal
head-hunt (to)	seleccionar directivos
head-hunter	profesional que hace selección de directivos
	cazador *(m)* de cabezas
hedge (to)	cubrirse
hedging	cobertura *(f)*
hello: golden ...	prima *(m)* de enganche
heuristics	heurística *(f)*
hidden agenda	objetivo *(m)* confidencial
hidden assets	bienes *(mpl)* ocultos
hierarchy of goals	jerarquía *(f)* de objetivos
high-flier	ejecutivo *(m)* de alto potencial
high-tech	tecnología *(f)* punta
hire (to)	contratar
hire: contract ...	alquiler *(m)* a largo plazo

hire: plant ...	alquiler *(m)* de equipo
hiring and firing	contratar y despedir
histogram	histograma *(m)*
hive off (to)	vender parte del negocio
hold margins (to)	mantener los márgenes
holding company	sociedad *(f)* "holding"
holidays: staggered ...	vacaciones *(fpl)* escalonadas
home country	país *(m)* de origen
horizontal integration	integración *(f)* horizontal
host country	país *(m)* anfitrión
hot money	inversiones *(fpl)* especulativas
house style	sello *(m)* de la empresa
HRD (human resource development)	desarrollo *(m)* de recursos humanos
HRM (human resource management)	GRH (gestión *(f)* de recursos humanos)
HRP (human resource planning)	planificación *(f)* de recursos humanos
human engineering	adaptación *(f)* del trabajo al hombre ergonómica *(f)*
human relations	relaciones *(fpl)* humanas
human resource development (HRD)	desarrollo *(m)* de recursos humanos
human resource management (HRM)	gestión *(f)* de recursos humanos
human resource planning (HRP)	planificación *(f)* de recursos humanos
human resources	recursos *(mpl)* humanos
hustle (to)	presionar
hygiene factors	condiciones *(fpl)* aceptables
hype	hipérbole *(f)*

I

idle capacity	capacidad *(f)* no utilizada
image: brand ...	imagen *(f)* de la marca
image: corporate ...	imagen *(f)* de la empresa
image: global ...	imagen *(f)* global
image: product ...	imagen *(f)* del producto
imaging	creación *(f)* de la imagen
imbalance: trade ...	desequilibrio *(m)* comercial
impact	impacto *(m)*
	efecto *(m)*
impact: profit ...	incidencia *(f)* sobre el beneficio
implement (to)	implementar
implementation: strategy ...	instrumentación *(f)* de estrategias
implication: profit ...	repercusión *(f)* sobre el beneficio
import: parallel ...	importación *(f)* paralela
improvement: job ...	mejora *(f)* del trabajo
improvement: product ...	mejora *(f)* del producto
improvement: profit ...	mejora *(f)* de la rentabilidad
impulse buying	compra *(f)* impulsiva
impulse goods	productos *(mpl)* de consumo por impulso
impulse sale	venta *(f)* por impulso
in-company	interno (de orden interno)
in-depth interview	entrevista *(f)* a fondo
in-house	interno (de orden interno)
in-plant training	formación *(m)* dentro de la empresa
incentive	incentivo *(m)*
incentive scheme	sistema *(m)* de incentivos
incentive wage	incentivo *(m)* (paga de)
incentive: financial ...	incentivo *(m)* financiero
incentive: group ...	incentivo *(m)* colectivo
incentive: tax ...	incentivo *(m)* fiscal
	incentivo *(m)* impositivo
income tax	impuesto *(m)* sobre la renta (IR)
income tax: negative	impuesto *(m)* sobre la renta negativo
income: disposable ...	ingresos *(mpl)* disponibles
income: real ...	ingresos *(mpl)* reales
increase: price ...	incremento *(m)* de precio
incremental	incremental
	marginal
incremental analysis	análisis *(m)* marginal

incremental cash flow	"cash flow " *(m)* marginal
index number	índice *(m)*
index: consumer price ...	índice *(m)* de precios de bienes al consumidor (IPC)
index: growth ...	índice *(m)* de crecimiento
index: retail price ... (RPI)	índice *(m)* de precios de venta al publico
indicator: performance ...	pauta *(f)* de rendimiento
indirect costs	coste *(m)* indirecto
indirect expenses	gastos *(mpl)* indirectos
indirect labour	mano *(f)* de obra indirecta
induction	iniciación *(f)* de empleados
industrial action	acción *(f)* laboral (huelga)
industrial democracy	democracia *(f)* industrial
industrial dispute	conflicto *(m)* laboral
industrial dynamics	dinámica *(f)* industrial
industrial engineering	ingeniería *(f)* industrial
industrial espionage	espionaje *(m)* industrial
industrial goods	bienes *(mpl)* industriales
industrial injury	accidente *(m)* laboral
industrial psychology	psicología *(f)* industrial
industrial relations	relaciones *(mpl)* industriales
industrial safety	seguridad *(f)* industrial
industrial security	contra-espionaje *(m)* industrial
industrial waste	residuos *(mpl)* industriales
industry: growth ...	industria *(f)* en desarrollo
industry: sunrise ...	industria *(f)* en crecimiento
	industria *(f)* floreciente
industry: sunset ...	industria *(f)* en declive
industry: training within ... (TWI)	formación *(f)* dentro de la empresa
inflation: cost-push ...	inflación *(f)* de costes
inflation: demand-pull ...	inflación *(f)* por exceso de demanda
inflationary pressure	presión *(f)* inflacionaria
informal organization	organización *(f)* informal
informatics	informática *(f)*
information flow	circulación *(f)* de datos
information handling	utilización *(f)* de datos
information network	red *(f)* de información
information processing	proceso *(m)* de datos
	sistematización *(f)* de datos
information retrieval	recuperación *(f)* de datos
information system	sistema *(m)* de información

information technology	informática *(f)*
	tecnología *(f)* de la información
information theory	teoría *(f)* de la información
information: computerized ... system (COINS)	sistema *(f)* mecanizado de información
information: control ...	información *(f)* de control
information: management ...	información *(f)* para la dirección
information: management ... system (MIS)	sistema *(m)* de información para la dirección
infrastructure	infraestructura *(f)*
injury: industrial ...	accidente *(m)* laboral
innovate (to)	innovar
innovative	innovador
	innovativo
input	entrada *(f)*
input (data)	entrar (datos)
input-output analysis	análisis *(m)* de entradas y salidas
input-output table	tabla *(f)* de entradas y salidas
input: computer ...	entrada *(f)* al ordenador
insider dealing	trato *(m)* con información privilegiada
insider trading	comercio *(m)* con información privilegiada
instruction: programmed ...	enseñanza *(f)* programada
intangible assets	activo *(m)* inmaterial
integrate (to)	integrar
integrated management system	sistema *(m)* integrado de gestión
integrated project management (IPM)	gestión *(f)* integrada
integrated: computer-... manufacturing (CIM)	fabricación *(f)* integrada por ordenador
integration	integración *(f)*
intensive production	producción *(f)* intensiva
intensive: labour ...	alta utilización de mano de obra
interactive	interactivo
interest: controlling ...	participación *(f)* mayoritaria
interest: job ...	interés *(m)* en el trabajo
interest: majority ...	participación *(f)* mayoritaria
interest: minority ...	participación *(f)* minoritaria
interest: vested ...	participación *(f)* propia
interface	"interface" *(f)*
interface (to)	poner interfaces
inter-firm comparison	comparación *(f)* entre empresas
interlocking directorate	dirección *(f)* entrelazada

internal audit	auditoría *(f)* interna
internal rate of return (IRR)	tasa *(f)* de rendimiento interno
internalize (to)	hacer propio
internationalize (to)	internacionalizar
interview: in-depth ...	entrevista *(f)* a fondo
intuitive management	gestión *(f)* intuitiva
inventory control	control *(m)* del inventario
inventory management	gestión *(f)* del inventario
inventory turnover	giro *(m)* de existencias
inventory: perpetual ...	inventario *(m)* perpetuo
investment analysis	análisis *(f)* de inversiones
investment appraisal	evaluación *(f)* de inversiones
investment bank	banco *(m)* de inversiones
investment budget	presupuesto *(m)* de inversiones
investment criteria	criterios *(mpl)* de inversión
investment goods	bienes *(mpl)* de inversión
investment management	gestión *(f)* de inversión
investment mix	combinación *(f)* de inversiones
investment policy	política *(f)* de inversiones
investment programme	programa *(m)* de inversión
investment: offshore ...	inversión *(f)* en el exterior
investment: return on ... (ROI)	rendimiento *(m)* de las inversiones
invisibles	partidas *(fpl)* invisibles
involvement: financial ...	relación *(f)* financiera
IPM (integrated project management)	gestión *(f)* integrada
IRR (internal rate of return)	tasa *(f)* de rendimiento interno
issue	emisión *(f)*
issue: rights ...	derecho *(m)* preferente de suscripción
issued capital	capital *(m)* emitido
IT (information technology)	informática *(f)*
iterative	iterativo
iterative process	proceso *(m)* iterativo

J

JIT (just in time)	justo a tiempo
job analysis	análisis *(m)* de puestos de trabajo
job assignment	asignación *(f)* de tareas
job breakdown	responsabilidades *(fpl)* del puesto
job challenge	incentivo *(m)* del puesto
job characteristics	características *(fpl)* del puesto
job classification	clasificación *(f)* de puestos de trabajo
job competence	aptitud *(f)* en el trabajo
job content	contenido *(m)* del puesto
job description	descripción *(f)* del trabajo
job design	objetivo *(m)* del trabajo
job enlargement	ampliación *(f)* de las tareas
job enrichment	valoración *(f)* del puesto
job evaluation	evaluación *(f)* de puestos de trabajo
	clasificación *(f)* de tareas
job expectations	expectativas *(fpl)* del puesto
job improvement	mejora *(f)* del trabajo
job interest	interés *(m)* en el trabajo
job performance	ejecución *(f)* del trabajo
	rendimiento *(m)* del trabajo
job profile	perfil *(m)* del puesto
job requirements	exigencias *(fpl)* del puesto
job rotation	rotación *(f)* de trabajos
job satisfaction	satisfacción *(f)* en el empleo
job security	seguridad *(f)* en el empleo
job security agreement	acuerdo *(m)* sobre seguridad en el empleo
job-sharing	reparto *(f)* del trabajo
job simplification	simplificación *(f)* del puesto
job specification	especificación *(f)* de un puesto de trabajo
job title	nombre *(m)* del puesto
job: off-the-... training	formación *(f)* fuera del trabajo
job: on-the-... training	formación *(f)* sobre la práctica
jobbing	agiotaje *(m)*
joint consultation	consultación *(f)* conjunta
joint negotiation	negociación *(f)* conjunta
joint representation	representación *(f)* conjunta
joint venture	aventura *(f)* común
	empresa *(f)* conjunta

joint-venture company	sociedad *(f)* en participación conjunta
junk bond	obligación *(f)* desvalorizada
	bono *(m)* basura
jurisdiction	zona *(f)* de responsabilidad
	zona *(f)* de competencia
just in time (JIT)	justo a tiempo

K

key buying factor factor *(m)* clave de compra
key success factor factor *(m)* clave de éxito
know-how pericia *(f)*

L

labour cost: unit	coste (m) unitario de la mano de obra
labour dispute	conflicto (m) laboral
labour-intensive	predominio (m) de la mano de obra
labour mobility	movilidad (f) laboral
labour relations	relaciones (fpl) laborales
	relaciones (fpl) empresariales
labour turnover	rotación (f) de personal
labour: direct ...	mano (f) de obra directa
labour: indirect ...	mano (f) de obra indirecta
labour: semi-skilled ...	mano (f) de obra semicualificada
labour: skilled ...	mano (f) de obra cualificada
labour: unit ... costs	coste (m) unitario de la mano de obra
labour: unskilled ...	trabajo (m) no cualificado
	mano (f) de obra no cualificada
lag	desfase (m)
lag response	respuesta (f) retrasada
lag: time ...	desfase (m) de tiempo
LAN (local area network)	red (f) de área local
landing: hard ...	entrada (f) en la depresión (economía)
landing: soft ...	evitación (f) de la depresión (economía)
language: common ...	lenguaje (m) común
language: computer ...	lenguaje (m) de ordenadores
language: machine ...	lenguaje (m) de máquinas
laptop computer	ordenador (m) portátil
laser printer	impresora (f) laser
lateral thinking	pensamiento (m) lateral
latest date	última fecha (f)
launch: product ...	lanzamiento (m) de un producto
launching	presentación (m)
launder (to)	blanquear (dinero)
laundering	blanqueado (m)
lay-off	despido (m) del trabajo
	cese (m) de empleo
lay off (to)	despedir (m) obreros
layout: functional ...	disposición (f) funcional
layout: plant ... study	estudio (m) de proyecto de una planta industrial
layout: process equipment ...	producción (f) agrupada
LBO (leveraged buyout)	LBO (compra (f) con apalancamiento)
LDC (less-developed country)	país (m) menos desarrollado

lead time	tiempo *(m)* de ejecución
leader merchandising	comercialización *(f)* con líder
	venta *(f)* de objetos-reclamos
leader: loss-...	venta *(f)* a pérdida
	venta *(f)* reclamo (con pérdida)
leader: market ...	líder *(m)* del mercado
leader: price ...	pauta *(f)* de precio
leader: team ...	jefe *(m)* de equipo
leadership	don *(m)* de mando
	jefatura *(f)*
leading edge	tecnología *(f)* punta
leak: security ...	divulgación *(f)* de información secreta
leap-frog (to)	saltar por encima de
learning curve	curva *(f)* de aprendizaje
learning: computer-aided ... (CAL)	aprendizaje *(m)* asistido por ordenador (CAL)
learning: distance ...	aprendizaje *(f)* a distancia
learning: programmed ...	enseñanza *(f)* programada
lease (to)	arrendar
lease or buy (to)	arrendar o comprar
lease-lend	préstamo *(m)* para arrendamiento
leasing	"leasing" *(m)*
	arrendamiento *(m)*
leasing: equipment ...	arrendamiento *(m)* de medios de producción
least-cost	coste *(m)* mínimo
less-developed country (LDC)	país *(m)* menos desarrollado
level playing-field	ventajas *(fpl)* iguales
level: wage ...	nivel *(m)* salarial
leverage	apalancamiento *(m)*
leveraged bid	licitación *(f)* con apalancamiento
leveraged buyout (LBO)	compra *(f)* con apalancamiento (LBO)
liabilities	pasivo *(m)*
	obligaciones *(fpl)*
	deudas *(fpl)*
liabilities: current ...	pasivo *(m)* circulante
	pasivo *(m)* real
liability: asset ... management	gestión *(f)* del circulante
liberalization	liberalización *(f)*
licence	licencia *(f)*
licence: under ...	bajo licencia
	por concesión
licensing: cross-...	concesión *(f)* recíproca de licencias

life cycle (*of a product*)	ciclo *(m)* de la vida (de un producto)
life: economic ...	vida *(f)* económica
life: product ...	vida *(f)* del producto
life: product ... expectancy	previsión *(f)* de vida del producto
life: shelf-...	vida *(f)* de un producto
lifestyle	estilo *(m)* de vida
limitation: damage ...	limitación *(f)* de daños
line and staff	estructura *(f)* jerárquica
line and staff organization	organización *(f)* jerárquica
line assistant	auxiliar *(m/f)* de línea
line authority	autoridad *(f)* lineal
line executive	directivo *(m)* de línea
line management	dirección *(f)* lineal
line manager	jefe *(m)* de línea
line of command	línea *(f)* de mando
line organization	organización *(f)* lineal
line production	producción *(f)* en cadena
line relations	relaciones *(fpl)* jerárquicas
line responsibility	responsabilidad *(f)* jerárquica
line: assembly ...	línea *(f)* de montaje
line: down the ...	subordinados *(mpl)*
line: flow ...	cadena *(f)* de producción
line: on ...	conectado (al ordenador)
line: product ...	serie *(m)* de productos
line: production ...	producción *(m)* en cadena
line: up the ...	más alto en la jerarquía
linear programming	programación *(f)* lineal
linear responsibility	responsabilidad *(f)* lineal
liquid assets	activo *(m)* disponible
	activo *(m)* líquido
liquidate (to)	liquidar
	saldar
	cancelar
liquidating: self-...	autoamortizable
liquidation	liquidación *(f)*
liquidity ratio	índice *(m)* de liquidez
listing	listado *(m)*
literate: computer-...	con conocimientos de informática
load factor	factor *(m)* de carga
	grado *(m)* de saturación
load: work ...	cantidad *(f)* de trabajo
loan capital	créditos *(mpl)* bancarios

loan stock	créditos *(mpl)* financieros a largo plazo
loan: parallel ...	créditos *(mpl)* paralelos
local area network (LAN)	red *(f)* de área local
local content rules	normas *(fpl)* de contenido local
localization	localización *(f)*
location: plant ...	localización *(f)* de la fábrica
lock-out	"lock out" *(m)*
	cierre *(m)* por los patrones
logistic process	proceso *(m)* logístico
logistical	logística
logistics	logística *(f)*
logo	logotipo *(m)*
	logo *(m)*
logo: company ...	logotipo *(m)* de la empresa
long-range planning	planificación *(f)* a largo plazo
long-term planning	planificación *(f)* a largo plazo
loop: closed ...	ciclo *(m)* cerrado
	lazo *(m)*
loss-leader	venta *(f)* reclamo (con pérdida)
loss-maker	producto *(m)* no rentable
loss: capital ...	pérdida *(f)* de capital
	minusvalía *(f)*
losses: bad-debt ...	deudas *(fpl)* incobrables
low-flier	ejecutivo *(m)* con potencial limitado
low-tech	tecnología *(f)* baja
loyalty: brand ...	lealtad *(f)* a la marca
lump sum	suma *(f)* global
	tanto *(m)* alzado

M

M & A (mergers and acquisitions)	F y A (fusiones y adquisiciones)
machine language	lenguaje *(m)* de máquina
macro	macro *(m)*
mailbox	buzón *(m)*
mail merge	sistema *(m)* automático de mailing personalizado
mail order	pedido *(m)* por correo
mail: direct ...	correo *(m)* directo
mail: electronic ... (e-mail)	correo *(m)* electrónico
mailing	publicidad *(f)* directa
	mailing *(m)*
mainframe	ordenador *(m)* central
	unidad *(f)* central
maintenance: planned ...	mantenimiento *(m)* planificado
maintenance: preventive ...	mantenimiento *(m)* prevenido
maintenance: productive ...	mantenimiento *(m)* productivo
maintenance: resale price ... (RPM)	mantenimiento *(m)* de precios de reventa
maintenance: total plant ...	mantenimiento *(m)* total de los talleres
majority interest	participación *(f)* mayoritaria
make-or-buy decision	opción *(f)* de fabricar o comprar
maker: market ...	creador *(m)* de mercado
malfunction	malfuncionamiento *(m)*
	fallo *(m)*
manage (to)	dirigir
	administrar
managed costs	costes *(mpl)* controlados
managed: system ... company	empresa *(f)* dirigida de forma sistematizada
management	dirección *(f)* general
	gestión *(f)* directiva
	organización *(f)*
	"management" *(m)*
	política *(f)* directiva
	gerencia *(f)*
	jefatura *(f)*
	dirección *(f)*
management accounting	contabilidad *(f)* gerencial
management audit	valoración *(f)* de gestión

management buyout (MBO)	compra *(f)* de una empresa por sus directivos
management by exception	dirección *(f)* por excepción
management by objectives (MBO)	dirección *(f)* por objetivos
management by walking around	gestión *(f)* de alta participación de los ejecutivos
management chart	esquema *(m)* de gestión
management competence	competencia *(f)* de la gerencia
management consultancy	consultoría *(f)* de empresas
management consultant	consultor *(m)* de empresas
management contract	contrato *(m)* de directivos
management development	formación *(f)* de la dirección
management game	simulación *(f)* de gestión
management information	información *(m)* para la gestión
management information system (MIS)	sistema *(m)* de información para la dirección
management potential	potencial *(m)* de directivos
management practices	normas *(fpl)* de gestión
management ratio	"ratios" *(m)* de gestión
management science	ciencia *(f)* de política directiva organización *(f)* científica del trabajo
management services	servicios *(mpl)* de dirección
management staff	personal *(m)* directivo
management style	estilo *(m)* de dirección
management succession planning	planificación *(f)* de sucesión de directivos
management system	dirección *(f)* sistematizada gestión *(f)* por sistemas
management team	equipo *(m)* de dirección
management technique	técnicas *(fpl)* de gestión
management theory	teoría *(f)* de política directiva
management training	formación *(f)* de directivos
management: asset ...	gestión *(f)* del activo
management: asset liability ...	gestión *(f)* del circulante
management: business ...	dirección *(f)* comercial
management: cash ...	gestión *(f)* del activo disponible
management: change ... (management of change)	gestión *(f)* de cambios
management: computerized ...	gestión *(f)* informatizada
management: credit ...	gestión *(f)* de crédito
management: crisis ...	gestión *(f)* de crisis
management: decentralized ...	gestión *(f)* descentralizada

management: departmental ...	gestión *(f)* por departamentos
management: divisional ...	gestión *(f)* por secciones
management: dynamic ... model	modelo *(m)* dinámico de administración
management: effective ...	dirección *(f)* eficaz
management: financial ...	dirección *(f)* financiera
management: functional ...	gestión *(f)* funcional
management: general ...	dirección *(f)* general
management: human resource ... (HRM)	gestión *(f)* de recursos humanos (GRH)
management: integrated ... system	sistema *(m)* integrado de gestión
management: integrated project ...	gestión *(f)* integrada de proyectos
management: intuitive ...	gestión *(f)* intuitiva
management: investment ...	gestión *(f)* de inversiones
management: line ...	dirección *(f)* lineal
management: manpower ...	administración *(f)* de mano de obra
management: market ...	gestión *(f)* comercial
management: matrix ...	organización *(f)* en matríz
management: middle ...	cuadros *(mpl)* medios
management: multiple ...	dirección *(f)* múltiple
management: office ...	dirección *(f)* administrativa
management: operating ...	dirección *(f)* operativa
management: operations ...	gestión *(f)* de operaciones
management: participative ...	dirección *(f)* participativa
management: personnel ...	dirección *(f)* de personal
management: physical distribution	gestión *(f)* de la distribución física
management: portfolio ...	gestión *(f)* de cartera (de valores mobiliarios)
management: product ...	gestión *(f)* del producto
management: production ...	administración *(f)* de producción
management: programmed ...	gestión *(f)* programada
management: project ...	gestión *(f)* de proyectos
management: quality ...	gestión *(f)* de la calidad
management: resource ...	gestión *(f)* de recursos
management: safety ...	gestión *(f)* de seguridad
management: sales ...	dirección *(f)* de ventas
management: scientific ...	organización *(f)* científica del trabajo
management: staff ...	dirección *(f)* del personal
management: supervisory ...	gestión *(f)* supervisora

management: systems ...	dirección (f) sistematizada
	gestión (f) por sistemas
management: time ...	organización (f) del tiempo
management: top ...	alta (f) dirección
management: top ... approach	enfoque (m) según la alta dirección
management: total quality ... (TQM)	gestión (f) total de la calidad
management: venture ...	gestión (f) de riesgos
manager	director (m)
	jefe (m)
	gerente (m)
manager: advertising ...	jefe (m) de publicidad
manager: area ...	director (m) de área
manager: assistant ...	director (m) adjunto
manager: assistant to ...	adjunto (m) al director
manager: brand ...	jefe (m) de marca
manager: departmental ...	director (m) de departamento
manager: deputy ...	subdirector (m)
manager: distribution ...	jefe (m) de distribución
manager: first-line ...	jefe (m) de primera línea
manager: general ...	director (m) general
manager: line ...	jefe (m) de línea
manager: marketing ...	director (m) de márketing
manager: operations ...	director (m) de operaciones
manager: owner-...	director (m) propietario
manager: personnel ...	director (m) de personal
manager: plant ...	jefe (m) de fábrica
manager: procurement ...	jefe (m) de compras
manager: product ...	jefe (m) de producto
manager: production ...	jefe (m) de producción
manager: project ...	director (m) de proyectos
manager: purchasing ...	jefe (m) de compras
manager: sales ...	jefe (m) de ventas
manager: works ...	jefe (m) de fábrica
managerial	directivo
	directorial
managerial control	control (m) directivo
managerial effectiveness	eficacia (f) directiva
managerial function	función (f) directiva
managerial grid	plantilla (f) de dirección
managerial structure	jerarquía (f) directiva
managerial style	estilo (m) directivo
managing director (MD)	director (m) gerente

managing director: **deputy ... ...**	director *(m)* gerente adjunto
manning	plantilla *(f)*
manpower	mano *(f)* de obra
manpower audit	revisión *(f)* de la mano de obra
manpower forecast	previsión *(f)* de mano de obra
manpower forecasting	previsión *(f)* de mano de obra
manpower management	administración *(f)* de mano de obra
manpower planning	planificación *(f)* de mano de obra
manpower resourcing	reclutamiento *(m)* y gestión *(f)* del personal
manpower: executive ... **strategy**	estrategia *(f)* de personal directivo
manufacturing capacity	capacidad *(f)* de fabricación
manufacturing control	control *(m)* de fabricación
manufacturing: computer- **aided ... (CAM)**	fabricación *(f)* asistida por ordenador (CAM)
manufacturing: computer- **integrated ... (CIM)**	fabricación *(f)* integrada por ordenador
manufacturing: economic ... **quantity**	tamaño *(m)* del lote económico de fabricación
margin of safety	margen *(m)* de seguridad
margin: gross ... (GM)	margen *(m)* bruto
margin: net ...	margen *(m)* neto
margin: profit ...	margen *(m)* de beneficios
marginal analysis	análisis *(f)* marginal
marginal costs	costes *(mpl)* marginales
marginal costing	contabilidad *(f)* marginal
	método *(m)* de costes marginales
marginal pricing	fijación *(f)* de precios marginales
marginalize (to)	marginar
	marginalizar
margins: hold ... (to)	mantener los márgenes *(mpl)*
mark-up	margen *(m)*
	sobre carga *(f)*
market appraisal	evaluación *(f)* del mercado
market awareness	percepción *(f)* del mercado
market drive	empuje *(m)* comercial
market dynamics	dinámica *(f)* del mercado
market exploration	investigación *(f)* del mercado
market forces	tendencias *(fpl)* del mercado
market forecast	previsión *(f)* del mercado
market intelligence	información *(f)* comercial

market leader	líder *(m)* del mercado
market maker	creador *(m)* de mercado
market management	gestión *(f)* comercial
market opportunity	oportunidad *(f)* comercial
market penetration	penetración *(f)* del mercado
market plan	plan *(m)* comercial
market planning	planificación *(f)* de mercados
market potential	potencial *(f)* del mercado
market price	precio *(m)* de mercado
market profile	perfil *(m)* del mercado
market prospects	perspectivas *(fpl)* comerciales
market rating	tipo *(m)* de mercado
market research	análisis *(m)* de mercados
market saturation	saturación *(f)* del mercado
market segmentation	fragmentación *(f)* de mercados
market segment	segmento *(m)* de mercado
market-sensitive	sensible al mercado
market share	parte *(f)* del mercado
market structure	estructura *(f)* del mercado
market study	estudio *(m)* del mercado
market survey	encuesta *(f)* sobre el mercado
market test	prueba *(f)* en el mercado
market thrust	empuje *(m)* comercial
market trend	tendencia *(f)* del mercado
market value	valor *(m)* de mercado
market: bear ...	mercado *(m)* con tendencia a bajar
market: bull ...	mercado *(m)* con tendencia a subir
market: buyers' ...	mercado *(m)* de oferta
market: commodity ...	mercado *(m)* de mercancías
market: down-...	mercado *(m)* abajo
market: equity ...	mercado *(m)* de acciones
market: financial ...	mercado *(m)* financiero
market: forward ...	mercado *(m)* futuro
market: fringe ...	mercado *(m)* marginal
market: grey ...	mercado *(m)* paralelo
market: mature ...	mercado *(m)* maduro
market: sellers' ...	mercado *(m)* de demanda
market: single ... (*of the EC*)	mercado *(m)* único (de la CE)
market: stock ...	bolsa *(f)*
market: target ...	mercado *(m)* objetivo
market: up-...	mercado *(m)* de élite
marketable	comercializable

marketing	comercialización *(f)* del producto
	márketing *(m)*
marketing appropriation	asignación *(f)* para márketing
marketing budget	presupuesto *(m)* de márketing
marketing department	departamento *(m)* de márketing
marketing manager	director *(m)* comercial
	director *(m)* de márketing
marketing mix	combinación *(f)* de medios de márketing
marketing research	investigación *(f)* de márketing
marketing strategy	estrategia *(f)* comercial
marketing: creative ...	márketing *(f)* creativo
marketing: direct ...	márketing *(m)* directo
marketing: global ...	márketing *(m)* global
marketing: test ...	prueba *(f)* del mercado
mass production	fabricación *(f)* en serie
mass: critical	masa *(f)* crítica
massage the figures (to)	disfrazar los resultados financieros
	maquillar las cifras
material: point-of-sale ...	material *(m)* publicitario en el punto de venta
materials handling	movimientos *(mpl)* de materiales
mathematical programming	programación *(f)* matemática
matrix management	organización *(f)* en matriz
matrix organization	organización *(f)* matricial
mature market	mercado *(m)* maduro
maximization: profit ...	maximización *(f)* de beneficios
maximize (to)	maximizar *(f)*
MBO (management buyout)	compra *(f)* de una empresa por sus directivos
MBO (management by objectives)	dirección *(f)* por ojetivos
MD (managing director)	director *(m)* gerente
mean	promedio *(m)*
	medio *(m)*
meaningful	significativo
measurement: clerical work... (CWM)	medición *(f)* del trabajo administrativo
measurement: performance ...	medición *(f)* del rendimiento
measurement: productivity ...	medición *(f)* de productividad
measurement: work ...	medición *(f)* del trabajo
media	medios *(mpl)* de comunicación

media analysis	análisis *(f)* de los medios de comunicación
media selection	selección *(f)* de medios de comunicación
media: advertising ...	medios *(mpl)* de publicidad
median	punto *(m)* medio
	mediana *(f)*
mediate (to)	mediar
mediation	mediación *(f)*
meeting: board ...	reunión *(f)* del consejo de dirección
memory	memoria *(f)*
memory: computer ...	memoria *(f)* de ordenador
memory: random-access ... (RAM)	memoria *(f)* RAM
memory: read-only ... (ROM)	memoria *(f)* ROM
merchandising	técnica *(f)* de mercancías
	comercialización *(f)* del producto
merchandising: leader ...	comercialización *(f)* con líder
	venta *(f)* de objetos-reclamo
	venta *(f)* a pérdida
merchant bank	banco *(m)* mercantíl
merge (to)	fusionarse
merger	fusión *(f)*
mergers and acquisitions (M & A)	fusiones *(fpl)* y adquisiciones *(fpl)*
merit rating	clasificación *(f)* por méritos
message: advertising ...	tema *(m)* publicitario
methectics	dinámica *(f)* de grupos
method: critical path (CPM)	método *(m)* del punto crítico
method: full cost ...	método *(m)* analítico de costes
method: points rating ...	método *(m)* de calificación por puntos
method: present value ...	método *(m)* del valor actual
method: random observation ...	método *(m)* de observación aleatoria
method: simplex ...	método *(m)* simplex
methods engineering	estudio *(m)* de métodos
methods study	estudio *(m)* de métodos
methods study department	departamento *(m)* de estudio de métodos
methods: organization and ... (O & M)	organización *(m)* y métodos *(mpl)* (O and M)
methods: time and ... study	estudio *(m)* de métodos y tiempo
micro	micro *(m)*
microchip	microchip *(m)*

middle management	cuadros *(mpl)* medios
milestone chart	diagrama *(m)*
minimize risks (to)	minimizar los riesgos
minimum wage	salario *(m)* mínimo
minority interest	participación *(f)* minoritaria
MIS (management information system)	sistema *(m)* de la información para la dirección
mission statement	declaración *(f)* de la misión
mission: corporate ...	misión *(f)* de la empresa
mission: economic ...	misión *(f)* económica
mix: investment ...	combinación *(f)* de inversiones
mix: marketing ...	combinación *(f)* de medios de márketing
mix: product ...	combinación *(f)* de productos
mix: promotional ...	combinación *(f)* de medios de promoción
mix: sales ...	combinación *(f)* de medios de venta
mobile phone	teléfono *(m)* portátil
mobile: upwardly ...	dinámico
	que mejora siempre en su posición social
mobility: staff ...	movilidad *(f)* del personal
mode	modo *(m)*
model	modelo *(m)*
model: accounting ...	modelo *(m)* de contabilidad
model: corporate ...	modelo *(m)* de la empresa
model: decision ...	modelo *(m)* de decisión
model: dynamic management ...	modelo *(m)* dinámico de administración
modem	módem *(m)*
modular production	producción *(f)* modular
modularity	modularidad *(f)*
monetarism	monetarismo *(m)*
monetary policy	política *(f)* monetaria
money supply	provisión *(f)* de fondos
	provisión *(f)* de dinero
monitor (to)	controlar
monitor performance (to)	controlar *(m)* el funcionamiento
monitoring: performance ...	control *(m)* del funcionamiento
moonlighting	pluriempleo *(m)*
morphological analysis	análisis *(m)* morfológico
motion economy	economía *(f)* de movimientos

motion study	estudio *(m)* de movimientos
motion: predetermined ... time system (PMTS)	sistema *(m)* de movimientos predeterminados (PMTS)
motion: time and ... study	estudio *(m)* de tiempos *(mpl)* y movimientos *(mpl)*
motivate (to)	motivar
motivation	motivación *(f)*
motivation: self-...	automotivación *(f)*
motivational	motivador
motivational research	investigación *(f)* de la motivación
motivator	motivador *(m)*
motivator: purchasing ...	motivo *(m)* de compra
motive: profit ...	motivación *(f)* por el beneficio
mouse	ratón *(m)*
MRA (multiple regression analysis)	análisis *(m)* de regresión múltiple
multi-access	entrada *(f)* múltiple
multimedia training	formación *(f)* multimedia
multiple management	dirección *(f)* múltiple
multiple regression analysis (MRA)	análisis *(m)* de regresión múltiple
mutual recognition	reconocimiento *(m)* mutuo

N

name of the game	las reglas *(fpl)* del juego
natural wastage	amortización *(f)* de puestos de trabajo por jubilación
need-to-know basis	información *(f)* de base (para un trabajo)
needs analysis	análisis *(m)* de necesidades
needs analysis: training	análisis *(m)* de necesidades de formación
negative cash flow	"cash flow" *(m)* negativo
	flujo *(m)* de caja negativo
negative income tax	impuesto *(m)* negativo sobre la renta
negotiate (to)	negociar
negotiation strategy	estrategia *(f)* de negociación
negotiation: joint ...	negociación *(f)* conjunta
net assets	activo *(m)* neto
net current assets	activo *(m)* circulante neto
net margin	margen *(m)* neto
net present value (NPV)	valor *(m)* neto actualizado
net profit	beneficio *(m)* neto
net worth	valor *(m)* neto
network (to)	relacionarse
network analysis	análisis *(m)* de la red
network: communications ...	red *(f)* de comunicaciones
network: distribution ...	red *(f)* de distribución
network: information ...	red *(f)* de información
network: wide area ... (WAN)	red *(f)* de área extendida
networking	explotación *(f)* de contactos profesionales
new-product development	desarrollo *(m)* de nuevos productos
new-product launching	lanzamiento *(m)* de nuevos productos
newly industrialized country (NIC)	país *(m)* de reciente industrialización
niche	nicho *(m)*
night shift	turno *(m)* de noche
non-durable goods	productos *(mpl)* perecederos
non-executive director	vocal *(m)*
	consejero *(m)*
non-linear programming	programación *(f)* no lineal
non-profit-making	no rentable
non-tariff barrier (NTB)	barrera *(f)* no arancelaria

non-verbal communication	comunicación *(f)* no verbal
NPV (net present value)	valor *(m)* neto actualizado
NTB (non-tariff barrier)	barrera *(f)* arancelaria
number-crunching	cálculos *(mpl)* básicos
numerical control	control *(m)* numérico

O

O & M (organization and methods)	organización *(f)* y métodos *(mpl)*
objective	objetivo *(m)*
objective-setting	definición *(f)* de objetivos
objective: company ...	objetivos *(mpl)* empresariales
objectives: management by ... (MBO)	dirección *(f)* por objetivos
objectives: overall company ...	objetivos *(mpl)* globales de la empresa
objectives: performance against ...	relación *(f)* resultados
	relación *(f)* objetivos
observation: random ... method	método *(m)* de observación aleatoria
obsolescence	obsolencia *(f)*
obsolescence: built-in ...	obsolencia *(f)* interna
obsolescence: planned ...	obsolencia *(f)* planificada
occupational hazard	riesgo *(m)* ocupacional
off line	fuera de línea
off-the-job training	formación *(f)* fuera del trabajo
office automation	ofimática *(f)*
office management	dirección *(f)* administrativa
office planning	planificación *(f)* de la oficina
office: branch ...	sucursal *(f)*
	delegación *(f)*
office: electronic ...	oficina *(f)* electrónica
office: head ...	central *(f)*
	oficina *(f)* principal
officer: training ...	jefe *(m)* de formación
official strike	huelga *(f)* oficial
offshore	extraterritorial *(f)*
offshore investment	inversión *(f)* en el exterior
on cost	gastos *(mpl)* generales
on line	conectado
	en línea
on stream	en curso *(m)*
on-the-job training	formación *(f)* sobre la práctica
one-off	fuera de gama *(f)* especial
ongoing	continuo
	ininterrumpido
open-ended	sin límites *(mpl)* fijos
open-plan	plan *(m)* abierto

open shop	empresa *(f)* de representación sindical múltiple
operating division	división *(f)* operacional
operating expenses	gastos *(mpl)* de operación
operating management	dirección *(f)* operacional
operational	operativo
operational planning	planificación *(f)* operacional
operational research (OR)	investigación *(f)* operativa
operations	operaciones *(fpl)*
operations analysis	análisis *(m)* de operación
operations audit	evaluación *(f)* de operaciones
operations breakdown	desglose *(m)* de operaciones
operations management	gestión *(f)* de operaciones
operations manager	director *(m)* de operaciones
operations planning	planificación *(f)* de operaciones
operations research (OR)	investigación *(f)* de operaciones
operations: ancillary ...	servicios *(mpl)* auxiliares
operations: hedging ...	operaciones *(fpl)* de cobertura
opinion survey	encuesta *(f)* de opiniones
opportunity costs	coste *(m)* de oportunidad
opportunity: equal employment ...	igualdad *(f)* de oportunidad en el empleo
opportunity: market ...	oportunidad *(f)* comercial
opportunity: window of ...	marco *(m)* de negociación favorable
optimization: profit ...	optimización *(f)* de beneficios
optimize (to)	optimizar
option: stock ...	opción *(f)* de compra de acciones
option: stock ... plan	plan *(m)* de compra opcional de acciones
option: traded ...	opción *(f)* de mercado
OR (operational research, operations research)	investigación *(f)* operativa
order: economic ... quantity	magnitud *(f)* económica de un pedido
organic growth	crecimiento *(m)* orgánico
organization and methods (O & M)	organización *(f)* y métodos *(mpl)* (O and M)
organization chart	organógrama *(m)*
organization culture	cultura *(f)* empresarial
organization planning	planificación *(f)* de la organización
organization structure	estructura *(f)* de la organización
organization theory	teoría *(f)* organizativa
organization: functional ...	organización *(f)* funcional
organization: informal ...	organización *(f)* informal
organization: line ...	organización *(f)* lineal

organization: line and staff ...	organización (f) jerárquica
organization: matrix ...	organización (f) matricial
organization: staff ...	organización (f) "staff"
organizational behaviour	conducta (f) del hombre en la organización
organizational change	transformación (f) de la organización
organizational development	desarrollo (m) de la organización
organizational effectiveness	eficacia (f) de la organización
organogram	organógrama (m)
orientation: consumer ...	orientación (f) del consumidor
orientation: customer ...	orientación (f) del consumidor
out of stock	agotado
out-house	externo
outlook: business ...	perspectiva (f) comercial
outlook: profit ...	perspectivas (fpl) de beneficio
outplacement	trabajo (m) externo
output	salida de datos (f)
	producción (f)
output budgeting	control (m) de producción
output: capital-... ratio	"ratio" (f) rendimiento
	"ratio" (f) capital
output: input-... analysis	análisis (m) de entradas y salidas
output: input-... table	tabla (f) de entradas y salidas
outside director	director (m) suplente
outsourcing	fuentes (fpl) externas de suministro
	aprovisionamiento (m) externo
overall company objectives	objetivos (mpl) globales de la empresa
overall company philosophy	filosofía (f) global de la empresa
overcapacity	sobre capacidad (f)
overcapitalized	sobrecapitalizado
overextended	sobre extendido
overheads	gastos (mpl) generales
overheads recovery	recuperación (f) de gastos generales
overheads: administrative ...	gastos (mpl) generales de administración
overheads: factory ...	gastos (mpl) generales de fabricación
overmanned	con exceso (m) de mano de obra
overmanning	exceso (m) de mano de obra
overprice (to)	sobrepreciar
overstaffed	exceso (m) de personal
overstaffing	exceso (m) de personal
overtime	horas (fpl) extras
owner-manager	director (m) propietario

P

P/E (price-earnings ratio)	PER
	tasa *(f)* de capitalización de beneficios (TCB)
P/V (profit-volume ratio)	tasa *(f)* de beneficio sobre ventas
package deal	oferta *(f)* combinada
package: software ...	paquete *(m)* de software
packaging	embalaje *(m)*
palletization	utilización *(f)* de 'pallets'
panel: consumers' ...	"panel" *(m)* de consumidores
par	par *(f)*
par: above ...	por encima de la par
par: at ...	a la par *(f)*
par: below ...	por debajo de la par
parachute: golden ...	indemnización *(f)* por despido
parallel currency	moneda *(f)* paralela
parallel import	importación *(f)* paralela
parallel loan	crédito *(m)* paralelo
parameter	parámetro *(m)*
parametric programming	programación *(f)* paramétrica
parent company	empresa *(f)* matriz
part-analysis training	formación *(f)* por etapas
part-time employment	trabajo *(m)* por horas
part-timer	empleado *(m)* a tiempo parcial
participation	participación *(f)*
participation: worker ...	participación *(f)* obrera
participative management	dirección *(f)* participativa
partner	socio *(m)*
partnership	sociedad *(f)*
party: working ...	comisión *(f)* investigadora
patent	patente *(f)*
patent trading	comercio *(m)* de patentes
pay-as-you-earn (PAYE)	retención *(f)* en origen del impuesto sobre la renta
pay-as-you-go	sistema *(m)* de retención de impuestos en origen
	anticipos *(mpl)* a cuenta
pay-off	rentabilidad *(f)*
	resultado *(m)*
pay pause	congelación *(f)* de salarios
pay talks	negociaciones *(fpl)* sobre salarios

pay: equal ...	igualdad *(f)* de salarios
pay: profit-related ...	salarios *(mpl)* vinculados a beneficios
pay: severance ...	indemnización *(f)* por despido
pay: take-home ...	salario *(m)* neto
payback	"payback" *(m)*
	reembolso *(m)*
payback period	período *(m)* de recuperación de la inversión
PAYE (pay-as-you-earn)	retención *(f)* en origen del impuesto sobre la renta
payment by results	destajo *(m)*
payment: *ex gratia* ...	paga *(f)* voluntaria
payroll	nómina *(f)*
PC (personal computer)	ordenador *(m)* personal
penetration pricing	fijación *(f)* de precios de penetración
penetration: market ...	penetración *(f)* del mercado
per-share earnings	beneficios *(mpl)* por acción
perform (to)	rendir
performance against objectives	relación *(f)* resultados/objetivos
performance appraisal	evaluación *(f)* del rendimiento
performance budgeting	control *(m)* de rendimiento
performance evaluation	evaluación *(f)* del rendimiento
performance indicator	pauta *(f)* de rendimiento
performance measurement	medición *(f)* del rendimiento
performance monitoring	control *(m)* del rendimiento
performance rating	valoración *(f)* del rendimiento
performance review	evaluación *(f)* del rendimiento
performance standard	estándar *(m)* de rendimiento
performance: earnings ...	rentabilidad *(f)*
performance: job ...	ejecución *(f)* del trabajo
	rendimiento *(m)* del trabajo
performance: monitor ... (to)	controlar el rendimiento
performance: product ...	rendimiento *(m)* del producto
performance: profit ...	rendimiento *(m)*
	beneficio *(m)*
performance: share price ...	comportamiento *(m)* del precio de la acción
performance: standard ...	estándares *(mpl)* de rendimiento
period: accounting	ejercicio *(m)* contable
peripheral equipment	equipo *(m)* periférico
peripherals	periféricos *(mpl)*
perpetual inventory	inventario *(m)* perpetuo
personal computer (PC)	ordenador *(m)* personal

personal growth	formación *(f)* personal
personalize (to)	personalizar
personnel department	departamento *(m)* del personal
personnel management	dirección *(f)* del personal
	administración *(f)* de personal
personnel manager	director *(m)* de personal
personnel policy	política *(f)* de personal
personnel rating	clasificación *(f)* de personal
personnel specification	especificación *(f)* de personal
PERT (programme evaluation and review technique)	técnica *(f)* de evaluación y revisión *(f)* de programas (PERT)
pertinence tree	árbol *(m)* de pertinencia
petty cash	caja *(f)* para gastos menores
petty expenses	gastos *(mpl)* menores
phase in (to)	añadir por etapas
phase out (to)	eliminar por etapas
philosophy: company ...	filosofía *(f)* de la empresa
physical distribution management	gestión *(f)* de la distribución física
picket	piquete *(m)* (de huelga)
pie chart	gráfico *(m)* redondo
piecework	trabajo *(m)* a destajo
piggyback	apoyarse para una actividad en una estructura existente
pilot production	producción *(f)* piloto
pilot run	serie *(f)* piloto
pioneer (to)	iniciar
pioneer product	producto *(m)* pionero
piracy	piratería *(f)*
plan	plan *(m)*
plan: action ...	plan *(m)* de acción
plan: departmental	plan *(m)* departamental
plan: market ...	plan *(m)* comercial
plan: open-...	plan *(m)* abierto
plan: share-of-production ...	plan *(m)* de participación en la producción
plan: stock option ...	plan *(m)* de compra opcional de acciones
plan: tactical ...	plan *(m)* táctico
planned maintenance	mantenimiento *(m)* planificado
planned obsolescence	obsolencia *(f)* planificada
planning	planificación *(f)*

planning department	departamento *(m)* de planificación
planning, programming, budgeting system (PPBS)	sistema *(m)* de programación y planificación de presupuesto
planning: career ...	planificación *(f)* del desarrollo profesional
planning: company ...	planificación *(f)* empresarial
planning: contingency ...	plan *(m)* para lo imprevisto
planning: corporate ...	planificación *(f)* empresarial
planning: distribution ...	planificación *(f)* de distribución
planning: financial ...	planificación *(f)* financiera
planning: forward ...	planificación *(f)* a largo plazo
planning: human resource ... (HRP)	planificación *(f)* de recursos humanos
planning: long-range ...	planificación *(f)* a largo plazo
planning: long-term ...	planificación *(f)* a largo plazo
planning: management succession ...	planificación *(f)* de sucesión de directivos
planning: manpower ...	planificación *(f)* de la mano de obra
planning: market ...	planificación *(f)* de mercados
planning: office ...	planificación *(f)* de oficinas
planning: operational ...	planificación *(f)* operacional
planning: organization ...	planificación *(f)* de la organización
planning: product ...	planificación *(f)* del producto
planning: production ...	planificación *(f)* de la producción
planning: production ... and control	planificación *(f)* y control *(m)* de la producción
planning: profit ...	planificación *(f)* de beneficios
planning: project ...	planificación *(f)* de proyectos
planning: sales ...	planificación *(f)* de ventas
planning: short-term ...	planificación *(f)* a corto plazo
planning: staff ...	planificación *(f)* de personal
planning: strategic ...	planificación *(f)* estratégica
planning: systems ...	planificación *(f)* de sistemas
plant bargaining	negociación *(f)* a nivel de fábrica
plant capacity	capacidad *(f)* de planta
plant hire	alquiler *(m)* de equipo
plant layout study	estudio *(m)* de proyecto de una planta industrial
plant location	localización *(f)* de la fábrica
plant maintenance	mantenimiento *(m)* de la planta
plant maintenance: total	mantenimiento *(m)* total del taller
plant manager	jefe *(m)* de fábrica

player: team ...	jugador *(m)* de equipo
playing: role ...	desempeño *(m)* de funciones
ploughback	autofinanciación *(f)*
	beneficios *(mpl)* reinvertidos
PMTS (predetermined motion time system)	sistema *(f)* de movimientos predeterminados (PMTS)
point of sale (POS)	lugar *(m)* de venta
point-of-sale advertising (POS)	publicidad *(f)* en el lugar de venta (PLV)
point-of-sale material	material *(m)* de publicidad en el lugar de venta
point: break-even ...	punto *(m)* de equilibrio
	umbral *(m)* de rentabilidad
point: unique selling ... (USP)	punto *(m)* único de venta
points-rating method	método *(m)* de calificación por puntos
poison pill	falsear la situación de la empresa para que no se venda
policy execution	ejecución *(f)* de la política
policy formulation	formulación *(f)* de la política
policy statement	establecimiento *(m)* de la política
policy: business ...	política *(f)* comercial
policy: company ...	política *(f)* de la empresa
policy: distribution ...	política *(f)* de distribución
policy: dividend ...	política *(f)* de dividendos
policy: investment ...	política *(f)* de inversión
policy: personnel ...	política *(f)* de personal
policy: pricing ...	política *(f)* de precios
policy: promotional ...	política *(f)* de promoción
policy: remittance ...	política *(f)* de remesas
policy: sales ...	política *(f)* de ventas
policy: selling ...	política *(f)* de ventas
policy: wage ...	política *(f)* salarial
pooling arrangements	acuerdos *(mpl)* consorciales
poor: cash ...	falta *(f)* de liquidez
	escasez *(f)* de tesorería
portfolio management	gestión *(f)* de cartera (de valores mobiliarios)
portfolio selection	selección *(f)* de cartera
portfolio: asset ...	cartera *(f)* de valores
portfolio: balanced ...	cartera *(f)* equilibrada
portfolio: brand ...	cartera *(f)* comercial
	fondo *(m)* de comercio
portfolio: business ...	cartera *(f)* de negocios

portfolio: product ...	cartera *(f)* de productos
portfolio: stock ...	cartera *(f)* de acciones
POS (point of sale)	punto *(m)* de venta
position: competitive ...	situación *(f)* competitiva
position: financial ...	situación *(f)* financiera
positioning	posicionamiento *(m)*
positioning: brand ...	posicionamiento *(m)* de marcas comerciales
positive discrimination	discriminación *(f)* positiva
potential buyer	comprador *(m)* potencial
potential: development ...	potencial *(m)* de explotación
potential: growth ...	potencial *(m)* de crecimiento
potential: management ...	potencial *(m)* de directivos
potential: market ...	potencial *(m)* de mercado
potential: sales ...	potencial *(m)* de ventas
power: earning ...	capacidad *(f)* de beneficio
PPBS (planning, programming, budgeting system)	sistema *(m)* de programación y planificación de presupuestos
PR (public relations)	relaciones *(fpl)* públicas
practices: management ...	prácticas *(fpl)* de gestión
practices: restrictive ... (*industrial*)	prácticas *(fpl)* restrictivas
practices: restrictive ... (*legal*)	prácticas *(fpl)* restrictivas
predator	predador *(m)*
predetermined motion time system (PMTS)	sistema *(m)* de movimientos predeterminados
pre-emptive bid	licitación *(f)* preferente
premium	prima *(f)*
premium bonus	prima *(f)* por rendimiento
present value method	método *(m)* del valor actual
president	presidente *(m)*
president: vice-...	vicepresidente *(m)*
pressure	presión *(f)*
prestige pricing	fijación *(f)* de precio de prestigio
preventive maintenance	mantenimiento *(m)* preventivo
price (to)	fijar el precio
price-cutting	abaratamiento *(m)* de precios
price determination	fijación *(f)* de precios
price differential	escalado *(m)* de precios
price discrimination	discriminación *(f)* de precios
price-earnings ratio (P/E)	PER tasa *(f)* de capitalización de beneficios (TCB)

price escalation	escalada *(f)* de precios
price-fixing	fijación *(f)* de precios
price increase	aumento *(m)* de precio
price index	índice *(m)* de precios
price index: consumer	índice *(m)* de precios al consumidor
price index: retail ... ... (RPI)	índice *(m)* de precios al detalle
price leader	pauta *(f)* de precio
price range	escala *(f)* de precios
price structure	estructura *(f)* de precios
price: competitive ...	precio *(m)* competitivo
price: differential ...	diferencia *(f)* de precios
price: market ...	precio *(m)* de mercado
price: resale ... maintenance (RPM)	mantenimiento *(m)* del precio de venta mantenimiento *(m)* del precio al detalle
price: spot ...	precio *(m)* al contado
price: standard ...	precio *(m)* estándar
prices: cut ... (to)	abaratar los precios *(mpl)*
pricing	precio *(m)* en lugar de venta
pricing policy	política *(f)* de precios
pricing strategy	estrategia *(f)* de precios
pricing: differential ...	escalado *(m)* de precios
pricing: marginal ...	determinación *(f)* del precio marginal
pricing: penetration ...	política *(f)* de fijación de precios de penetración
pricing: prestige ...	política *(f)* de fijación de precios para dar prestigio al producto
pricing: transfer ...	fijación *(f)* de precios de transferencia
primary commodity	producto *(m)* de primera necesidad
print out (to)	imprimir (informática)
printout	impresión *(f)* de salida
prioritize (to)	establecer prioridades
private enterprise	empresa *(f)* privada
privatization	privatización *(f)*
privatize (to)	privatizar
pro rata	pro rata
proactive	proactivo
proactive strategy	estrategia *(f)* proactiva
probability theory	teoría *(f)* de la probabilidad
problem analysis	análisis *(m)* del problema
problem area	zona *(f)* problemática
problem assessment	evaluación *(f)* de problemas
problem solving	resolución *(f)* de problemas

procedural	procedimental
procedure	procedimiento *(m)*
	método *(m)* de trabajo
procedure: administrative control ...	proceso *(m)* de control administrativo
procedure: grievance ...	tramitación *(f)* de quejas
procedures: systems and ...	procedimientos *(mpl)* administrativos
process (to)	procesar (informática)
process control	control *(m)* del proceso
process costing	contabilidad *(f)* de producción
process equipment layout	producción *(f)* agrupada
process: decision ...	procedimientos *(mpl)* de decisión
process: flow ... chart	diagrama *(m)* de flujos del proceso
process: logistic ...	proceso *(m)* logístico
process: production ...	proceso *(m)* de producción
processing: automatic data ... (ADP)	proceso *(m)* automático de datos
processing: batch ...	elaboración *(f)* por lotes
processing: central ... unit	unidad *(f)* de proceso central
processing: data ...	procesado *(m)* de datos
processing: electronic ...	procesado *(m)* electrónico
processing: electronic data ... (EDP)	procesado *(m)* electrónico de datos
processing: information ...	procesado *(m)* de datos
	sistematización *(f)* de datos
processing: word ...	procesador *(m)* de textos (PT)
processor: word ... (WP)	procesador *(m)* de textos
procurement	obtención *(f)*
procurement manager	jefe *(m)* de abastecimiento
product abandonment	abandono *(m)* del producto
product advertising	publicidad *(f)* de productos
product analysis	análisis *(m)* del producto
product area	sector *(m)* de productos
product conception	concepción *(f)* de productos
product costing	evaluación *(f)* del coste de productos
product design	diseño *(m)* del producto
product development	desarrollo *(m)* de productos
product differentiate (to)	diferenciar productos
product differentiation	diferenciación *(f)* entre productos
product diversification	diversificación *(f)* de productos
product dynamics	dinámica *(f)* de productos
product engineering	estudio *(m)* de productos
product generation	creación *(f)* de productos

product group	grupo *(m)* de productos
product image	imagen *(m)* del producto
product improvement	mejora *(f)* del producto
product introduction	introducción *(f)* de un producto
product launch	lanzamiento *(m)* de un producto
product life	ciclo *(m)* de la vida de un producto
product life cycle	ciclo *(m)* de vida de un producto
product life expectancy	previsión *(f)* de vida de un producto
product line	serie *(f)* de productos
product management	gestión *(f)* de producto
product manager	jefe *(m)* de productos
product mix	combinación *(f)* de productos
product performance	rendimiento *(m)* del producto
product planning	planificación *(f)* del producto
product portfolio	cartera *(f)* de productos
product profile	perfil *(m)* del producto
product profitability	rentabilidad *(f)* del producto
product range	gama *(f)* de productos
product reliability	fiabilidad *(f)* de un producto
product research	investigación *(f)* de productos
product strategy	estrategia *(f)* de productos
product testing	"test" *(m)* de productos
product: by-...	subproducto *(m)*
	derivado *(m)*
product: core ...	producto *(m)* clave
product: new-... development	desarrollo *(m)* de nuevos productos
product: pioneer ...	inovación *(f)*
product: star ...	producto *(m)* estrella
production	producción *(f)*
production complex	parque *(m)* de producción
production control	control *(m)* de producción
production costs	costes *(mpl)* de producción
production director	director *(m)* de producción
production engineering	técnicas *(fpl)* de producción
production line	producción *(f)* en cadena
production management	administración *(f)* de producción
production manager	jefe *(m)* de producción
production planning	planificación *(f)* de la producción
production planning and control	planificación *(f)* y control *(m)* de la producción
production process	proceso *(m)* de producción
production run	fase *(f)* de ejecución
production schedule	programa *(m)* de producción

production scheduling	programación *(f)* de la producción
production standard	estándares *(mpl)* de la producción
production target	objetivo *(m)* de producción
production technique	técnica *(f)* de producción
production: batch ...	producción *(f)* por lotes
production: continuous-flow ...	producción *(f)* contínua
production: factors of ...	elementos *(mpl)* de producción
production: flow ...	fabricación *(f)* en cadena
production: intensive ...	producción *(f)* intensiva
production: line ...	producción *(f)* en cadena
production: mass ...	fabricación *(f)* en serie
production: modular ...	producción *(f)* modular
production: pilot ...	producción *(f)* piloto
production: share of ... plan	plan *(m)* de participación en la producción
productive maintenance	mantenimiento *(m)* productivo
productivity	productividad *(f)*
productivity agreement	convenio *(m)* de productividad
productivity bargaining	negociación *(f)* de productividad
productivity campaign	campaña *(f)* de productividad
productivity drive	campaña *(f)* de productividad
productivity measurement	medición *(f)* de productividad
professionalization	profesionalización *(f)*
profile: acquisition ...	perfil *(m)* de adquisición
profile: company ...	perfil *(m)* de la empresa
profile: customer ...	perfil *(m)* del consumidor
profile: job ...	perfil *(m)* del puesto
profile: product ...	perfil *(m)* del producto
profile: risk ...	perfil *(m)* de riesgos
profit	beneficio *(m)*
profit centre	centro *(m)* de beneficio
profit centre accounting	contabilidad *(f)* por centros de beneficio
profit-factor analysis	análisis *(m)* de centros de beneficio
profit goal	objetivo *(m)* de beneficio
profit impact	incidencia *(f)* sobre el beneficio
profit implication	repercusión *(f)* sobre el beneficio
profit improvement	mejora *(f)* de la rentabilidad
profit margin	margen *(m)* de beneficios
profit maximization	maximización *(f)* de beneficios
profit motive	motivación *(f)* por el beneficio
profit optimization	optimización *(f)* de beneficios
profit outlook	perspectivas *(fpl)* de beneficio

profit performance	rendimiento *(m)*
	beneficio *(m)*
profit planning	planificación *(f)* de beneficios
profit projection	proyección *(f)* del beneficio
profit-related pay	pago *(m)* de beneficios
profit-sharing	participación *(f)* en los beneficios
profit strategy	estrategia *(f)* de beneficios
profit target	objetivo *(m)* de beneficio
profit-volume ratio (P/V)	tasa *(f)* de beneficio sobre ventas
profit: cost-volume-... analysis	análisis *(m)* de coste volumen y beneficio
profit: distributed ...	distribución *(f)* de beneficio
profit: gross ...	beneficio *(m)* bruto
profit: net ...	beneficio *(m)* neto
profit: undistributed ...	beneficio *(m)* no distribuido
profitability	rentabilidad *(f)*
profitability analysis	análisis *(m)* de rentabilidad
profitability: product ...	rentabilidad *(f)* del producto
profits tax	impuesto *(m)* sobre beneficios
program (to)	programar
program: computer ...	programa *(m)* de ordenador
programme	programa *(m)*
programme (to)	programar *(m)*
programme budgeting	sistema *(m)* de presupuestos programados
programme evaluation and review technique (PERT)	método *(m)* PERT
	técnica *(f)* de evaluación de programas y revisión
programme package	sistema *(m)* de programación
	paquete *(m)* de sistemas
programme: development ...	programa *(m)* de desarrollo
programme: investment ...	programa *(m)* de inversión
programme: trading ...	programa *(m)* de comercialización
programmed instruction	enseñanza *(f)* programada
programmed learning	enseñanza *(f)* programada
programmed management	gestión *(f)* programada
programmer: computer ...	programador *(m)* informático
programming: computer ...	programación *(f)*
programming: dynamic ...	programación *(f)* dinámica
programming: linear ...	programación *(f)* lineal
programming: mathematical ...	programación *(f)* matemática
programming: non-linear ...	programación *(f)* no lineal
programming: parametric ...	programación *(f)* paramétrica

programming: scientific ...	programación *(f)* científica
progress control	control *(m)* de la marcha del trabajo
progress: work in ...	trabajo *(m)* en proceso
progression: salary ... curve	curva *(f)* de incremento de salarios
project analysis	estudio *(m)* de proyectos
project assessment	evaluación *(f)* de proyectos
project management	gestión *(f)* de proyectos
project manager	director *(m)* de proyecto
project planning	planificación *(f)* de proyectos
project: capital ... evaluation	evaluación *(f)* de proyectos de inversión
project: chunk a ... (to)	dividir un proyecto en partes
project: integrated ... management (IPM)	gestión *(f)* de proyectos integrales (IPM)
projection	proyección *(f)*
projection: profit ...	proyección *(f)* del beneficio
promotion (*personnel*)	promoción *(f) (del personal)*
promotion: executive ...	ascenso *(m)* de directivos
promotion: sales	promoción *(f)* de ventas
promotional	promocional
promotional mix	combinación *(f)* de medios de promoción
promotional policy	política *(f)* de promoción
proposal: value ...	propuesta *(f)* de valoración
proposition: business	propuesta *(f)* de negocios
proposition: unique selling ... (USP)	argumento *(m)* de venta único
prospective customer	cliente *(m)* potencial
prospects: market ...	perspectivas *(fpl)* comerciales
protection: consumer ...	protección *(f)* del consumidor
protection: data ...	protección *(f)* de datos
protection: turf ...	protección *(f)* del territorio
psychology: industrial ...	psicología *(f)* industrial
psychometric testing	prueba *(f)* psicométrica
public enterprise	empresa *(f)* pública
public: go ... (to)	salir a bolsa
public relations (PR)	relaciones *(fpl)* públicas
public utility	empresa *(f)* de utilidad pública
publicly listed company	empresa *(f)* cotizada en bolsa
publishing: desk-top ...	autoedición *(f)*
purchasing	compras *(fpl)*
purchasing manager	jefe *(m)* de compras
purchasing motivator	motor *(m)* de compra

purchasing power	poder *(m)* adquisitivo
purchasing power parity	paridad *(f)* de poder adquisitivo

Q

QC (quality control)	control *(m)* de calidad
quality assessment	valoración *(f)* de la calidad
quality assurance	aseguramiento *(m)* de la calidad
quality circle	círculo *(m)* de calidad
quality control (QC)	control *(m)* de calidad
quality control: total ... ... (TQC)	gestión *(f)* total de calidad
quality management	gestión *(f)* de calidad
quality management: total .. (TQM)	gestión *(f)* total de calidad
quantitative analysis	análisis *(m)* cuantitativo
quantity: break-even ...	cantidad *(f)* necesaria para alcanzar el punto de equilibrio
quantity: economic batch ...	tamaño *(m)* del lote económico
quantity: economic manufacturing ...	tamaño *(m)* del lote económico de fabricación
quantity: economic order ...	cantidad *(f)* necesaria para alcanzar el punto económico de un pedido
queuing theory	teoría *(f)* de colas
	teoría *(f)* de líneas de espera
quick assets	activo *(m)* disponible a corto plazo
	fondos *(mpl)*
quick fix	arreglo *(m)* rápido
	(poner) un parche
quota: sales ...	cupo *(m)* de ventas
quoted company	empresa *(f)* cotizada en bolsa
quotient	cociente *(m)*

R

R & D (research and development)	investigación (f) y desarrollo (m)
raid a company (to)	hacer la compra (f) hóstil de acciones de una empresa
raider: corporate ...	predador (m)
raising: capital ...	movilización (f) de fondos
RAM (random-access memory)	RAM (memoria (f) RAM)
random access	entrada (f) aleatoria
random-access memory (RAM)	RAM (memoria (f) RAM)
random observation method	método (m) de observación aleatoria
random sampling	muestreo (m) al azar
range: price ...	escala (f) de precios
range: product ...	gama (f) de productos
ranking	clasificación (f)
rat race	(estar) en la rueda
rate of return	tasa (f) de rendimiento
rate of return: internal ... ... (IRR)	tasa (f) de rendimiento interno
rate: bank ...	tipo (m) bancario
rate: base ...	tasa (f) base
	tipo (m) base
rate: forward ...	cambio (m) a plazo
rate: going ...	tasa (f) en vigor
	tipo (m) vigente
rating: credit ...	clasificación (f) de solvencia
rating: market ...	tipo (m) de mercado
rating: merit ...	clasificación (f) por méritos
rating: performance ...	valoración (f) del rendimiento
rating: personnel ...	clasificación (f) de personal
rating: points-... method	método (m) de clasificación por puntos
ratio: accounting ...	"ratio" (m) contable
ratio: administration-production ...	"ratio" (m) administración producción
ratio: capital-output ...	"ratio" (m) rendimiento/capital
ratio: cash ...	proporción (f) de valores disponibles
ratio: cover ...	proporción (f) de cobertura
ratio: current ...	índice (m) de liquidez
ratio: debt ...	índice (m) de deuda

ratio: debt-equity ...	"ratio" *(m)* deuda-activo
ratio: financial ...	coeficiente *(m)* financiero
ratio: gearing ...	"ratio" *(m)* de endeudamiento
ratio: liquidity ...	índice *(m)* de liquidez
ratio: management ...	"ratio" *(m)* de gestión
ratio: price-earnings ... (P/E)	PER
	tasa *(f)* de capitalización de beneficios (TCB)
ratio: profit-volume ... (P/V)	tasa *(f)* de beneficio sobre ventas
rationale	razón *(f)* fundamental
	la lógica *(f)*
rationalization	racionalización *(f)*
rationalize (to)	organizar lógicamente
	simplificar
rationing: capital ...	racionamiento *(m)* de capital
re-evaluation of assets	revalorización *(f)* del activo
re-image (to)	cambiar la imagen *(f)*
reach a deal (to)	llegar a un acuerdo
reactive	reactivo *(m)*
reactive strategy	estrategia *(f)* reactiva
read-only memory (ROM)	memoria *(f)* ROM (memoria de lectura)
real income	ingresos *(mpl)* reales
real time	tiempo *(m)* real
realize (to) *(profit)*	alcanzar *(beneficio)*
recentring	recentrar
recognition: brand ...	identificación *(f)* de la marca
recognition: mutual ...	reconocimiento *(m)* mutuo
reconfiguration	reconfiguración *(f)*
reconstruction: company ...	reconstitución *(f)* de la empresa
record: track ...	registro *(m)* de antecedentes *(mpl)*
recovery of expenses	recuperación *(f)* de gastos
recovery: overhead ...	recuperación *(f)* de gastos generales
recruit (to)	reclutar
recruitment	reclutamiento *(m)*
recycle (to)	reciclar
recycling	reciclaje *(m)*
redeploy (to)	desplazar
redeployment	desplazamiento *(m)*
reduction: cost ...	reducción *(f)* de costes
reduction: variety ...	reducción *(f)* de la variedad
redundancy	desempleo *(m)*
	exceso *(m)* de mano de obra

refocusing	reenfocado *(m)*
registered trademark	marca *(f)* registrada
regression analysis	análisis *(m)* de regresión
regression analysis: multiple ... ... (MRA)	análisis *(m)* de regresión multiple
regulate (to)	regular
regulation	reglamento *(m)*
	regulación *(f)*
reinvent the wheel (to)	reinventar la rueda
relations: business ...	relaciones *(fpl)* comerciales
relations: employee ...	relaciones *(fpl)* con el personal
relations: external ...	relaciones *(fpl)* externas
relations: functional ...	relaciones *(fpl)* funcionales
relations: human ...	relaciones *(fpl)* humanas
relations: industrial ...	relaciones *(fpl)* empresariales
	relaciones *(fpl)* industriales
relations: labour ...	relaciones *(fpl)* laborales
	relaciones *(fpl)* empresariales
relations: line ...	relaciones *(fpl)* de línea
	jerarquización *(f)*
relations: public ... (PR)	relaciones *(fpl)* públicas
reliability	fiabilidad *(f)*
reliability: product ...	fiabilidad *(f)* del producto
relief: tax ...	desgravación *(f)* fiscal
remittance policy	política *(f)* de remesas
remuneration	remuneración *(f)*
remuneration: executive ...	remuneración *(f)* de ejecutivos
reorganization	reorganización *(f)*
replacement costs	coste *(m)* de sustitución
representation: analog(ue) ...	representación *(f)* análoga
representation: joint ...	representación *(f)* conjunta
representation: worker ...	representación *(f)* del personal
representative: trade union ...	representante *(m/f)* sindical
requirements: job ...	exigencias *(fpl)* del puesto
rerun (to)	repetir la ejecución
resale price maintenance (RPM)	mantenimiento *(m)* del precio de venta
	mantenimiento *(f)* del precio al detalle
research and development (R & D)	investigación *(f)* y desarrollo *(m)*
research department	departamento *(m)* de investigación
research: advertising ...	investigación *(f)* publicitaria
research: blue-sky ...	investigación *(f)* de base

research: consumer ...	investigación *(f)* de consumidores
research: desk ...	investigación *(f)* de gabinete
research: economic ...	investigación *(f)* económica
research: field ...	investigación *(f)* de campo
research: market ...	investigación *(f)* de mercado
research: marketing ...	investigación *(f)* de márketing
research: motivational ...	investigación *(f)* de la motivación
research: operational ... (OR)	investigación *(f)* operativa (OR)
research: operations ... (OR)	investigación *(f)* de operaciones (OR)
research: product ...	investigación *(f)* de productos
reserve: contingency ...	reserva *(f)* para imprevistos
resistance: consumer ...	resistencia *(f)* del consumidor
resource allocation	asignación *(f)* de recursos
resource appraisal	evaluación *(f)* de recursos
resource management	gestión *(f)* de recursos
resourcing: manpower ...	reclutamiento *(m)* y gestión *(f)* de personal
resourcing: staff ...	recursos *(mpl)* de personal
response: anticipatory ...	respuesta *(f)* anticipada
	conducta *(f)* anticipada
response: lag ...	respuesta *(f)* retrasada
responsibilities: allocation of ...	asignación *(f)* de responsabilidades
responsibility accounting	responsabilidad *(f)* contable
responsibility centre	centro *(m)* de responsabilidad
responsibility: functional ...	responsabilidad *(f)* funcional
responsibility: linear ...	responsabilidad *(f)* lineal
responsive: consumer-...	de respuesta *(f)* al consumidor
restriction: trade ...	restricción *(f)* comercial
	cupo *(m)* comercial
restrictive practices (*industrial*)	prácticas *(fpl)* restrictivas
restrictive practices (*legal*)	prácticas *(fpl)* restrictivas
restructure (to)	reestructurar *(m)*
restructuring	re-estructuración *(f)*
results: payment by ...	destajo *(m)*
retail price index (RPI)	índice *(m)* de precios al consumidor
retained profits	beneficios *(mpl)* retenidos
retire (to)	jubilarse
retirement	retiro *(m)*
	jubilación *(f)*
retirement: early ...	jubilación *(f)* anticipada
retraining	reeducación *(f)* profesional
retrieval: data ...	recuperación *(f)* de datos
retrieval: information ...	recuperación *(f)* de datos

return	beneficio *(m)*
	rendimiento *(m)*
return on assets	rendimiento *(m)* del activo
return on capital	rendimiento *(m)* del capital
	renta *(f)* del capital
return on capital employed (ROCE)	rendimiento *(m)* del capital invertido
return on equity (ROE)	rendimiento *(m)* de las acciones
return on investment (ROI)	rendimiento *(m)* de las inversiones
	rentabilidad *(f)* de las inversiones
return on sales	rentabilidad *(f)* de ventas
return: fair ...	beneficio *(m)* justo
	rendimiento *(m)* justo
return: internal rate of ... (IRR)	tasa *(f)* de rendimiento interno
return: rate of ...	tasa *(f)* de rendimiento
revaluation of assets	revalorización *(f)* del activo
revenue: average ...	ingresos *(mpl)* medios
review (to)	revisar
review: financial ...	análisis *(m)* financiero
review: performance ...	revisión *(f)* del comportamiento
review: salary ...	revisión *(f)* salarial
revolving credit	crédito *(m)* abierto
rich: cash-...	exceso *(m)* de tesorería
rights issue	derecho *(m)* preferente de suscripción
risk analysis	análisis *(m)* de riesgos
risk assessment	apreciación *(f)* de riesgos
risk capital	capital *(m)* de riesgo
risk management	gestión *(f)* de riesgos
risk profile	perfil *(m)* de riesgos
risks: minimize ... (to)	minimizar los riesgos
robot	robot *(m)*
robotics	robótica *(f)*
robotize (to)	robotizar
robust	sólido
ROCE (return on capital employed)	rendimiento *(m)* del capital invertido
ROE (return on equity)	rendimiento *(m)* del capital invertido
ROI (return on investment)	rendimiento *(m)* de las inversiones
	rentabilidad *(f)* de las inversiones
role-playing	desempeño *(m)* de funciones
role set	conjunto *(m)* de atribuciones
roll out (to)	introducir un producto

ROM (read-only memory)	memoria *(f)* ROM
	memoria *(f)* de lectura
rotation: job ...	rotación *(f)* de trabajos
round figures: in ...	en números *(mpl)* redondos
round off (to)	redondear
route (to)	hacer la ruta
routine	rutina *(f)*
routine: diagnostic ...	rutina *(f)* del diagnóstico
routing	circulación *(f)*
royalty	derechos *(mpl)*
RPI (retail price index)	índice *(m)* de precios al consumo (IPC)
RPM (resale price maintenance	mantenimiento *(m)* del precio de venta
	mantenimiento *(m)* del precio al detalle
running expenses	gastos *(mpl)* corrientes

S

safety management	gestión (f) de la seguridad
safety stock	stock (m) de seguridad
safety: industrial ...	seguridad (f) industrial
safety: margin of ...	margen (m) de seguridad
salary grade	nivel (m) salarial
salary progression curve	curva (f) de incrementos de salarios
salary review	revisión (f) salarial
salary structure	estructura (f) salarial
sale: impulse ...	venta (f) por impulso
sale: point-of-... (POS)	lugar (m) de venta
sale: point-of-... advertising	publicidad (f) en el lugar de venta
sales analysis	análisis (m) de ventas
sales appeal	atracción (f) comercial
	garra (f) comercial
sales area	zona (f) de ventas
sales budget	presupuesto (m) de ventas
sales coverage	alcance (m) del servicio de ventas
sales department	departamento (m) de ventas
sales drive	empuje (m) de ventas
sales engineer	ingeniero (m) de ventas
sales estimate	prevision (f) de ventas
sales expansion effort	esfuerzo (m) para el desarrollo de ventas
sales expectations	expectativas (fpl) de venta
sales force	equipo (m) de vendedores
sales forecast	previsión (f) de ventas
sales goal	objetivo (m) de ventas
sales management	dirección (f) de ventas
sales manager	jefe (m) de ventas
sales mix	combinación (f) de medios de venta
sales planning	planificación (f) de ventas
sales policy	política (f) de ventas
sales potential	potencial (m) de ventas
sales promotion	promoción (f) de ventas
sales quota	cupo (m) de ventas
sales slump	bajón (m) de ventas
sales talk	argumentos (mpl) de venta
sales target	objetivo (m) de ventas
sales territory	territorio (m) de ventas
sales test	prueba (f) de ventas

sales turnover	cifra *(f)* de ventas
	ventas *(fpl)* totales
sales volume	volumen *(m)* de ventas
sales: return on ...	rentabilidad *(f)* de ventas
sampling: activity ...	muestreo *(m)* de actividades
sampling: random ...	muestreo *(m)* al azar
sampling: statistical ...	muestreo *(m)* estadístico
satisfaction: consumer ...	satisfacción *(f)* del consumidor
satisfaction: job ...	satisfacción *(f)* en el trabajo
saturation: market ...	saturación *(f)* del mercado
scab	esquirol *(m)*
scale: diseconomy of ...	deseconomía *(f)* de escala
scale: economy of ...	economía *(f)* de escala
scale: sliding ...	escala *(f)* móvil
scan: environmental ...	control *(m)* medioambiental
scanning	análisis *(m)*
	exploración *(f)*
scatter diagram	diagrama *(f)* de dispersión
scenario	escenario *(m)*
scenario: best-case ...	hipótesis *(f)* optimista
scenario: worst-case ...	hipótesis *(f)* pesimista
schedule (to)	programar
schedule	programa *(m)*
	plan *(m)* de trabajo
schedule: production ...	programa *(m)* de producción
schedule: work ...	programa *(m)* de trabajo
scheduling	programación *(f)*
scheduling: production ...	programación *(f)* de la producción
scheme: bonus ...	sistema *(m)* de primas
scheme: incentive ...	sistema *(m)* de incentivos
scheme: suggestion ...	esquema *(m)* de sugerencias
science: behavioural ...	ciencia *(f)* de la conducta
science: management ...	teoría *(f)* de política directiva
	organización *(f)* científica del trabajo
scientific management	organización *(f)* científica del trabajo
scientific programming	programación *(f)* científica
screen (to)	tamizar
	seleccionar
search: executive ...	reclutamiento *(m)* de ejecutivos
second guess (to)	anticipar lo que alguien va hacer
	decidir contra el consejo de alguien
securities	valores *(m)*
securitization	titularización *(f)*

securitize (to)	titularizar
security leak	divulgación *(f)* de información secreta
	fallo *(m)* en la seguridad
security: collateral ...	garantía *(f)* subsidiaria
	aval *(m)* personal
security: gilt-edged ...	bonos *(mpl)* del Estado
security: industrial ...	contra-espionaje *(m)* industrial
security: job ...	seguridad *(f)* de empleo
security: unlisted ...	valor *(m)* no admitido a cotización
seed money	inversión *(f)* inicial
seeking: goal-...	identificación *(f)* de objetivos
segment (to)	segmentar
segmentation	segmentación *(f)*
segmentation: market ...	fragmentación *(f)* de mercados
segment: market ...	segmento *(m)* de mercado
selection: media ...	selección *(f)* de medios de
	comunicación
selection: portfolio ...	selección *(f)* de cartera
self-actualization	autorealización *(f)*
self-appraisal	autoevaluación *(f)*
self-liquidating	autoamortizable
self-motivation	automotivación *(f)*
sell out (to)	liquidar
sell-by date	fecha *(f)* límite de venta
sell: hard ...	venta *(f)* agresiva
sell: soft ...	venta *(f)* suave
sellers' market	mercado *(m)* de demanda
selling policy	política *(f)* de ventas
selling: direct ...	venta *(f)* directa
selling: switch ...	desviación *(f)* de marcas
semiconductor	semiconductor *(m)*
semi-skilled labour	mano *(f)* de obra semicualificada
semi-variable costs	costes *(mpl)* semi-variables
sensitive: cost-...	sensible al coste
sensitive: market-...	sensible al mercado
sensitivity analysis	análisis *(m)* de sensibilidad
sensitivity training	enseñanza *(f)* para la sensibilidad
sensitize (to)	sensibilizar
sequential analysis	análisis *(m)* secuencial
series: time ...	series *(fpl)* de tiempos
service: after-sales ...	servicio *(m)* postventa
services: advisory ...	asesores *(mpl)*
	consultores *(mpl)*

services: computer ... department	departamento *(m)* de proceso de datos
services: customer ...	servicio *(m)* al cliente
services: extension ...	servicios *(mpl)* logísticos
services: management ...	servicios *(mpl)* de dirección
set-up costs	gastos *(mpl)* de constitución
severance pay	indemnización *(f)* por despido
sexual harassment	acoso *(m)* sexual
share capital	capital *(m)* en acciones
share of production plan	plan *(m)* de participación en la producción
share price performance	rendimiento *(m)* de precios de acciones
share: earnings per ... (EPS)	beneficio *(m)* por acción
share: golden ...	acción *(f)* preferencial
share: market ...	parte *(f)* del mercado
shareholding	tenencia *(f)* de acciones
sharing: job-...	compartir un mismo trabajo (dos personas)
sharing: profit-...	participación *(f)* en los beneficios
sharing: time-...	compartición *(f)* de tiempo
shelf-life	duración *(f)* de vida
shift: day ...	turno *(m)* de día
shift: night ...	turno *(m)* de noche
shiftwork	trabajo *(m)* por turnos
shipping	expedición *(f)*
shop : closed ...	empresa *(m)* de representación sindical única
shop-floor	taller *(m)*
	personal *(m)* obrero
shop: open ...	empresa *(f)* de representación sindical múltiple
short-range planning	planificación *(f)* a corto plazo
short-term planning	planificación *(f)* a corto plazo
shortfall	déficit *(m)*
	insuficiencia *(f)*
shortlist (to)	seleccionar candidatos
	hacer la lista final
shortlist	lista *(f)* de candidatos escogidos
	lista *(f)* abreviada
shut-down	inactividad *(f)*
	cierre *(m)*
significant	significante
simplex method	método *(m)* simplex

simplification: job ...	simplificación *(f)* del puesto
simplification: work ...	simplificación *(f)* del trabajo
simulate (to)	simular
simulation	simulación *(f)*
simulation: computer ...	simulación *(f)* por computador
single currency	moneda *(f)* única
single market	mercado *(m)* único
single market (*of the EC*)	mercado *(m)* único (de la CE)
single sourcing	aprovisionamiento *(m)* de fuente única
sinking fund	fondo *(m)* de amortización
sit-down strike	huelga *(f)* de brazos caídos
skilled labour	mano *(f)* de obra cualificada
skills analysis	análisis *(m)* de pericias
slack	infrautilización *(f)*
sliding scale	escala *(f)* móvil
slim down (to)	adelgazar
slot	ranura *(f)*
slump	depresión *(f)*
slump: sales ...	bajón *(m)* de ventas
slush fund	caja *(f)* negra
	caja *(f)* dos
smart card	tarjeta *(f)* multi-funcional
	tarjeta *(f)* inteligente
social analysis	análisis *(m)* social
socio-cultural	socio-cultural
socio-economic	socioeconómico
sociometric	sociométrico
soft landing	evitación *(f)* de la depresión *(f)* (economía)
soft sell	venta *(f)* suave
software	software *(m)*
	programas *(mpl)*
software applications	aplicaciones *(fpl)* de software
software company	empresa *(f)* de software
software engineer	ingeniero *(m)* de programas
software package	paquete *(m)* de software
sole agent	agente *(m)* en exclusiva
solving: problem ...	resolución *(f)* de problemas
source and disposition of funds	origen *(m)* y aplicación de recursos
sourcing	aprovisionamiento *(m)*
sourcing: dual ...	aprovisionamiento *(m)* de dos fuentes
sourcing: single ...	aprovisionamiento *(m)* de fuente única
span of control	organización *(f)* del mando

span: time ... of discretion	tiempo *(m)* máximo discrecional
spare capacity	capacidad *(f)* ociosa
specification: job ...	especificación *(f)* de un puesto de trabajo
specification: personnel ...	especificación *(f)* de personal
spellcheck	diccionario *(m)* en procesador de textos
spill-over effects	efectos *(mpl)* secundarios
spin-off effects	efectos *(mpl)* secundarios
spirit: entrepreneurial ...	espíritu *(m)* empresarial
sponsorship	patrocinio *(m)*
spot price	precio *(m)* en el lugar de venta
spreadsheet	hoja *(f)* de cálculo
squeeze: credit ...	restricción *(f)* crediticia
staff	plantilla *(f)*
staff and line	estructura *(f)* "line-staff"
staff appraisal	evaluación *(f)* del personal
staff assistant	auxiliar *(m)* consultivo
staff audit	auditoría *(f)* de personal
staff commitment	compromiso *(m)* del personal
staff cut-back	reducción *(f)* del personal
staff forecasting	previsión *(f)* de personal
staff management	dirección *(f)* del personal
staff manager	gerente *(m)*
staff mobility	movilidad *(f)* de personal
staff organization	organización *(f)* "staff"
staff planning	planificación *(f)* de personal
staff resourcing	reclutamiento *(m)* y gestión *(f)* de personal
staff strategy	estrategia *(f)* de personal
staff transfer	traslados *(mpl)* del personal
staff turnover	rotación *(f)* de personal
staff: line and ... organization	organización *(f)* jerárquica
staff: management ...	gestión *(f)* de personal
stag	especulador *(m)* (de acciones)
stagflation	estancamiento *(m)* con inflación
stagger	escalonar
staggered holidays	vacaciones *(fpl)* escalonadas
stake	participación *(f)*
	paquete *(m)* accional
stand-alone	autónomo
	independiente
stand-alone word processor	procesador *(m)* de texto independiente

standard	estándar *(m)*
standard costing	método *(m)* de costes estándares
standard costs	costes *(mpl)* estándares
standard deviation	desviación *(f)* estándar
standard of living	nivel *(m)* de vida
standard performance	estándar *(m)* de rendimiento
standard price	precio *(m)* estándar
standard time	tiempo *(m)* estándar
standard: budget ...	estándar *(m)* de presupuesto
standard: cost ...	estándar *(m)* de costes
standard: financial ...	estándar *(m)* financiero
standard: performance ...	rendimiento *(m)* estándar
standard: production ...	estándar *(m)* de producción
standardization	estandarización *(f)*
standardize (to)	estándarizar
star product	producto *(m)* estrella
start-up	comienzo *(m)*
	puesta *(f)* en marcha
start-up costs	gastos *(mpl)* de instalación
state of the art	de vanguardia
statement: financial ...	balance *(m)*
statement: mission ...	declaración *(f)* de la misión
statement: policy ...	establecimiento *(m)* de la política
statement: vision ...	declaración *(f)* de la visión del futuro
statistical control	verificación *(f)* estadística
statistical sampling	muestreo *(m)* estadístico
status report	informe *(m)* sobre situación actual
stimulus: competitive ...	estímulo *(m)* competitivo
stock control	control *(m)* de existencias
stock market	bolsa *(f)*
stock option	opción *(f)* de compra de acciones
stock option plan	plan *(m)* de compra opcional de acciones
stock portfolio	cartera *(f)* de valores
stock turnover	rotación *(f)* de existencias
stock valuation	valoración *(f)* de existencias
stock: blue chip ...	valor *(m)* solidísimo
stock: buffer ...	stock *(m)* regulador
stock: gilt-edged ...	valores *(mpl)* de bolsa
stock: safety ...	stock *(m)* de seguridad
stockbroker	corredor *(m)* de bolsa
stockbroking	correduría *(f)* de bolsa
stocktaking	inventario *(m)* de existencias

stocktaking: continuous ...	inventario *(m)* continuo de existencias
storage	almacenaje *(m)*
storage: computer ...	almacenaje *(m)* del ordenador
strategic alliance	alianza *(f)* estratégica
strategic business unit	unidad de actividad estratégica
strategic interdependence	interdependencia *(f)* de estrategias
strategic plan	plan *(m)* estratégico
strategic planning	planificación *(f)* estratégica
strategy formulation	elaboración *(f)* de estrategias
strategy implementation	instrumentación *(f)* de estrategias
strategy: brand ...	estrategia *(f)* de marca
strategy: business ...	estrategia *(f)* de negocios
	estrategia *(f)* comercial
strategy: competitive ...	estrategia *(f)* competitiva
strategy: corporate ...	estrategia *(f)* empresarial
strategy: defensive ...	estrategia *(f)* defensiva
strategy: diversification ...	estrategia *(f)* de diversificación
strategy: executive manpower ...	estrategia *(f)* de personal directivo
strategy: expansion ...	estrategia *(f)* de desarrollo
strategy: financial ...	estrategia *(f)* financiera
strategy: growth ...	estrategia *(f)* de crecimiento
strategy: marketing ...	estrategia *(f)* comercial
strategy: negotiation ...	estrategia *(f)* de negocios
strategy: pricing ...	estrategia *(f)* de precios
strategy: proactive ...	estrategia *(f)* pro-activa
strategy: product ...	estrategia *(f)* de productos
strategy: profit ...	estrategia *(f)* de beneficios
strategy: reactive ...	estrategia *(f)* reactiva
strategy: staff ...	estrategia *(f)* de personal
strategy: survival ...	estrategia *(f)* de supervivencia
strategy: user ...	estrategia *(f)* del consumidor
stream: business ...	flujo *(m)* de negocios
	flujo *(m)* empresarial
stream: on ...	en curso
	en cascada
streamline (to)	racionalizar
strengths, weaknesses, opportunities and threats (SWOT) analysis	análisis *(m)* de fuerzas, debilidades, oportunidades y amenazas
stress: work ...	estrés *(m)* laboral
strike: official ...	huelga *(f)* oficial
strike: sit-down ...	huelga *(f)* de brazos caídos
strike: sympathy ...	huelga *(f)* de solidaridad

strike: unofficial ...	huelga (f) no oficial
strike: wildcat ...	huelga (f) no negociada
stripping: asset-...	liquidación (f) de activos
structure (to)	estructurar
structure	estructura (f)
structure: authority ...	estructura (f) de autoridad
structure: capital ...	estructura (f) del capital
structure: cost ...	estructura (f) de costes
structure: grid ...	estructura (f) de red
structure: managerial ...	jerarquía (f) directiva
structure: market ...	estructura (f) del mercado
structure: organization ...	estructura (f) de la organización
structure: price ...	estructura (f) de precios
structure: salary ...	estructura (f) salarial
structure: wage ...	estructura (f) de sueldos
structured	estructurado
structuring	estructuración (f)
structuring: work ...	estructuración (f) del trabajo
study: case ...	estudio (m) de casos
study: feasibility ...	estudio (m) de viabilidad
study: gap ...	análisis (f) de las varianzas
study: market ...	estudio (m) del mercado
study: methods ...	estudio (m) de métodos
study: motion ...	estudio (m) de movimientos
study: plant layout ...	estudio (m) de proyectos de una planta industrial
study: time ...	estudio (m) de tiempos
study: time-and-methods ...	estudio (m) de tiempos y métodos
study: time-and-motion ...	estudio (m) de tiempos y movimientos
study: work ...	estudio (m) del trabajo
style: house ...	estilo (m) de la empresa
style: management ...	plan (m) de sucesión de directivos
sub-optimization	sub-optimización (f)
subcontract (to)	subcontratar
subcontracting	subcontratación (f)
subliminal advertising	publicidad (f) subliminal
subsidiarity	subsidiaridad (f)
subsidiary company	filial (f)
	sucursal (f)
succession planning: management ...	planificación (f) de sucesión
suggestion scheme	esquema (m) de sugerencias

summary dismissal	despedida *(f)* sumária
sunrise industry	industria *(f)* floreciente
sunset industry	industria *(f)* en declive
supervise (to)	supervisar
supervision	supervisión *(f)*
supervisor	supervisor *(m)*
	revisor *(m)*
supervisory board	consejo *(m)* supervisor
supervisory management	gestión *(f)* supervisora
supply	suministro *(m)*
support activities	actividades *(fpl)* de apoyo
survey: attitude ...	encuesta *(f)* de actitudes
	encuesta *(f)* de opiniones
survey: market ...	encuesta *(f)* sobre el mercado
survival strategy	estrategia *(f)* de supervivencia
swap	canje *(m)*
swap: forward ...	acciones *(fpl)* canjeables con fecha futura
switch selling	desviación *(f)* de marcas
switch trading	comercialización *(f)* aplazada
SWOT (strengths, weaknesses, opportunities & threats) analysis	análisis *(m)* de fuerzas, debilidades, oportunidades y amenazas
sympathy strike	huelga *(f)* de solidaridad
symposium	coloquio *(m)*
syndicate	sindicato *(m)*
synergism	sinergismo *(m)*
synergy	sinergía *(f)*
system	sistema *(m)*
system-managed company	empresa *(f)* dirigida de forma sistematizada
system: business ...	sistema *(m)* empresarial
system: computerized information (COINS)	sistema *(m)* mecanizado de información (COINS)
system: expert ...	sistema *(m)* experto
system: information ...	sistema *(m)* de información
system: integrated management ...	sistema *(m)* integrado de gestión
system: management ...	sistema *(m)* de gestión
system: management information ... (MIS)	sistema *(m)* de información para la dirección
system: planning, programming, budgeting ... (PPBS)	sistema *(m)* de programación y planificación de presupuestos

system: predetermined-motion-time... (PMTS)	sistema *(m)* de movimientos predeterminados (PMTS)
system: wage ...	sistema *(m)* salarial
systematize (to)	sistematizar
systems analysis	análisis *(m)* de sistemas
systems and procedures	procedimientos *(mpl)* administrativos
systems approach	enfoque *(m)* sistemático
	enfoque *(m)* según la teoría de sistemas
systems design	elaboración *(f)* de sistemas
systems engineer	ingeniero *(m)* de sistemas
systems engineering	elaboración *(f)* de sistemas
systems management	dirección *(f)* sistematizada
	gestión *(f)* por sistemas
systems planning	planificación *(f)* de sistemas
systems theory	teoría *(f)* de sistemas
systems: estimating ... costs	evaluación *(f)* de costes de sistemas

T

T-group training	diagnóstico *(m)* de grupos
TA (transactional analysis)	análisis *(m)* transaccional
table: input-output	tabla *(f)* de entradas y salidas
tactical plan	plan *(m)* táctico
tactical planning	planificación *(f)* táctica
tactics: competitive ...	tácticas *(fpl)* competitivas
take-home pay	salario *(m)* neto
take-off	despegue *(m)*
takeover	toma *(f)* de posesión
	absorción *(f)*
takeover bid (TOB)	oferta *(f)* pública de compra
talk: sales ...	argumentos *(mpl)* de venta
talks: pay ...	negociaciones *(fpl)* salariales
tangible assets	activo *(m)* material
target (to)	marcar objetivos
target	objetivo *(m)*
target market	mercado *(m)* objetivo
target-setting	fijación *(f)* de objetivos
target: production ...	objetivo *(m)* de producción
target: profit ...	objetivo *(m)* de beneficio
targeting	fijar objetivos
tariff barrier	barrera *(f)* arancelaria
tariff barrier: non-... ... (NTB)	barrera *(f)* no arancelaria
task force	personal *(m)* para misión especial
tax-deductible	deducible fiscalmente
tax incentive	incentivo *(m)* fiscal
tax relief	desgravación *(f)* fiscal
tax: corporation ...	impuesto *(m)* de sociedades
tax: income ...	impuesto *(m)* sobre la renta
tax: profits ...	impuesto *(m)* sobre beneficios
tax: value added ... (VAT)	impuesto *(m)* sobre el valor agregado (IVA)
taxation relief: double	desgravación *(f)* de impuestos duplicados
teaching: computer-aided ... (CAT)	enseñanza *(f)* asistida por ordenador (CAT)
team-building	desarrollo *(m)* de equipos
	formación (f) de equipos
team leader	líder *(m)* del equipo
team player	buen trabajador *(m)* en equipo

tech: high-...	alta *(f)* tecnología
tech: low-...	baja *(f)* tecnología
technical manager	director *(m)* técnico
technique: management ...	técnicas *(fpl)* de gestión
technique: production ...	técnica *(f)* de producción
technique: programme evaluation and review (PERT)	técnica *(f)* de evaluación y revisión de programas (PERT)
technological forecasting	previsión *(f)* tecnológica
technology transfer	transferencia *(f)* de tecnología
technology: information ...	tecnología *(f)* de la información
	tecnología *(f)* de datos
	informática *(f)*
teleconference	teleconferencia *(f)*
telemarketing	telemárketing *(m)*
telematics	telemática *(f)*
telesales	televentas *(fpl)*
	ventas *(fpl)* por teléfono
teletext	teletexto *(m)*
tender (to)	concursar (a un contrato)
tender	oferta *(f)*
tendering: competitive ...	oferta *(f)* competitiva
terminal	terminal *(f)*
	borne *(m)*
terminal: computer ...	terminal *(f)* de ordenador
test marketing	prueba *(f)* del mercado
test run	serie *(f)* piloto
test: aptitude ...	prueba *(f)* de aptitud
test: market ...	prueba *(f)* en el mercado
testing: field ...	pruebas *(fpl)* (en el mercado etc)
testing: product ...	"test" *(m)* de productos
testing: psychometric ...	prueba *(f)* psicométrica
T-group training	diagnóstico *(m)* de grupos
theme: advertising ...	tema *(m)* de publicidad
theory: administrative ...	teoría *(f)* de la administración
theory: communications ...	teoría *(f)* de la comunicación
theory: contingency ...	teoría *(f)* de las contingencias
theory: decision ...	teoría *(f)* de decisiones
theory: game ...	teoría *(f)* de juegos
theory: information ...	teoría *(f)* de la información
theory: management ...	teoría *(f)* de política directiva
theory: organization ...	teoría *(f)* organizadora
theory: probability ...	teoría *(f)* de la probabilidad

theory: queueing ...	teoría (f) de colas
	teoría (f) de líneas de espera
theory: systems ...	teoría (f) de sistemas
think-tank	grupo (m) investigador
think the unthinkable (to)	pensar lo impensable
thinking: creative ...	espíritu (m) creativo
thinking: lateral ...	pensamiento (m) lateral
third party	tercera parte (f)
throughput	cantidad (f) tratada
	producción (f) total
thrust: competitive ...	empuje (m) competitivo
time and methods study	estudio (m) de métodos y tiempos
time and motion study	estudio (m) de tiempos y movimientos
time frame	plazo (m) de tiempo
time-lag	retraso (m)
	desfase (m)
time management	gestión (f) del tiempo
time series	series (fpl) de tiempos
time-sharing	compartición (f) de tiempo
time sheet	hoja (f) de devengos
time span of discretion	tiempo (m) máximo discrecional
time study	estudio (m) de tiempos
time: down ...	tiempo (m) inactivo
	horas (fpl) bajas
time: lead ...	tiempo (m) de ejecución
time: predetermined motion ... system (PMTS)	sistema (m) de movimientos predeterminados (PMTS)
time: real ...	tiempo (m) real
time: standard ...	tiempo (m) estándar
time: turnaround ...	plazo (m) de ejecución
title: job ...	nombre (m) del puesto
TOB (takeover bid)	oferta (f) pública de compra (OPA)
toolbox	caja (f) de herramientas
	cuadro (m) de herramientas
top management	alta (f) dirección
top management approach	enfoque (m) según la alta dirección
top up (to)	reforzar (la inversión)
top-down	de la cumbre para abajo
total plant maintenance	mantenimiento (m) total de los talleres
total quality control (TQC)	control (m) total de calidad
total quality management (TQM)	gestión (f) total de calidad
TQC (total quality control)	control (m) total de calidad

TQM (total quality management)	gestión *(f)* total de calidad
track record	registro *(m)* de antecedentes *(mpl)*
trade association	asociación *(f)* de comerciantes
trade cycle	ciclo *(m)* comercial
trade imbalance...	desequilibrio *(m)* comercial
trade name	nombre *(m)* comercial
trade off (to)	llegar a una transacción
trade-off	sustitución *(f)*
trade restriction	restricción *(f)* comercial
trade union	sindicato *(m)*
trade union representative	representante *(m/f)* del sindicato
trade: barter ...	permuta *(f)*
traded option	opción *(f)* negociable
trademark: registered ...	marca *(f)* registrada
trading area	zona *(f)* comercial
trading programme	programa *(m)* comercial
trading: insider ...	comercio *(m)* de iniciado
trading: patent ...	comercio *(m)* de patentes
trading: switch ...	comercialización *(f)* aplazada
trainee turnover	rotación *(f)* de aprendices
training	formación *(f)*
	capacitación *(f)*
training needs	necesidades *(fpl)* de formación
training needs analysis	análisis *(m)* de necesidades de formación
training officer	jefe *(m)* de formación
training within industry (TWI)	formación *(f)* dentro de la industria
training: analytical ...	formación *(f)* analítica
training: booster ...	reeducación *(f)* profesional
	readaptación *(f)* profesional
training: computer-based ...	formación *(f)* asistida por ordenador
training: executive ...	formación *(f)* de ejecutivos
training: group ...	formación *(f)* en grupos
training: hands-on ...	formación *(f)* práctica
training: in-plant ...	formación *(f)* dentro de la empresa
training: management ...	formación *(f)* de directivos
training: multimedia ...	formación *(f)* multimedia
training: off-the-job ...	formación *(f)* fuera del trabajo
training: on-the-job ...	formación *(f)* sobre la práctica
training: part-analysis ...	formación *(f)* por etapas
training: sensitivity ...	enseñanza *(f)* para la sensibilidad
training: T-group ...	diagnóstico *(m)* de grupos

training: vocational ...	formación *(f)* vocacional
transactional	transaccional
transactional analysis (TA)	análisis *(m)* transaccional
transfer pricing	fijación *(f)* de precios de transferencia
transfer: technology ...	transferencia *(f)* de tecnología
transfer: staff ...	traslado *(m)* del personal
transitional	transitorio
transportation	transporte *(m)*
tree: decision ...	árbol *(m)* de decisiones
	esquema *(f)* de decisiones
tree: family ...	árbol *(m)* genealógico
tree: pertinence ...	árbol *(m)* de pertinencia
trend	tendencia *(f)*
trend: economic ...	tendencia *(f)* económica
trend: exponential ...	tendencia *(f)* exponencial
trend: market ...	tendencia *(f)* del mercado
trickle-down theory	teoría *(f)* de la filtración
troubleshooter	conciliador *(m)*
	experto *(m)* en fallos
troubleshooting	investigación *(f)* de fallos
turf protection	protección *(f)* del territorio
turn around (to)	arreglar
turnaround time	plazo *(m)* de ejecución
turnover	cifra *(f)* de negocios
turnover: asset ...	rotación *(f)* del activo
turnover: inventory ...	giro *(m)* de existencias
turnover: sales ...	cifra *(f)* de ventas
	ventas *(fpl)* totales
turnover: staff ...	rotacion *(f)* de personal
turnover: stock ...	rotación *(f)* de existencias
turnover: trainee ...	rotación *(f)* de aprendices
TWI (training within industry)	formación *(f)* dentro de la industria

U

unbundle (to)	desglosar
unbundling	separación *(f)* de aranceles
under licence	bajo licencia
undercapacity	por debajo de la capacidad
undercapitalized	descapitalizado
undercut (to)	vender más barato
undermanned	escasez *(f)* de mano de obra
undermanning	escasez *(f)* de mano de obra
underperform (to)	bajar el rendimiento
underprice (to)	tirar los precios
understaffed	escasez *(f)* de personal
understaffing	escasez *(f)* de personal
undistributed profit	beneficios *(mpl)* no distribuidos
unfair competition	competencia *(f)* desleal
unfair dismissal	despido *(m)* injusto
unique selling point/proposition (USP)	argumento *(m)* de venta único
unit labour costs	coste *(m)* unitario de mano de obra
unlisted company	empresa *(f)* no cotizada en Bolsa
unlisted security	valores *(mpl)* no admitidos a cotización
unofficial action	acción *(f)* no sindicada
unofficial strike	huelga *(f)* no sindicada
unscramble (to)	descifrar
unskilled labour	mano *(f)* de obra no cualificada
unstructured	no estructurado
up the line	en ascenso (jerárquico)
update (to)	poner al día
	actualizar
update	actualización *(f)*
up-market	artículos *(mpl)* de alta calidad
upstream	río *(m)* arriba
upswing	en alza *(f)*
uptime	tiempo *(m)* productivo
upturn	mejora *(f)*
upwardly mobile	que mejora siempre en su posición social
	dinámico
use-by date	fecha *(f)* de caducidad
user attitude	actitud *(f)* de los usuarios

user-friendly	fácil de utilizar
	amigable (informática)
user strategy	estrategia *(f)* del consumidor
user-unfriendly	difícil de utilizar
USP (unique selling point/ proposition)	argumento (m) de venta único
utility: public ...	empresa *(f)* de utilidad pública
utilization: capacity ...	utilización *(f)* de la capacidad

V

VA (value analysis)	análisis *(m)* de valor
valuation: stock ...	valoración *(f)* de existencias
value added	valor *(m)* añadido
value added tax (VAT)	impuesto *(m)* sobre el valor agregado
value analysis (VA)	análisis *(m)* del valor
value chain	cadena *(f)* de valor
value concept	concepto *(m)* del valor
value engineering	análisis *(m)* de costes
	análisis *(m)* de valores
value proposal	propuesta *(f)* de valorización
value: asset ...	valor *(m)* del activo
	valor *(m)* contable
value: book ...	valor *(m)* según balance
	valor *(m)* en libros
value: break-up ...	valor *(m)* en liquidación
	valor *(m)* de recuperación
value: market ...	valor *(m)* de mercado
value: net present ... (NPV)	valor *(m)* neto actualizado
value: present ... method	método *(m)* del valor actual
variable costs	costes *(mpl)* variables
variable costs: semi-... ...	costes *(mpl)* semivariables
variable expenses	gastos *(mpl)* variables
variance	varianza *(f)*
variance analysis	análisis *(m)* de varianza
variance: cost ...	varianza *(f)* de costes
variety reduction	reducción *(f)* de la variedad
VAT (value added tax)	impuesto *(m)* sobre el valor agregado
VDU (visual display unit)	unidad *(f)* de representación visual
venture capital	capital *(m)* arriesgado
venture capitalist	inversor *(m)* de riesgo
venture management	gestión *(f)* de riesgos
venture: joint ...	aventura *(f)* común
	empresa *(f)* conjunta
venture: joint-... company	sociedad *(f)* en participación conjunta
verbal communication	comunicación *(f)* verbal
verbal communication: non-... ...	comunicación *(f)* no verbal
verify (to)	verificar
vertical integration	integración *(f)* vertical
vested interest	intereses *(mpl)* creados

viability	viabilidad *(f)*
viable	viable
vice-chairman	vicepresidente *(m)*
vice-president	vicepresidente *(m)*
video	video *(m)*
viewdata	datos *(mpl)* de pantalla
virus: computer ...	virus *(m)* de ordenador
vision	visión *(f)*
vision statement	declaración *(f)* de visión
visual display unit (VDU)	unidad *(f)* de representación visual
vocational guidance	orientación *(f)* profesional
vocational training	formación *(f)* profesional
volume	volumen *(m)*
volume: cost-...-profit analysis	análisis *(m)* de coste volumen y beneficio
volume: profit-... ratio (P/V)	tasa *(f)* de beneficio sobre ventas
volume: sales ...	volumen *(m)* de ventas

W

wage ceiling	techo *(m)* salarial
wage differential	escalado *(m)* de salarios
wage drift	desviación *(f)* salarial
wage freeze	congelación *(f)* salarial
wage level	nivel *(m)* salarial
wage policy	política *(f)* salarial
wage structure	estructura *(f)* salarial
wage system	sistema *(m)* salarial
wage: incentive ...	incentivo *(m)* salarial
wage: minimum ...	salario *(m)* mínimo
walking around: management by	gestión *(f)* de alta participación de los ejecutivos
walkout	huelga *(f)*
WAN (wide area networked)	red *(f)* de área extendida
warehousing	almacenaje *(m)*
wastage: natural ...	salida *(f)* del mercado de trabajo
waste: industrial ...	residuos *(mpl)* industriales
wasting assets	activo *(m)* amortizable
weighted average	media *(f)* ponderada
weighting	ponderación *(f)*
well-packaged	bien empaquetado
wheeling and dealing	maquinaciones *(fpl)*
white-collar (worker)	cuello *(m)* blanco
	oficinista *(m)*
white goods	electrodomésticos *(mpl)* de la línea blanca
white knight	empresa *(f)* preferente (en una adquisición)
whiz-kid	ejecutivo *(m)* dinámico
wide area network (WAN)	red *(f)* de área extendida
wildcat strike	huelga *(f)* no negociada
Winchester disk	disco *(m)* winchester
wind down (to)	disminuir
	reducir
wind up (to)	cancelar
	terminar
winding up	liquidación *(f)*
window	ventana *(f)*
window-dressing	camuflaje *(m)* (del balance)
	contabilidad *(f)* trucada

window of opportunity	marco *(m)* de oportunidad
word processing	procesamiento *(m)* de textos
word processor (WP)	procesador *(m)* de textos
word processor:	procesador *(m)* de textos
stand-alone	independiente
work by contract	trabajo *(m)* por contrato
work content	contenido *(m)* del trabajo
work cycle	ciclo *(m)* de trabajo
work in progress	trabajo *(m)* en progreso
workload	cantidad *(f)* de trabajo
work measurement	medición *(f)* del trabajo
work schedule	plan *(m)* de trabajo
work simplification	simplificación *(f)* del trabajo
work station	puesto *(m)* de trabajo
	entorno *(m)* autosuficiente
	(informática)
work stress	estrés *(m)* laboral
work structuring	estructuración *(f)* del trabajo
work study	estudio *(m)* del trabajo
work-to-rule	huelga *(f)* de trabajo lento
	huelga *(f)* de celo
worker buyout	compra *(f)* por los trabajadores
worker participation	participación *(f)* obrera
worker representation	representación *(f)* obrera
working capital	capital *(m)* circulante
	fondo *(m)* de maniobra
working hours	horario *(m)* de trabajo
working hours: flexible	horario *(m)* de trabajo flexible
working party	comisión *(f)* investigadora
workplace	lugar *(m)* de trabajo
works committee	comité *(m)* de la empresa
works council	consejo *(m)* de obreros
works manager	jefe *(m)* de fábrica
world-class	clase *(f)* mundialmente reconocida
worst-case scenario	hipótesis *(f)* pesimista
worth: net ...	valor *(m)* neto
WP (word processor)	procesador *(m)* de textos
write off (to)	cancelar
	anular (apuntes contables)
write-off	sin valor *(m)* contable
	anulación *(f)*

Y

yardstick	criterio *(m)*
	norma *(f)*
year: base ...	año *(m)* base
year: financial ...	ejercicio *(m)* financiero
year: fiscal ...	año *(m)* fiscal
	ejercicio *(m)* fiscal
yield	rendimiento *(m)*
yield: average ...	rendimiento *(m)* medio
yield: earnings ...	rédito *(m)*
yuppie	joven ejecutivo *(m)* en alza

Z

Z chart	gráfico *(m)* Z
zero-base budget	presupuesto *(m)* de base cero
zero defects	sin defectos
zero-rating	exento de impuestos de tasa *(f)* cero
zero-sum game	juego *(m)* de suma cero

ESPAÑOL-INGLÉS

A

a la par	at par
a medida *(f)* del usuario	customized
abajo: de la cumbre para ...	top-down
abajo: más ...	downstream
abajo: mercado *(m)* ...	down-market
abajo: viraje *(m)* ...	downswing
abandono *(m)* del producto	product abandonment
abaratamiento *(m)* de precios	price-cutting
abaratar *(mpl)* precios	cut prices (to)
abastecimiento: jefe *(m)* de ...	procurement manager
abierto: crédito *(m)* ...	revolving credit
abierto: plan *(m)* ...	open-plan
abreviada: lista *(f)* ...	shortlist
absentismo *(m)*	absenteeism
absorción *(f)*	absorption
	takeover
absorción *(f)* de costes	absorption cost
acaparar el mercado	corner the market (to)
acceder	access (to)
accidente *(m)* laboral	industrial injury
acción *(f)* de primera clase	blue-chip stock
acción *(f)* laboral (huelga)	industrial action
acción *(f)* no sindicada	unofficial action
acción *(f)* preferencial	golden share
acción: beneficios *(mpl)* por ...	EPS (earnings per share), per-share earnings
acción: plan *(m)* de ...	action plan
accionable	actionable
accionariado: dilución *(f)* de ...	dilution of equity
acciones *(fpl)* canjeables con fecha futura	forward swap
acciones *(fpl)* de dividendo no fijo	equity
acciones de empresas: predador *(m)* de ...	corporate raider
acciones de una empresa: hacer la compra *(f)* hóstil de ...	raid a company (to)
acciones: capital *(m)* en ...	share capital

acciones: mercado *(m)* **de ...**	equity market
acciones: opción *(f)* **de compra de ...**	stock option
acciones: plan *(m)* **de compra opcional de ...**	stock option plan
acciones: rendimiento *(m)* **de las ...**	return on equity (ROE)
acciones: rendimiento *(m)* **de precios de ...**	share price performance
acciones: tenencia *(f)* **de ...**	shareholding
aceptación *(f)* **de marca**	brand acceptance
aceptación *(m)* **por parte del consumidor**	consumer acceptance
acoso *(m)* **sexual**	sexual harassment
actitud *(f)* **de los usuarios**	user attitude
actitudes: encuesta *(f)* **de ...**	attitude survey
activar	activate (to)
actividad *(f)* **artificial**	dummy activity
actividad estratégica: unidad de ...	strategic business unit
actividades *(fpl)* **de apoyo**	support activities
actividades: esquema *(m)* **de ...**	activity chart
actividades: muestreo *(m)* **de ...**	activity sampling
activo *(m)*	assets
activo *(m)* **amortizable**	wasting assets
activo *(m)* **circulante**	current assets
activo *(m)* **circulante neto**	net current assets
activo *(m)* **disponible**	liquid assets
activo *(m)* **disponible a corto plazo**	quick assets
activo *(m)* **fijo**	fixed assets
activo *(m)* **líquido**	liquid assets
activo *(m)* **material**	tangible assets
activo *(m)* **neto**	net assets
activo *(m)* **realizable**	current assets
activo: cartera *(f)* **del ...**	asset portfolio
activo: derechos *(mpl)* **sobre el ...**	equity
activo: gestión *(f)* **del ...**	asset management
activo: reducción *(f)* **del ...**	divestment
activo: rendimiento *(m)* **del ...**	earnings on assets
	return on assets
activo: revalorización *(f)* **del ...**	re-evaluation of assets
	revaluation of assets

activo: rotación *(f)* del ...	asset turnover
activo: valor *(m)* del ...	asset value
activos: liquidación *(f)* de ...	asset-stripping
actual: informe *(m)* sobre situación ...	status report
actual: método *(m)* del valor ...	present value method
actuales: gastos *(mpl)* ...	current expenditure
actualización *(f)*	update
actualizado: "cash flow" ...	discounted cash flow (DCF)
actualizado: valor *(m)* neto ...	net present value (NPV)
actualizar	update (to)
acuerdo *(m)* al contado	cash deal
acuerdo *(m)* de caballeros	gentleman's agreement
acuerdo *(m)* escrito	agreement (written ...)
acuerdo *(m)* sobre seguridad en el empleo	job security agreement
acuerdo: llegar a un ...	reach a deal (to)
acuerdos *(mpl)* consorciales	pooling arrangements
adaptación *(f)* del trabajo al hombre	ergonomics human engineering
adaptivo: control *(m)* ...	adaptive control
adelantamiento *(m)*	advancement
adelgazar	slim down (to)
adjudicar	allocate (to) award (to)
adjunto *(m)* al director	assistant to manager
adjunto: director *(m)* ...	assistant director assistant manager
adjunto: director *(m)* gerente ...	deputy managing director
administración *(f)* de mano de obra	manpower management
administración *(f)* de personal	personnel management
administración *(f)* de producción	production management
administración *(f)* financiera	financial administration
administración: consejo *(m)* de ...	board of directors executive board
administración: control *(m)* del consejo de ...	board control
administración: gastos *(mpl)* de ...	administrative expenses
administración: gastos *(mpl)* generales de ...	administrative overheads

administración: índice *(m)* ... producción	administration-production ratio
administración: modelo *(m)* dinámico de ...	dynamic management model
administración: reunión *(f)* del consejo de ...	board meeting
administración: teoría *(f)* de la ...	administrative theory
administrar	manage (to)
administrativa: dirección *(f)* ...	office management
administrativo: medición *(f)* del trabajo ...	clerical work measurement (CWM)
administrativo: proceso *(m)* de control ...	administrative control procedure
administrativos: procedimientos *(mpl)* ...	systems and procedures
admitidos a cotización: valores *(mpl)* no ...	unlisted security
ADP (proceso *(m)* automático de datos)	ADP (automatic data processing)
adquisición *(f)*	acquisition
adquisición *(f)* de datos	data acquisition
adquisición: perfil *(m)* de ...	acquisition profile
adquisiciones *(fpl)*: fusiones *(fpl)* y ...	mergers and acquisitions (M & A)
adquisitivo: paridad *(f)* de poder ...	purchasing power parity
adquisitivo: poder *(m)* ...	purchasing power
afiliada: empresa *(f)* ...	associate company
agencia *(f)* de colocaciones	employment bureau
agente *(m)* de despacho	forwarding agent
agente *(m)* de publicidad	advertising agent
agente *(m)* en exclusiva	sole agent
agiotaje *(m)*	jobbing
agotado	out of stock
agregado: impuesto *(m)* sobre el valor ...	value added tax (VAT)
agrupación *(f)*	bundling
(al) alcance de la mano	(at) arm's length
alcance *(m)* del servicio de ventas	sales coverage
alcanzar (beneficio)	realize (to) (profit)

alcanzar el punto de equilibrio	break-even (to)
alcista *(m)*	bull
alcista: mercado *(m)* ...	bull market
aleatoria: entrada *(f)* ...	random access
aleatoria: método *(m)* **de observación** ...	random observation method
algoritmo *(m)*	algorithm
alianza *(f)* **estratégica**	strategic alliance
alimentar gota a gota	drip-feeding
almacenaje *(m)*	storage
	warehousing
almacenamiento *(m)* **del ordenador**	computer storage
alquiler *(m)* **de equipo**	plant hire
alta calidad: artículos *(mpl)* **de** ...	up-market
alta *(f)* **dirección**	top management
alta dirección: enfoque *(m)* **según la** ...	top management approach
alta participación de los ejecutivos: gestión *(f)* **de** ...	management by walking around
alta peligrosidad: productos *(mpl)* **químicos de** ...	hazchem (hazardous chemicals)
alto nivel: jefe *(m)* **de** ...	first-line manager
alto potencial: ejecutivo *(m)* **de** ...	high-flier
alza *(f)*	boom
alza *(f)*: **en** ...	upswing
alzado: tanto *(m)* ...	lump sum
amañar (los libros)	fiddle (to)
ambiente *(m)* **económico**	economic climate
ambiente: análisis *(m)* **del medio** ...	environmental analysis
ambiente: temas *(mpl)* **del medio** ...	environmental scan
	green issues
amenazas: análisis *(m)* **de fuerzas, debilidades, oportunidades y** ...	strengths, weaknesses, opportunities and threats (SWOT) analysis
amigable (informática)	user-friendly
amortizable: activo *(m)* ...	wasting assets
amortización *(f)* **de puestos de trabajo por jubilación**	natural wastage

amortización: fondo *(m)* de ...	sinking fund
amortización: reserva *(f)* para ...	depreciation allowance
ampliación *(f)* de las tareas	job enlargement
añadir por etapas	phase in (to)
análisis *(m)*	scanning
análisis *(m)* a fondo	depth analysis
análisis *(m)* coste-beneficio	cost-benefit analysis (CBA)
análisis *(m)* cuantitativo	quantitative analysis
análisis *(f)* de aportaciones	contribution analysis
análisis *(m)* de centros de beneficio	profit-factor analysis
análisis *(m)* de coste volumen y beneficio	cost-volume-profit analysis
análisis *(m)* de costes	cost analysis
	value engineering
análisis *(m)* de decisiones	decision analysis
análisis *(m)* de entradas y salidas	input-output analysis
análisis *(f)* de equilibrio	break-even analysis
análisis *(m)* de formación por étapas	part-analysis training
análisis *(m)* de fuerzas, debilidades, oportunidades y amenazas	SWOT (strengths, weaknesses, opportunities & threats) analysis
análisis *(f)* de inversiones	investment analysis
análisis *(m)* de la competencia	competitor analysis
análisis *(m)* de la red	network analysis
análisis *(m)* de las varianzas	gap study
	variance analysis
análisis *(f)* de los medios de comunicación	media analysis
análisis *(m)* de mercado	market research
análisis *(m)* de necesidades	needs analysis
análisis *(m)* de necesidades de formación	training needs analysis
análisis *(m)* de operación	analysis operations
	operations analysis
análisis *(m)* de pericias	skills analysis
análisis *(m)* de puestos de trabajo	job analysis

análisis *(m)* **de regresión**	regression analysis
análisis *(m)* **de regresión múltiple**	multiple regression analysis (MRA)
análisis *(m)* **de rentabilidad**	profitability analysis
análisis *(m)* **de riesgos**	risk analysis
análisis *(m)* **de sensibilidad**	sensitivity analysis
análisis *(m)* **de sistemas**	systems analysis
análisis *(m)* **de valor**	value analysis (VA)
análisis *(m)* **de valores**	value engineering
análisis *(m)* **de varianza**	variance analysis
análisis *(m)* **de ventas**	sales analysis
análisis *(m)* **del camino crítico**	critical path analysis (CPA)
análisis *(m)* **del medio ambiente**	environmental analysis
análisis *(m)* **del problema**	problem analysis
análisis *(m)* **del producto**	product analysis
análisis *(m)* **financiero**	financial analysis
	financial review
análisis *(m)* **funcional**	functional analysis
análisis *(m)* **intensivo de grupo**	brainstorming
análisis *(m)* **marginal**	incremental analysis
	marginal analysis
análisis *(m)* **morfológico**	morphological analysis
análisis *(m)* **secuencial**	sequential analysis
análisis *(m)* **social**	social analysis
análisis *(m)* **transaccional**	transactional analysis (TA)
analítica: contabilidad *(f)* ...	analytic accounting
analítica: formación *(f)* ...	analytical training
analógica: representación *(f)* ...	analog(ue) representation
analógico: ordenador *(m)* ...	analog computer
anfitrión: país *(m)* ...	host country
año *(m)* **base**	base year
año *(m)* **fiscal**	fiscal year
anónima: sociedad *(f)* ...	business corporation
antecedentes *(mpl)***: registro** *(m)* **de ...**	track record
anteproyecto *(m)*	blueprint
anticipada: respuesta *(f)* ...	anticipatory response
anticipos *(mpl)* **a cuenta**	pay-as-you-go
anulación *(f)*	write-off
anular (apuntes contables)	write off (to)
anuncios: tablón *(m)* **de ...**	bulletin board
apagando fuegos	fire-fighting

apalancamiento *(m)*	leverage
apalancamiento: compra *(f)* con ... (LBO)	leveraged buyout (LBO)
apalancamiento: licitación *(f)* con ...	leveraged bid
aplazada: comercialización *(f)* ...	switch trading
aplicación de recursos: origen *(m)* y ...	source and disposition of funds
aplicaciones *(fpl)* de software	software applications
aportaciones: análisis *(f)* de ...	contribution analysis
aporte *(m)* de capital	capital formation
apoyarse para una actividad en una estructura existente	piggyback
apoyo: actividades *(fpl)* de ...	support activities
apreciación *(f)*	assessment
apreciación *(f)* de riesgos	risk assessment
aprendices: rotación *(f)* de ...	trainee turnover
aprendizaje *(m)* a distancia	distance learning
aprendizaje *(m)* asistido por ordenador (CAL)	computer-aided learning (CAL)
aprendizaje: curva *(f)* de ...	learning curve
aprovisionamiento *(m)*	sourcing
aprovisionamiento *(m)* de fuente única	single sourcing
aprovisionamiento *(m)* externo	outsourcing
aproximación *(f)* exponencial	exponential smoothing
aproximado: cálculo *(m)* ...	guesstimate
aptitud *(f)* del ejecutivo	executive competence
aptitud *(f)* en el trabajo	job competence
aptitud: prueba *(f)* de ...	aptitude test
arancel *(m)*	tariff
arancelaria: barrera *(f)* ...	tariff barrier
arancelaria: barrera *(f)* no ...	non-tariff barrier (NTB)
aranceles: separación *(f)* de ...	separation of tariffs
arbitraje *(m)*	arbitration
árbol *(m)* de decisiones	decision tree
árbol *(m)* de pertinencia	pertinence tree
árbol *(m)* genealógico	family tree
arbitrador *(m)*	arbitrageur
área de actividad estratégica	strategic business unit
área extendida: red *(f)* de ...	wide area network (WAN)
área: director *(m)* de ...	area manager
área local: red *(f)* de ...	local area network (LAN)

argumento *(m)* de venta único	unique selling point/proposition (USP)
argumentos *(mpl)* de venta	sales talk
armonización *(f)*	harmonization
armonizar	harmonize (to)
arreglo *(m)* rápido	quick fix
arrendamiento *(m)*	leasing
arrendamiento *(m)* de medios de producción	equipment leasing
arrendamiento: préstamo *(m)* para ...	lease-lend
arrendar	lease (to)
arrendar o comprar	lease or buy (to)
arriba: río *(m)* ...	upstream
arriesgado: capital *(m)* ...	venture capital
artículo *(m)* de comercio	commodity
artículos *(mpl)* de alta calidad	up-market
artículos *(mpl)* de consumo	consumer goods
artificial: actividad *(f)* ...	dummy activity
artificial: inteligencia *(f)* ...	artificial intelligence
ascenso *(m)*	advancement
ascenso *(m)* de directivos	executive advancement
	executive promotion
ascenso *(m)* vertiginoso	fast-track
ascenso: en ... (jerárquico)	up the line
aseguramiento *(m)* de la calidad	quality assurance
asesor *(m)*	consultant
asesorar	consult (to)
asesores *(mpl)*	advisory services
asignación *(f)* de costes	allocation of costs
	cost allocation
asignación *(f)* de gastos	assignment of expenditure
asignación *(f)* de recursos	resource allocation
asignación *(f)* de responsabilidades	allocation of responsibilities
asignación *(f)* de tareas	job assignment
asignación *(f)* del presupuesto	budget appropriation
asignación *(f)* para márketing	marketing appropriation
asignación *(f)* para publicidad	advertising appropriation
asignar	allocate (to)
	appropriate (to)

asistida por ordenador: enseñanza *(f)* ... **(CAT)**	computer-aided teaching (CAT)
asistida por ordenador: fabricación *(f)* ... **(CAM)**	computer-aided manufacturing (CAM)
asistida por ordenador: formación *(f)* ...	computer-based training (CBT)
asistido por ordenador: aprendizaje *(m)* ... **(CAL)**	computer-aided learning (CAL)
asociación *(f)* **de comerciantes**	trade association
atención *(f)* **al cliente**	customer care
atracción *(f)* **comercial**	sales appeal
atribuciones: conjunto *(m)* **de** ...	role set
atribuir	allocate (to)
audiovisuales: saportes *(mpl)* ...	audiovisual aids
auditor *(m)*	auditor
auditoría *(f)*	audit
auditoría *(f)* **de personal**	staff audit
auditoría *(f)* **interna**	internal audit
auge *(m)*	boom
aumento *(m)* **de precio**	price increase
aumento *(m)* **lineal de salarios**	across-the-board increase
autoamortizable	self-liquidating
autoedición *(f)*	desktop publishing
autoeditar	desktop publish (to)
autoevaluación *(f)*	self-appraisal
autofinanciación *(f)*	ploughback
automático de datos: proceso *(m)* ...	automatic data processing (ADP)
automático: proceso *(m)* ... **de datos (ADP)**	automatic data processing (ADP)
automatización *(f)*	automation
automatizada: gerencia *(f)* ...	computerized management
automatizar	automate (to) computerize (to)
automotivación *(f)*	self-motivation
autónomo	stand-alone
autorealización *(f)*	self-actualization
autoridad *(f)* **lineal**	line authority
autoridad: disminución *(f)* **de** ...	contraction of authority
autoridad: estructura *(f)* **de** ...	authority structure
autorizado: capital *(m)* **social** ...	authorized capital
autosuficiente: entorno *(m)* ... **(informática)**	work station

auxiliar *(m)* consultivo	staff assistant
auxiliar *(m/f)* de línea	line assistant
auxiliar: equipo *(m)* ...	add-on equipment
auxiliares: servicios *(mpl)* ...	ancillary operations
avance *(m)* importante	breakthrough
ayudas *(fpl)* audiovisuales	audiovisual aids
azar: muestreo *(m)* al ...	random sampling

B

baja: mercado *(m)* bursátil a la ...	bear market
baja: tecnología *(f)* ...	low-tech
bajada *(f)*	downturn
bajar el rendimiento	underperform (to)
bajas: horas *(fpl)* ...	down time
bajista *(m)*	bear
bajo licencia	under licence
bajo par	below par
bajón *(m)* de ventas	sales slump
balance *(m)*	financial statement
balance *(m)* de situación	balance sheet
balance: valor *(m)* según ...	book value
balance: verificación *(f)* del ...	balance sheet auditing
bancario: tipo *(m)* ...	bank rate
bancarios: créditos *(mpl)* ...	loan capital
banco *(m)* comercial	commercial bank
banco *(m)* de datos	data bank
banco *(m)* de datos del ordenador	computer bank
banco *(m)* de inversiones	investment bank
banco *(m)* mercantíl	merchant bank
barato: vender más ...	undercut (to)
barras: gráfico *(m)* de ...	bar chart
barrera *(f)* arancelaria	tariff barrier
barrera *(f)* no arancelaria	non-tariff barrier (NTB)
base cero: presupuesto *(m)* de ...	zero-base budget
base *(f)* de datos	database
base: año *(m)* ...	base year
base: investigación *(f)* de ...	blue-sky research
base: tasa *(f)* ...	base rate
base: tipo *(m)* ...	base rate
básicos: mercado *(m)* de productos ...	commodity market
basura: bono *(m)* ...	junk bond
beneficio *(m)*	profit
	profit performance
	return

beneficio *(m)* **bruto**	gross profit
beneficio *(m)* **neto**	net profit
beneficio *(m)* **por acción**	earnings per share (EPS)
beneficio sobre ventas: tasa *(f)* **de ...**	profit-volume ratio (P/V)
beneficio: análisis *(m)* **de centros de ...**	profit-factor analysis
beneficio: análisis *(m)* **de coste volumen y ...**	cost-volume-profit analysis
beneficio: centro *(m)* **de ...**	profit centre
beneficio: contabilidad *(f)* **por centros de ...**	profit centre accounting
beneficio: incidencia *(f)* **sobre el ...**	profit impact
beneficio: motivación *(f)* **por el ...**	profit motive
beneficio: objetivo *(m)* **de ...**	profit goal profit target
beneficio: perspectivas *(fpl)* **de ...**	profit outlook
beneficio: proyección *(f)* **del ...**	profit projection
beneficio: repercusión *(f)* **sobre el ...**	profit implication
beneficios *(mpl)* **por acción**	earnings per share (EPS) per-share earnings
beneficios *(mpl)* **reinvertidos**	ploughback
beneficios *(mpl)* **repartidos**	distributed profit
beneficios *(mpl)* **retenidos**	retained profits
beneficios: capacidad *(f)* **de ...**	earning power
beneficios: estrategia *(f)* **de ...**	profit strategy
beneficios: impuesto *(m)* **sobre ...**	profits tax
beneficios: margen *(m)* **de ...**	profit margin
beneficios: maximización *(f)* **de ...**	profit maximization
beneficios: optimización *(f)* **de ...**	profit optimization
beneficios: pago *(m)* **de ...**	profit-related pay
beneficios: participación *(f)* **en los ...**	profit-sharing
beneficios: planificación *(f)* **de ...**	profit planning
beneficios: tasa *(f)* **de capitalización de ... (TCB)**	price-earnings ratio (P/E)
bien *(m)* **de primera necesidad**	commodity

bien empaquetado	well-packaged
bienes *(mpl)* de capital	capital goods
bienes de capital: desgravación *(f)* sobre ...	capital allowance
bienes *(mpl)* de consumo de venta fácil	fast-moving consumer goods (FMCG)
bienes *(mpl)* de consumo no perecederos	consumer durables
bienes *(mpl)* de equipo	capital goods
bienes *(mpl)* de inversión	investment goods
bienes *(mpl)* industriales	industrial goods
bienes *(mpl)* ocultos	hidden assets
blanca: electrodomésticos *(mpl)* de la línea ...	white goods
blanco: cuello *(m)* ...	white-collar (worker)
blanqueado *(m)*	laundering
blanquear (dinero)	launder (to)
bloquear	freeze (to)
bolsa *(f)*	stock market
bolsa: corredor *(m)* de ...	dealer
	stockbroker
bolsa: correduría *(f)* de ...	stockbroking
bolsa: cotizar en la ...	go public (to)
bolsa: empresa *(f)* cotizada en ...	quoted company
	publicly listed company
bolsa: empresa *(f)* no cotizada en ...	unlisted company
bono *(m)* basura	junk bond
boom *(m)*	boom
borne *(m)*	terminal
botella: cuello *(m)* de ...	bottleneck
brazos caídos: huelga *(f)* de ...	sit-down strike
bruto: producto *(m)* ... interior (PIB)	gross domestic product (GDP)
bruto: beneficio *(m)* ...	gross profit
bruto: margen *(m)* ...	gross margin (GM)
buen trabajador *(m)* en equipo	team player
buzón *(m)*	mailbox
byte *(m)*	byte

C

caballeros: acuerdo *(m)* **de ...**	gentleman's agreement
cabezas: cazador *(m)* **de ...**	head-hunter
CAD (diseño *(m)* **asistido por ordenador)**	CAD (computer-aided design)
cadena *(f)* **de distribución**	chain of distribution
cadena *(f)* **de mando**	chain of command
cadena *(f)* **de producción**	chain of production
cadena *(f)* **de valor**	value chain
cadena: fabricación *(f)* **en ...**	flow production
cadena: producción *(f)* **en ...**	chain production
	line production
	production line
caducidad: fecha *(f)* **de ...**	use-by date
caídos: huelga *(f)* **de brazos ...**	sit-down strike
caja *(f)*	cash
caja *(f)* **de herramientas**	toolbox
caja *(f)* **dos**	slush fund
caja negativo: flujo *(m)* **de ...**	negative cash flow
caja *(f)* **negra**	slush fund
caja *(f)* **para gastos menores**	petty cash
caja: control *(m)* **presupuestario de ...**	cash budgeting
caja: falta *(f)* **de ...**	cash-poor
	cash-strapped
caja: presupuesto *(m)* **de ...**	cash budget
caja: rico de ...	cash-rich
CAL (aprendizaje *(m)* **asistido por ordenador)**	CAL (computer-aided learning)
calcular	assess (to)
cálculo *(m)* **aproximado**	guesstimate
cálculo: hoja *(f)* **de ...**	spreadsheet
calidad: artículos *(mpl)* **de alta ...**	up-market
calidad: aseguramiento *(m)* **de la ...**	quality assurance
calidad: círculo *(m)* **de ...**	quality circle
calidad: control *(m)* **de ...**	quality control (QC)
calidad: control *(m)* **total de ...**	total quality control (TQC)
calidad: gestión *(f)* **de ...**	quality management
calidad: gestión *(f)* **total de ...**	total quality management (TQM)

calidad: valoración *(f)* de la ...	quality assessment
calificación por puntos: método *(m)* de ...	points-rating method
CAM (fabricación *(f)* asistida por ordenador)	CAM (computer-aided manufacturing)
cámara *(f)* de compensación	clearing house
cambiar la imagen *(f)*	re-image (to)
cambio *(m)* a plazo	forward rate
cambio en fecha futura: tasa *(f)* de ...	forward exchange rate
cambio: gestión *(f)* de ...	change management (management of change)
cambio: mecanismo *(m)* de tasas de ...	Exchange Rate Mechanism (ERM)
cambio: tasa *(f)* de ...	exchange rate
camino crítico: análisis *(m)* del ...	critical path analysis (CPA)
camino crítico: método *(m)* del ...	critical path method (CPM)
campaña *(f)* de productividad	productivity campaign productivity drive
campaña *(f)* de publicidad	advertising campaign
campo: investigación *(f)* de ...	field research
campo: prueba *(f)* de ...	field testing
camuflaje *(m)* *(del balance)*	window-dressing
canal *(m)* de distribución	distribution channel
canales *(mpl)* de comunicación	channels of communication
cancelar	liquidate (to) wind up (to) write off (to)
candidatos escogidos: lista *(f)* de ...	shortlist
candidatos: seleccionar ...	shortlist (to)
canje *(m)*	swap
canjeables con fecha futura: acciones *(fpl)* ...	forward swap
cantidad *(f)* de trabajo	workload
cantidad *(f)* necesaria para alcanzar el punto de equilibrio	break-even quantity
cantidad *(f)* tratada	throughput
capacidad *(f)*	capability competency
capacidad *(f)* de beneficios	earning power

capacidad *(f)* **de fabricación**	manufacturing capacity
capacidad *(f)* **de planta**	plant capacity
capacidad *(f)* **excesiva**	excess capacity
capacidad *(f)* **no utilizada**	idle capacity
capacidad *(f)* **ociosa**	full capacity
capacidad: plena ...	spare capacity
capacidad: sobre ...	overcapacity
capacidad: utilización *(f)* **de la ...**	capacity utilization
capacitación *(f)*	training
capacitada: corporación *(f)* **de imano de obra no ...**	dilution of labour
capataz *(m)*	foreman
capital *(m)* **arriesgado**	venture capital
capital *(m)* **circulante**	circulating capital
	working capital
capital *(m)* **de riesgo**	risk capital
capital *(m)* **disponible**	capital assets
capital *(m)* **emitido**	issued capital
capital *(m)* **en acciones**	share capital
capital *(m)* **invertido**	capital employed
capital invertido: rendimiento *(m)* **del ...**	return on capital employed (ROCE)
	return on equity (ROE)
capital *(m)* **social autorizado**	authorized capital
capital: aporte *(m)* **de ...**	capital formation
capital: bienes *(mpl)* **de ...**	capital goods
capital: control *(m)* **presupuestario de gastos de ...**	capital budgeting
capital: crecimiento *(m)* **de ...**	capital appreciation
capital: desgravación *(f)* **sobre bienes de ...**	capital allowance
capital: estructura *(f)* **del ...**	capital structure
capital: evaluación *(f)* **de gastos de ...**	capital expenditure appraisal
capital: evaluación *(f)* **de proyectos de ...**	capital project evaluation
capital: ganancia *(f)* **de ...**	capital gain
capital: gastos *(mpl)* **en ...**	capital expenditure
capital: movimiento *(m)* **de ...**	funds flow
capital: pérdida *(f)* **de ...**	capital loss
capital: presupuesto *(m)* **de gastos de ...**	capital budget

capital: racionamiento *(f)* de ...	capital rationing
capital: "ratio" *(m)* rendimiento ...	capital-output ratio
capital: rendimiento *(m)* del ...	return on capital
capital: renta *(f)* del ...	return on capital
capitalización *(f)*	capitalization
capitalización de beneficios: tasa *(f)* de ... (TCB)	price-earnings ratio (P/E)
capitalizar	capitalize (to)
características *(fpl)* del puesto	job characteristics
carga: factor *(m)* de ...	load factor
carga *(f)*: sobre	mark-up
cartel *(m)*	cartel
cartera *(f)* de compensación	balanced portfolio
cartera *(f)* de marcas	brand portfolio
cartera *(f)* de negocios	business portfolio
cartera *(f)* de productos	product portfolio
cartera *(f)* de valores	stock portfolio
cartera *(f)* del activo	asset portfolio
cartera: gestión *(f)* de ... *(de valores mobiliarios)*	portfolio management
cartera: selección *(f)* de ...	portfolio selection
"cash flow" *(m)*	cash flow
"cash flow" *(m)* actualizado	discounted cash flow (DCF)
"cash flow" *(m)* marginal	incremental cash flow
"cash flow" *(m)* negativo	negative cash flow
casos: estudio *(m)* de ...	case study
cazador *(m)* de cabezas	head-hunter
celo: huelga *(f)* de ...	work-to-rule
central *(f)*	head office
central: ordenador *(m)* ...	mainframe
central: unidad *(f)* ...	mainframe
central: unidad *(f)* de proceso ... (UPC)	central processing unit (CPU)
centralización *(m)*	centralization
centralizar	centralize (to)
centro *(m)* de beneficio	profit centre
centro *(m)* de coste	cost centre
centro *(m)* de responsabilidad	responsibility centre
centro *(m)* de tasación	assessment centre
centro *(m)* informático	computer centre
centros de beneficio: contabilidad *(f)* por ...	profit centre accounting

cero: juego *(m)* de suma ...	zero-sum game
cero: presupuesto *(m)* de base ...	zero-base budget
cerrado: ciclo *(m)* ...	closed loop
cese *(m)* de empleo	lay-off
chip *(m)*	chip
cibernética *(f)*	cybernetics
ciclo *(m)* cerrado	closed loop
ciclo *(m)* comercial	trade cycle
ciclo *(m)* de vida *(de un producto)*	life cycle *(of a product)*
	product life
ciclo *(m)* de trabajo	work cycle
ciclo *(m)* de vida de un producto	product life cycle
ciclo *(m)* económico	business cycle
ciencia *(f)* de la conducta	behavioural science
ciencia *(f)* de política directiva	management science
científica del trabajo: organización *(f)* ...	management science scientific management
científica: programación *(f)* ...	scientific programming
cierre *(m)*	shut-down
cierre *(m)* por los patrones	lock-out
cifra *(f)* de negocios	turnover
cifra *(f)* de ventas	sales turnover
cifra *(f)* orientativa	ballpark figure
cifras: maquillar las ...	massage the figures (to)
circulación *(f)*	routing
circulación *(f)* de datos	information flow
circulante: activo *(m)* ...	current assets
circulante: capital *(m)* ...	circulating capital working capital
circulante: gestión *(f)* del ...	asset liability management
circulante neto: activo *(m)* ...	net current assets
circulante: pasivo *(m)* ...	current liabilities
círculo *(m)* de calidad	quality circle
clase *(f)* mundialmente reconocida	world-class
clasificación *(f)*	ranking
clasificación *(f)* de personal	personnel rating
clasificación *(f)* de puestos de trabajo	job classification
clasificación *(f)* de solvencia	credit rating
clasificación *(f)* de tareas	job evaluation

clasificación *(f)* **por méritos**	merit rating
clave de compra: factor *(m)* ...	key buying factor
clave de éxito: factor *(m)* ...	key success factor
clave: función *(f)* ...	function key
clave: producto *(m)* ...	core product
cliente *(m)* **potencial**	prospective customer
cobertura *(f)*	hedging
cobertura: proporción *(f)* **de** ...	cover ratio
coche: teléfono *(m)* **de** ...	car phone
cociente *(m)*	quotient
cogestión *(f)*	co-determination
colaborativo	collaborative
colas: teoría *(f)* **de** ...	queuing theory
colateral	collateral
colateral: garantía *(f)* ...	collateral security
colectiva: negociación *(f)* ...	collective bargaining
colectiva: prima *(f)* ...	group bonus
colectivo: incentivo *(m)* ...	group incentive
colectivo negociado: convenio *(m)* ...	collective bargaining agreement
colocaciones: agencia *(f)* **de** ...	employment bureau
coloquio *(m)*	symposium
combinación *(f)* **de inversiones**	investment mix
combinación *(f)* **de medios de márketing**	marketing mix
combinación *(f)* **de medios de promoción**	promotional mix
combinación *(f)* **de medios de venta**	sales mix
combinación *(f)* **de productos**	product mix
combinada: oferta *(f)* ...	package deal
comercial: atracción *(f)* ...	sales appeal
comercial: banco *(m)* ...	commercial bank
comercial: cartera *(f)* ...	brand portfolio
comercial: ciclo *(m)* ...	trade cycle
comercial: director *(m)* ...	marketing manager
comercial: empuje *(m)* ...	market drive
	market thrust
comercial: estrategia *(f)* ...	business strategy
	marketing strategy
comercial: garra *(f)* ...	sales appeal
comercial: gestión *(f)* ...	market management
comercial: información *(f)* ...	market intelligence

comercial: nombre *(m)* ...	trade name
comercial: oportunidad *(f)* ...	market opportunity
comercial: plan *(m)* ...	market plan
comercial: política *(f)* ...	business policy
comercial: posicionamiento *(m)* ...	brand positioning
comercial: previsión *(f)* ...	business forecasting
comercial: programa *(m)* ...	trading programme
comercial: pronóstico *(m)* ...	business forecasting
comercial: restricción *(f)* ...	trade restriction
comercial: separación *(f)* ...	demerger
comercial: zona *(f)* ...	trading area
comerciales: perspectivas *(fpl)* ...	market prospects
comerciales: relaciones *(fpl)* ...	business relations
comercializable	marketable
comercialización *(f)* aplazada	switch trading
comercialización *(f)* con líder venta de objetos-reclamos	leader merchandising
comercialización *(f)* del producto	marketing merchandising
comerciantes: asociación *(f)* de ...	trade association
comercio *(m)* con información privilegiada	insider trading
comercio *(m)* de patentes	patent trading
comercio *(m)* de trueque	barter trade
comercio: artículo *(m)* de ...	commodity
comercio: fondo *(m)* de ...	brand portfolio goodwill
comienzo *(m)*	start-up
comisión *(f)* investigadora	working party
comisionista *(m)* corredor	broker
comité *(m)* de la empresa	works committee
comparación *(f)* entre empresas	inter-firm comparison
compartición *(f)* de tiempo	time-sharing
compartimentar	compartmentalize (to)
compatible	compatible
compensación: cámara *(f)* de ...	clearing house
compensación: cartera *(f)* de ...	balanced portfolio
competencia *(f)*	competition
competencia *(f)* de la gerencia	management competence
competencia *(f)* desleal	unfair competition
competencia *(f)* leal	fair competition

competencia: análisis *(m)* de la ...	competitor analysis
competencia: ventaja *(f)* sobre la ...	competitive edge
competencia: zona *(f)* de ...	jurisdiction
competitiva: estrategia *(f)* ...	competitive strategy
competitiva: situación *(f)* ...	competitive position
competitiva: ventaja *(f)* ...	competitive advantage
competitivas: tácticas *(fpl)* ...	competitive tactics
competitividad *(f)*	competitiveness
competitivo *(m)*	competitive
competitivo: empuje *(m)* ...	competitive thrust
competitivo: estímulo *(m)* ...	competitive stimulus
competitivo: precio *(m)* ...	competitive price
completos: método *(m)* de costes ...	full-cost method
compra *(f)*	buyout
compra *(f)* con apalancamiento (LBO)	leveraged buyout (LBO)
compra de acciones: opción *(f)* de ...	stock option
compra *(f)* de una empresa por los empleados	employee buyout
compra *(f)* de una empresa por sus directivos	management buyout (MBO)
compra *(f)* hóstil de acciones de una empresa: hacer la ...	raid a company (to)
compra *(f)* impulsiva	impulse buying
compra *(f)* por los trabajadores	worker buyout
compra: factor *(m)* clave de ...	key buying factor
compra: motor *(m)* de ...	purchasing motivator
compra: oferta *(f)* pública de ... (OPA)	takeover bid (TOB)
comprador *(m)* potencial	potential buyer
compradores: conducta *(f)* de los ...	buying behaviour
comprar *(parte mayoritaria del activo)*	buy out (to)
comprar: arrendar o ...	lease or buy (to)
comprar: opción *(f)* de fabricar o ...	make-or-buy decision
compras: jefe *(m)* de ...	chief buyer
	purchasing manager

comprobar sistemas (de ordenador)	debug (to)
compromiso *(m)* de inversión	capital commitment
compromiso *(m)* del personal	staff commitment
computador *(m)*	computer
común: empresa *(f)* ...	joint venture
común: lenguaje *(m)* ...	common language
Común: Mercado *(m)* ...	Common Market
comunicación *(f)* electrónica	electronic communication
comunicación *(f)* no verbal	non-verbal communication
comunicación *(f)* por rumor	grapevine
comunicación *(f)* verbal	verbal communication
comunicación: análisis *(f)* de los medios de ...	media analysis
comunicación: canales *(mpl)* de ...	channels of communication
comunicación: medios *(mpl)* de ...	media
comunicación: selección *(f)* de medios de ...	media selection
comunicación: teoría *(f)* de ...	communications theory
comunicaciones: red *(f)* de ...	communications network
Comunidad *(f)* Europea (CE)	European Community (EC)
con conocimientos *(mpl)* de informática	computer-literate
con exceso *(m)* de mano de obra	overmanned
concentrar	amalgamate (to)
concepción *(f)* de productos	product conception
concepto *(m)* del valor	value concept
concesión *(f)* recíproca de licencias	cross-licensing
conciencia *(f)* del coste	cost awareness
	cost consciousness
conciliación *(f)*	conciliation
conciliador *(m)*	troubleshooter
conciliar	conciliate (to)
concursar (a un contrato)	tender (to)
condiciones *(fpl)* de empleo	conditions of employment
conducta *(f)* del consumidor	consumer behaviour
conducta *(f)* del hombre en la organización	organizational behaviour
conducta *(f)* de los compradores	buying behaviour

conducta: ciencia (f) de la ...	behavioural science
conectado	on line
confabulación (f)	collusion
confidencial: objetivo (m) ...	hidden agenda
confidencialidad (f)	confidentiality
conflicto (m) laboral	industrial dispute
congelación (f) de salarios	pay pause
congelación (f) salarial	wage freeze
congelar	freeze (to)
conglomerado (m)	conglomerate
conjunta: consultación (f) ...	joint consultation
conjunta: empresa (f)	joint venture
conjunta: negociación (f) ...	joint negotiation
conjunta: representación (f) ...	joint representation
conjunta: sociedad (f) en participación ...	joint-venture company
conjunto (m) de atribuciones	role set
conocimiento (m) de marca	brand awareness
consejero (m)	non-executive director
consejero (m) delegado	executive director
consejo (m) de administración	board of directors
	executive board
consejo (m) de empleados	employee counselling
consejo (m) de obreros	works council
consejo (m) supervisor	supervisory board
consejo: control (m) del ... de administración	board control
consejo: reunión (f) del ... de administración	board meeting
consejos: sala (f) de ...	boardroom
consenso (m)	consensus
consolidación (f)	consolidation
consolidados: estados (mpl) financieros ...	consolidated accounts
consorciales: acuerdos (mpl) ...	pooling arrangements
consorcio (f)	consortium
constitución: gastos (mpl) de ...	set-up costs
consultación (f) conjunta	joint consultation
consultar	consult (to)
consultivo	consultative
consultivo: auxiliar (m) ...	staff assistant
consultor (m) de empresas	management consultant
consultor (m) informático	computer consultant

consultores *(mpl)*	advisory services
consultoría *(f)* de empresas	management consultancy
consultorio *(m)* de expertos	brains trust
consumidor: aceptación *(m)* del ...	consumer acceptance
consumidor: conducta *(f)* del ...	consumer behaviour
consumidor: estrategia *(f)* del ...	user strategy
consumidor: índice *(m)* de precios al ...	retail price index (RPI)
consumidor: orientación *(f)* al ...	consumer orientation
consumidor: protección *(f)* al ...	consumer protection
consumidor: resistencia *(f)* del ...	consumer resistance
consumidor: satisfacción *(f)* del ...	consumer satisfaction
consumidores: investigación *(f)* de ...	consumer research
consumidores: "panel" *(m)* de ...	consumers' panel
consumismo *(m)*	consumerism
consumista: de reacción ...	consumer-responsive
consumo de venta fácil: bienes *(mpl)* de ...	fast-moving consumer goods (FMCG)
consumo no perecederos: bienes *(mpl)* de ...	consumer durables
consumo por impulso: productos *(mpl)* de ...	impulse goods
consumo: artículos *(mpl)* de ...	consumer goods
consumo: índice *(m)* de precios al ... (IPC)	consumer price index retail price index (RPI)
contabilidad *(f)*	accounting
contabilidad *(f)* analítica	analytic accounting
contabilidad *(f)* de costes	cost accounting
contabilidad *(f)* de producción	process costing
contabilidad *(f)* gerencial	management accounting
contabilidad *(f)* marginal	marginal costing
contabilidad *(f)* por centros de beneficio	profit centre accounting
contabilidad *(f)* presupuestaria	budgeting
contabilidad *(f)* trucada	window-dressing

contabilidad: departamento *(m)* de ...	accounting department accounts department
contabilidad: jefe *(m)* de ...	chief accountant
contabilidad: modelo *(m)* de ...	accounting model
contabilidad: período *(m)* de ...	accounting period
contabilidad: sistema *(m)* electrónico de ...	electronic accounting system
contable: "ratio" *(m)* ...	accounting ratio
contable: responsabilidad *(f)* ...	responsibility accounting
contable: sin valor *(m)* ...	write-off
contable: valor *(m)* ...	asset value
contactos profesionales: explotación *(f)* de ...	networking
contado: acuerdo *(m)* al ...	cash deal
contado: ventas *(fpl)* al ...	countertrade cash sales
contante: dinero *(m)* ...	cash
contenedor *(m)*	container
contenedores: utilización *(f)* de ...	containerization
contenido *(m)* **del puesto**	job content
contenido *(m)* **del trabajo**	work content
contenido local: normas *(fpl)* de ...	local content rules
contestador telefónico	answerphone
contingencias: teoría *(f)* de las	contingency theory
contínua: producción *(f)* ...	continuous-flow production
continuo	ongoing
continuo de mercancías: inventario *(m)* ...	continuous stocktaking
contra-espionaje *(m)* **industrial**	industrial security
contratar	hire (to)
contratar y despedir	hiring and firing
contrato *(m)* **de directivos**	management contract
contrato: trabajo *(m)* por ...	work by contract
control *(m)*	control
control *(m)* **adaptivo**	adaptive control
control administrativo: proceso *(m)* de ...	administrative control procedure
control *(m)* **de calidad**	quality control (QC)
control *(m)* **de costes**	cost control
control *(m)* **de crédito**	credit control
control *(m)* **de existencias**	stock control

control *(m)* de fabricación	manufacturing control
control *(m)* de la producción: planificación *(f)* y ...	production planning and control
control *(m)* de producción	output budgeting
	production control
control *(m)* de rendimiento	performance budgeting
control *(m)* del consejo de administración	board control
control *(m)* del inventario	inventory control
control *(m)* del lote	batch control
control *(m)* del proceso	process control
control *(m)* del rendimiento	efficiency audit
	performance monitoring
control *(m)* directivo	managerial control
control *(m)* financiero	financial control
control *(m)* numérico	numerical control
control *(m)* presupuestario	budgetary control
	budgeting control
control *(m)* presupuestario de caja	cash budgeting
control *(m)* presupuestario de gastos de capital	capital budgeting
control *(m)* total de calidad	total quality control (TQC)
control: información *(f)* de ...	control information
control: participación *(f)* de ...	controlling interest
controlados: costes *(mpl)* ...	managed costs
controlar	monitor (to)
	control (to)
controlar *(m)* el funcionamiento	monitor performance (to)
convenio *(m)* colectivo negociado	collective bargaining agreement
convenio *(m)* de productividad	productivity agreement
coordinación *(f)*	coordination
corporal: lenguaje *(m)* ...	body language
corporativismo *(m)*	corporatism
corredor *(m)*	broker
corredor *(m)* de bolsa	dealer
	stockbroker
correduría *(f)* de bolsa	stockbroking
correlación *(f)*	correlation
correlacionar	correlate (to)
correo *(m)* electrónico	electronic mail (e-mail)
correo: pedido *(m)* por ...	mail order

corretaje: honorarios *(mpl)* de ...	brokerage fees
corretajes *(mpl)*	brokerage
corto plazo: activo *(m)* disponible a ...	quick assets
corto plazo: planificación *(f)* a ...	short-range planning
	short-term planning
coste *(m)* de distribución	distribution cost
coste *(m)* de la vida	cost of living
coste *(m)* de liquidación	closing-down costs
coste *(m)* de oportunidad	opportunity costs
coste *(m)* de producción	costs of production
coste *(m)* de productos: evaluación *(f)* del ...	product costing
coste *(m)* de sustitución	replacement costs
coste *(m)* directo	direct costs
coste *(m)* indirecto	indirect costs
coste *(m)* medio	average cost
coste *(m)* mínimo	least-cost
coste *(m)* unitario de mano de obra	unit labour costs
coste volumen y beneficio: análisis *(m)* de ...	cost-volume-profit analysis
coste-beneficio: análisis *(m)* ...	cost-benefit analysis (CBA)
coste: centro *(m)* de ...	cost centre
coste: conciencia *(f)* del ...	cost awareness
	cost consciousness
coste: eficaz en relación con el ...	cost-effective
coste: eficiente *(m)* en relación con el ...	cost-efficient
coste: elemento *(m)* de ...	cost factor
costes completos: método *(m)* de ...	full-cost method
costes *(mpl)* controlados	managed costs
costes *(mpl)* de producción	production costs
costes de sistemas: evaluación *(f)* de ...	estimating systems costs
costes directos: método *(m)* de ...	direct costing
costes *(mpl)* estándares	standard costs
costes estándares: método *(m)* de ...	standard costing

costes *(mpl)* fijos	fixed costs
costes *(mpl)* marginales	marginal costs
costes marginales: método *(m)* de ...	marginal costing
costes por función: metodo *(m)* de ...	functional costing
costes *(mpl)* semi-variables	semi-variable costs
costes *(mpl)* variables	variable costs
costes: absorción *(f)* de ...	absorption cost
costes: análisis *(m)* de ...	cost analysis
	value engineering
costes: asignación *(f)* de ...	allocation of costs
	cost allocation
costes: contabilidad *(f)* de ...	cost accounting
costes: control *(m)* de ...	cost control
costes: distribución *(f)* de ...	cost apportionment
costes: estándares *(mpl)* de ...	cost standard
costes: estructura *(f)* de ...	cost structure
costes: evaluación *(f)* de ...	costing
costes: inflación *(f)* de ...	cost-push inflation
costes: reducción *(f)* de ...	cost reduction
costes: sensible a los ...	cost-sensitive
costes: varianza *(f)* de ...	cost variance
cotización: valores *(mpl)* no admitidos a ...	unlisted security
cotizada en bolsa: empresa *(f)* ...	publicly listed company
	quoted company
cotizada en bolsa: empresa *(f)* no ...	unlisted company
cotizar en la bolsa	go public (to)
creación *(f)* de la imagen	imaging
creación *(f)* de productos	product generation
creador *(m)* de mercado	market maker
creados: intereses *(mpl)* ...	vested interest
creativo: espíritu *(m)* ...	creative thinking
creativo: márketing *(m)* ...	creative marketing
crecimiento *(m)* de capital	capital appreciation
crecimiento *(m)* de la empresa	corporate growth
crecimiento *(m)* orgánico	organic growth
crecimiento: estrategia *(f)* de ...	growth strategy
crecimiento: índice *(m)* de ...	growth index
crecimiento: potencial *(m)* de ...	growth potential
crecimiento: sector *(m)* de ...	growth area

crediticia: restricción *(f)* ...	credit squeeze
crédito *(m)*	goodwill
crédito *(m)* abierto	revolving credit
crédito *(m)* paralelo	parallel loan
crédito: control *(m)* de ...	credit control
crédito: línea *(f)* de ...	borrowing facility
créditos *(mpl)* bancarios	loan capital
créditos *(mpl)* financieros a largo plazo	loan stock
créditos *(m)* incobrables	bad debts
créditos: gestión *(f)* de ...	credit management
crisis: gestión *(f)* de ...	crisis management
criterio *(m)*	yardstick
criterios *(mpl)* de inversión	investment criteria
crítica: masa *(f)* ...	critical mass
crítico: análisis *(m)* del camino ...	critical path analysis (CPA)
crítico: método *(m)* del camino ...	critical path method (CPM)
cuadro *(m)* de herramientas	toolbox
cuadros *(mpl)* medios	middle management
cualificada: mano *(f)* de obra ...	skilled labour
cualificada: mano *(f)* de obra no ...	unskilled labour
cuantitativo: análisis *(m)* ...	quantitative analysis
cubrirse	hedge (to)
cuello *(m)* blanco	white-collar (worker)
cuello *(m)* de botella	bottleneck
cuenta *(f)* de gastos	expense account
cuenta propia: trabajar por ...	freelance (to go)
cuenta: anticipos *(mpl)* a ...	pay-as-you-go
cuentas *(fpl)*: censor *(m)* de ...	auditor
cuentas *(fpl)*: revisar ...	audit (to)
cuentas: verificador *(m)* de ...	comptroller
cuentas *(fpl)*: verificar ...	audit (to)
cultura *(f)*	culture
cultura *(f)* empresarial	corporate culture
	organization culture
cumbre para abajo: de la ...	top-down
cupo *(m)* de ventas	sales quota
curso *(m)*: en ...	on stream

cursor *(m)*	cursor
curva *(f)* **de aprendizaje**	learning curve
curva *(f)* **de incrementos de salarios**	salary progression curve

D

daños: limitación *(f)* de ...	damage limitation
datos (EDP): proceso *(m)* electrónico de ...	electronic data processing (EDP)
datos *(mpl)* de pantalla	viewdata
datos del ordenador: banco *(m)* de ...	computer bank
datos: adquisición *(f)* de ...	data acquisition
datos: banco *(m)* de ...	data bank
datos: base *(f)* de ...	database
datos: circulación *(f)* de ...	information flow
datos: departamento *(f)* de proceso de ...	computer services department
datos: diagrama *(m)* de flujo de ...	data flow chart
datos: proceso *(m)* automático de ... (ADP)	automatic data processing (ADP)
datos: proceso *(m)* de ...	data processing
	information processing
datos: proceso *(m)* electrónico de ...	electronic data processing (EDP)
datos: protección *(f)* de ...	data protection
datos: recogida *(f)* de ...	data gathering
datos: recuperación *(f)* de ...	data retrieval
	information retrieval
datos *(f)*: salida de ...	output
datos: sistematización *(f)* de ...	information processing
datos: utilización *(f)* de ...	information handling
de la cumbre para abajo	top-down
de reacción consumista	consumer-responsive
de vanguardia	state of the art
dealer *(m)*	dealer
decisión: procedimientos *(mpl)* de ...	decision process
decisiones: análisis *(m)* de ...	decision analysis
decisiones: árbol *(m)* de ...	decision tree
decisiones: modelo *(m)* de ...	decision model
decisiones: proceso *(m)* de tomar ...	decision-making process
decisiones: teoría *(f)* de ...	decision theory

declaración *(f)* de la misión	mission statement
declaración *(f)* de visión	vision statement
declive: industria *(f)* en ...	sunset industry
deducible fiscalmente	tax-deductible
defectos: sin ...	zero defects
defensiva: estrategia *(f)* ...	defensive strategy
déficit *(m)*	shortfall
déficit: financiación *(f)* de ...	deficit financing
definición *(f)* de objetivos	objective-setting
delegación *(f)*	branch office
delegación *(f)* de poderes	delegation
delegar	delegate (to)
demanda: evaluación *(f)* de la ...	demand assessment
demanda: inflación *(f)* por la ...	demand-pull inflation
demanda: mercado *(m)* de ...	sellers' market
demanda: previsión *(f)* de la ...	demand forecasting
democracia *(f)* industrial	industrial democracy
demotivante: elemento *(m)* ...	disincentive
dentro de la empresa: formación *(m)* ...	in-plant training
dentro de la industria: formación *(f)* ...	training within industry (TWI)
departamental: plan *(m)* ...	departmental plan
departamento *(m)* de contabilidad	accounts department
departamento *(m)* de diseño	design office
departamento *(m)* de estudio de métodos	methods study department
departamento *(m)* de investigación	research department
departamento *(m)* de márketing	marketing department
departamento *(m)* de planificación	planning department
departamento *(f)* de proceso de datos	computer services department
departamento *(m)* de ventas	sales department
departamento *(m)* del personal	personnel department
departamento *(m)* técnico y de proyectos	engineering and design department
departamento: director *(m)* de ...	departmental manager
departamento: gerencia *(f)* de ...	departmental management
departamento: jefe *(m)* de ...	departmental head

depreciar	depreciate (to)
depresión *(f)*	slump
depresión: entrada *(f)* en la ...	hard landing
(economía)	entry into economic depression
depresión: evitacíon de la ...	soft landing
(f) (economía)	avoidance of economic depression
derecho *(m)* preferente de	rights issue
suscripción	
derechos *(mpl)*	royalty
derechos *(mpl)* sobre el activo	equity
derivado *(m)*	by-product
desarrollado: país *(m)*	less-developed country (LDC)
menos ...	
desarrollo *(m)* de equipos	team-building
desarrollo *(m)* de la	organizational development
organización	
desarrollo *(m)* de nuevos	new-product development
productos	
desarrollo *(m)* de productos	product development
desarrollo *(m)* de recursos	human resource development (HRD)
humanos	
desarrollo de ventas: esfuerzo	sales expansion effort
(m) para el ...	
desarrollo profesional:	career planning
planificación *(f)* del ...	
desarrollo: estrategia *(f)* de ...	expansion strategy
desarrollo: industria *(f)* en ...	growth industry
desarrollo *(m)*: investigación *(f)*	research and development (R & D)
y ...	
desarrollo: programa *(m)* de ...	development programme
desatascar	debottleneck (to)
descapitalizado	undercapitalized
descentralización *(f)*	decentralization
descentralizada: dirección *(f)* ...	decentralized management
descentralizar	decentralize (to)
descifrar	unscramble (to)
descomposición *(f)* de las	breakdown operations
tareas	
descomposición *(f)* en factores	factoring
descripción *(f)* del trabajo	job description
deseconomía *(f)* de escala	diseconomy of scale
desembolsar	disburse (to)
desembolso *(m)*	disbursement

desempeño *(m)* **de funciones**	role-playing
desempleo *(m)*	redundancy
	unemployment
desfase *(m)*	lag
	time-lag
desglosar	unbundle (to)
desglose *(m)* **de operaciones**	operations breakdown
desgravación *(f)* **de impuestos duplicados**	double taxation relief
desgravación *(f)* **fiscal**	tax relief
desgravación *(f)* **sobre bienes de capital**	capital allowance
desindustrialización *(f)*	deindustrialization
desintegración *(f)*	disintegration
desinversión *(f)*	disinvestment
	divestment
desleal: competencia *(f)* ...	unfair competition
desmotivación *(f)*	demotivation
desmotivar	demotivate (to)
despacho: agente *(m)* **de** ...	forwarding agent
despedida *(f)* **sumária**	summary dismissal
despedir	fire (to)
despedir *(m)* **obreros**	lay off (to)
despedir: contratar y ...	hiring and firing
despegue *(m)*	take-off
despido *(m)*	dismissal
despido *(m)* **del trabajo**	lay-off
despido *(m)* **injusto**	unfair dismissal
despido: indemnización *(f)* **por** ...	golden handshake
	golden parachute
	severance pay
desplazamiento *(m)*	redeployment
desplazar	redeploy (to)
desplegar	deploy (to)
despliegue *(m)*	deployment
desregulación *(f)*	deregulation
desregular	deregulate (to)
destajo *(m)*	payment by results
destajo: trabajo *(m)* **a** ...	piecework
desvalorizada: obligación *(f)* ...	junk bond
desviación *(f)* **de marcas**	switch selling
desviación *(f)* **estándar**	standard deviation
desviación *(f)* **salarial**	wage drift

detalle: mantenimiento (f) del precio al ...	resale price maintenance (RPM)
deuda-activo: ratio (m) ...	debt-equity ratio
deuda: financiación (f) de la ...	debt financing
deuda: índice (m) de ...	gearing ratio
	debt ratio
deudas (fpl)	liabilities
deudas (f) incobrables	bad-debt losses
deudor (m)	debtor
deudores (mpl) morosos	bad debts
devengos: hoja (f) de ...	time sheet
día: poner al ...	update (to)
día: turno (m) de ...	day shift
diagnóstico (m) de grupos	T-group training
diagnóstico: rutina (f) del ...	diagnostic routine
diagrama (m)	milestone chart
diagrama (f) de dispersión	scatter diagram
diagrama (m) de flujo de datos	data flow chart
diagrama (m) de flujos	flow chart
	flow diagram
diagrama (m) de flujos del proceso	flow process chart
diccionario (m) en procesador de textos	spellcheck
diferencia (f) de precios	differential price
diferenciación (f) entre productos	product differentiation
diferencial: valoración (f)	differential pricing
diferenciar	differentiate (to)
diferenciar productos	differentiate between products (to)
difícil de utilizar	user-unfriendly
digital	digital
digital: ordenador (m) ...	digital computer
digitalizar	digitize (to)
dilución (f) de accionariado	dilution of equity
dinámica (f) de grupos	group dynamics
	methectics
dinámica (f) de productos	product dynamics
dinámica (f) del mercado	market dynamics
dinámica (f) industrial	industrial dynamics
dinámica: evaluación (f) ...	dynamic evaluation
dinámica: programación (f) ...	dynamic programming

dinámico de administración: modelo *(m)* ...	dynamic management model
dinámico: ejecutivo *(m)* ...	whiz-kid
dinero: provisión *(f)* **de** ...	money supply
dirección *(f)*	management
dirección *(f)* **administrativa**	office management
dirección *(f)* **comercial**	business management
dirección *(f)* **de ventas**	sales management
dirección *(f)* **del personal**	personnel management
	staff management
dirección *(f)* **descentralizada**	decentralized management
dirección *(f)* **eficaz**	effective management
dirección *(f)* **entrelazada**	interlocking directorate
dirección *(f)* **financiera**	financial management
dirección *(f)* **general**	(general) management
dirección *(f)* **lineal**	line management
dirección *(f)* **múltiple**	multiple management
dirección *(f)* **operacional**	operating management
dirección *(f)* **participativa**	participative management
dirección *(f)* **por excepción**	management by exception
dirección *(f)* **por objetivos**	management by objectives (MBO)
dirección *(f)* **sistematizada**	management system
	systems management
dirección: alta *(f)* ...	top management
dirección: enfoque *(m)* **según la alta** ...	top management approach
dirección: equipo *(m)* **de** ...	management team
dirección: estilo *(m)* **de** ...	management style
dirección: formación *(f)* **de la** ...	management development
dirección: plantilla *(f)* **de** ...	managerial grid
dirección: servicios *(mpl)* **de** ...	management services
dirección: sistema *(m)* **de información para la** ...	management information system (MIS)
directa: mano *(f)* **de obra** ...	direct labour
directa: publicidad *(f)* ...	mailing
	direct mail
directa: venta *(f)* ...	direct selling
directiva: ciencia *(f)* **de política** ...	management science
directiva: eficacia *(f)* ...	managerial effectiveness
directiva: función *(f)* ...	managerial function
directiva: gestión *(f)* ...	management
directiva: jerarquía *(f)* ...	managerial structure

directiva: política *(f)* ...	management policy
directiva: teoría *(f)* de política ...	management theory
directivo *(m)*	executive
directivo *(m)* de línea	line executive
directivo: aptitud *(f)* del ...	executive competence
directivo: control *(m)* ...	managerial control
directivo: estilo *(m)* ...	managerial style
directivo: estrategia *(f)* de personal ...	executive manpower strategy
directivo: personal *(m)* ...	management staff
directivos: ascenso *(m)* de ...	executive advancement
	executive promotion
directivos: compra *(f)* de una empresa por sus ...	management buyout (MBO)
directivos: contrato *(m)* de ...	management contract
directivos: formación *(f)* de ...	management training
directivos: planificación *(f)* de sucesión de ...	management succession planning
directivos: potencial *(m)* de ...	management potential
directivos: reclutamiento *(m)* de ...	executive search
directivos: recompensa *(f)* de ...	executive compensation
directivos: remuneración *(f)* de ...	executive remuneration
directivos: seleccionar ...	head-hunt (to)
directo: coste *(m)* ...	direct costs
directo: márketing *(m)* ...	direct marketing
director *(m)*	director
	executive
	manager
director *(m)* adjunto	assistant director
	assistant manager
director *(m)* comercial	business manager
director *(m)* de área	area manager
director *(m)* de departamento	departmental manager
director *(m)* de márketing	marketing manager
director *(m)* de operaciones	operations manager
director *(m)* de personal	personnel manager
director *(m)* de producción	production director
director *(m)* ejecutivo	executive director
director *(m)* general	chief executive
	general manager
director *(m)* gerente	managing director (MD)

director *(m)* gerente adjunto	deputy managing director
director *(m)* gerente: presidente *(m)* y ...	chairman and managing director
director *(m)* propietario	owner-manager
director *(m)* suplente	outside director
director *(m)* técnico	technical manager
director: adjunto *(m)* al ...	assistant to manager
directorial	managerial
directos: gastos *(mpl)* ...	direct expenses
directriz *(f)*	guideline
dirigida de forma sistematizada: empresa *(f)* ...	system-managed company
dirigir	manage (to)
disco *(m)*	disk
disco *(m)* duro	hard disk
disco *(m)* flexible	floppy disk (floppy)
disco *(m)* winchester	Winchester disk
discos: unidad *(f)* de ...	disk drive
discrecional: tiempo *(m)* máximo ...	time span of discretion
discriminación *(f)*	discrimination
discriminación *(f)* de precios	price discrimination
discriminación *(f)* positiva	positive discrimination
discriminar	discriminate (to)
diseño *(m)* del producto	product design
diseño: departamento *(m)* de ...	design office
disfrazar los resultados financieros	massage the figures (to)
disfunción *(f)*	dysfunction
disminución *(f)* de autoridad	contraction of authority
disminución *(f)* del número de empleados	demanning
disminuir	wind down (to)
disminuir las pérdidas propias	cut one's losses (to)
disolución *(f)*	dissolution
dispersión: diagrama *(f)* de ...	scatter diagram
disponible: activo *(m)* ...	liquid assets
disponible a corto plazo: activo *(m)* ...	quick assets
disponible: capital *(m)* ...	capital assets
disponibles: ingresos *(mpl)* ...	disposable income

disponibles: proporción *(f)* de valores ...	cash ratio
disposición *(f)* funcional	functional layout
distancia: aprendizaje *(m)* a ...	distance learning
distribución *(f)*	apportionment
	distribution
distribución *(f)* de costes	cost apportionment
distribución *(f)* de frecuencia	frequency distribution
distribución física: gestión *(f)* de la ...	physical distribution management
distribución: cadena *(f)* de ...	chain of distribution
distribución: canal *(m)* de ...	distribution channel
distribución: coste *(m)* de ...	distribution cost
distribución: jefe *(m)* de ...	distribution manager
distribución: planificación *(f)* de ...	distribution planning
distribución: política *(f)* de ...	distribution policy
distribución: red *(f)* de ...	distribution network
distribuidos: beneficios *(mpl)* no ...	undistributed profit
diversificación *(f)*	diversification
diversificación *(f)* de productos	product diversification
diversificación: estrategia *(f)* de ...	diversification strategy
diversificar	diversify (to)
dividendo no fijo: acciones *(fpl)* de ...	equity
dividendos *(mpl)*	dividend
dividendos: política *(f)* de ...	dividend policy
divisa *(f)* europea	eurocurrency
divisas *(fpl)*	common currency
división *(f)* operacional	operating division
divulgación *(f)* de información secreta	security leak
dominante: inversión *(m)* ...	controlling interest
don *(m)* de mando	leadership
dos: caja *(f)* ...	slush fund
dotación *(f)* presupuestaria	budget allotment
dotar	allocate (to)
	appropriate (to)
dumping *(m)*	dumping
duplicados: desgravación *(f)* de impuestos ...	double taxation relief

duración *(f)* **de vida**	shelf-life
duraderos: productos *(mpl)* ...	durables
duro: disco *(m)* ...	hard disk
duro: ecu *(m)* ...	hard ecu

E

econométrico	econometric
economía *(f)* de escala	economy of scale
economía *(f)* de movimientos	motion economy
económica de un pedido: magnitud *(f)* ...	economic order quantity
económica: información *(f)* ...	economic intelligence
económica: investigación *(f)* ...	economic research
económica: misión *(f)* ...	economic mission
económica: tendencia *(f)* ...	economic trend
económica: vida *(f)* ...	economic life
económico de fabricación: tamaño *(f)* del lote ...	economic manufacturing quantity
económico: ambiente *(m)* ...	economic climate
económico: ciclo *(m)* ...	business cycle
económico: tamaño *(m)* del lote ...	economic batch quantity
economista *(m)* empresarial	business economist
ecu *(m)* duro	hard ecu
ECU (European Currency Unit)	ecu (European Currency Unit)
efectivo *(m)*	cash
efectivo: índice *(m)* de ...	gearing ratio
efecto *(m)*	impact
efecto *(m)* de halo	halo effect
efectos *(mpl)* secundarios	spill-over effects
	spin-off effects
eficacia *(f)*	effectiveness
eficacia *(f)* de la organización	organizational effectiveness
eficacia *(f)* de publicidad	advertising effectiveness
eficacia *(f)* directiva	managerial effectiveness
eficacia *(f)* en relación con el coste	cost-effectiveness
eficaz en relación con el coste	cost-effective
eficaz: dirección *(f)* ...	effective management
eficiencia *(f)*	efficiency
eficiente	efficient
eficiente *(m)* en relación con el coste	cost-efficient
ejecución *(f)* de la política	policy execution
ejecución *(f)* del trabajo	job performance
ejecución: fase *(f)* de ...	production run

ejecución: plazo *(m)* de ...	turnaround time
ejecución: repetir la ...	rerun (to)
ejecución: tiempo *(m)* de ...	lead time
ejecutivo *(m)*	executive
ejecutivo *(m)* con potencial limitado	low-flier
ejecutivo *(m)* de alto potencial	high-flier
ejecutivo *(m)* dinámico	whiz-kid
ejecutivo: director *(m)* ...	executive director
ejecutivos: formación *(f)* de ...	executive development executive training
ejercicio *(m)*	financial year
ejercicio *(m)* fiscal	fiscal year
elaboración *(f)* de estrategias	strategy formulation
elaboración *(f)* de sistemas	systems design
elaboración *(f)* de sistemas	systems engineering
elaboración *(f)* por lotes	batch processing
elasticidad *(f)*	elasticity
electrodomésticos *(mpl)* *(que no forman parte de la línea blanca)*	brown goods
electrodomésticos *(mpl)* de la línea blanca	white goods
electrónica: comunicación *(f)* ...	electronic communication
electrónica: oficina *(f)* ...	electronic office
electrónico: correo *(m)* ...	electronic mail (e-mail)
electrónico: proceso *(m)* ...	electronic processing
electrónico de contabilidad: sistema *(m)* ...	electronic accounting system
electrónico de datos: proceso *(m)* ...	electronic data processing (EDP)
elemento *(m)* de coste	cost factor
elemento *(m)* demotivante	disincentive
eliminar por etapas	phase out (to)
embalaje *(m)*	packaging
emisión *(f)*	issue
emitido: capital *(m)* ...	issued capital
empaquetado: bien ...	well-packaged
empírico	empirical
empleado *(m)* a tiempo completo	full-timer
empleado *(m)* a tiempo parcial	part-timer
empleados *(mpl)* del terreno	front-line employees

empleados: compra *(f)* de una empresa por los ...	employee buyout
empleados: consejo *(m)* de ...	employee counselling
empleados: disminución *(f)* del número de ...	demanning
empleados: iniciación *(f)* de ...	induction
empleo: acuerdo *(m)* sobre seguridad en el ...	job security agreement
empleo: cese *(m)* de ...	lay-off
empleo: condiciones *(fpl)* de ...	conditions of employment
empleo: igualdad *(f)* de oportunidad en el ...	equal employment opportunity
empleo *(m)*: pleno ...	full-time employment
empleo: satisfacción *(f)* en el ...	job satisfaction
empleo: seguridad *(f)* en el ...	job security
emprendedor	enterprising
emprendedor: tener espíritu ...	go-getter: be a go-getter (to)
empresa *(f)*	enterprise
empresa *(f)* afiliada	associate company
empresa *(f)* con horario flexible	flexible hours firm
empresa *(f)* conjunta	joint venture
empresa *(f)* cotizada en bolsa	publicly listed company
	quoted company
empresa *(f)* de representación sindical múltiple	open shop
empresa *(f)* de software	software company
empresa *(f)* de utilidad pública	public utility
empresa *(f)* dirigida de forma sistematizada	system-managed company
empresa *(f)* filial	affiliate company
empresa *(f)* líder de precios	market maker
empresa *(f)* matriz	parent company
empresa *(f)* no cotizada en bolsa	unlisted company
empresa *(f)* preferente (en una adquisición)	white knight
empresa *(f)* privada	private enterprise
empresa *(f)* pública	public enterprise
empresa: comité *(m)* de la ...	works committee
empresa: crecimiento *(m)* de la ...	corporate growth
empresa: engranaje *(m)* financiero de la ...	gearing

empresa: estrategia *(f)* **de la ...**	company strategy
empresa: estructura *(f)* **de la ...**	company structure
empresa: filosofia de la ...	company philosophy
empresa: filosofía *(f)* **global de la ...**	overall company philosophy
empresa: formación *(m)* **dentro de la ...**	in-plant training
empresa: hacer la compra *(f)* **hóstil de acciones de una ...**	raid a company (to)
empresa: imagen *(f)* **de la ...**	corporate image
empresa: logotipo *(m)* **de ...**	company logo
empresa: misión *(f)* **de la ...**	corporate mission
empresa: modelo *(m)* **de la ...**	company model corporate model
empresa: objetivo *(m)* **de la ...**	company goal corporate goal corporate objective
empresa: objetivos *(mpl)* **globales de la ...**	overall company objectives
empresa: perfil *(m)* **de la ...**	company profile
empresa: política *(f)* **de la ...**	company policy corporate policy
empresa: reconstitución *(f)* **de la ...**	company reconstruction
empresa: sello *(m)* **de la ...**	house style
empresa: valor *(m)* **de prestigio de una ...**	goodwill
empresarial: cultura *(f)* **...**	corporate culture organization culture
empresarial: economista *(m)* **...**	business economist
empresarial: espíritu *(m)* **...**	entrepreneurial spirit
empresarial: estrategia *(f)* **...**	corporate strategy
empresarial: estructura *(f)* **...**	corporate structure
empresarial: flujo *(m)* **...**	business stream
empresarial: perspectiva *(f)* **...**	business outlook
empresarial: planificación *(f)* **...**	corporate planning company planning
empresarial: publicidad *(f)* **...**	corporate advertising
empresarial: sistema *(m)* **...**	business system
empresariales: objetivos *(mpl)* **...**	company objective

empresas: comparación *(f)* entre ...	inter-firm comparison
empresas: consultor *(m)* de ...	management consultant
empresas: consultoría *(f)* de ...	management consultancy
empresas: predador *(m)* de acciones de ...	corporate raider
empuje *(m)* comercial	market drive
	market thrust
empuje *(m)* competitivo	competitive thrust
empuje *(m)* de ventas	sales drive
empuje *(m)* publicitario	advertising drive
en alza *(f)*	upswing
en ascenso (jerárquico)	up the line
en curso *(m)*	on stream
en el mejor de los casos	best-case scenario
en línea	on line
encima de: saltar por ...	leap-frog (to)
encuesta *(f)* de actitudes	attitude survey
encuesta *(f)* de opiniones	attitude survey
	opinion survey
encuesta *(f)* sobre el mercado	market survey
endeudamiento: ratio *(m)* de ...	debt ratio
enfocar	focus (to)
enfoque *(m)*	focus
enfoque *(m)* funcional	functional approach
enfoque *(m)* según la alta dirección	top management approach
enfoque *(m)* según la teoría de sistemas	systems approach
enfoque *(m)* sistemático	systems approach
enganche: prima *(f)* de ...	golden hello
engranaje *(m)* financiero de la empresa	gearing
enseñanza *(f)* asistida por ordenador (CAT)	computer-aided teaching (CAT)
enseñanza *(f)* para la sensibilidad	sensitivity training
enseñanza *(f)* programada	programmed instruction
	programmed learning
entorno *(m)* autosuficiente (informática)	work station
entrada *(f)*	input
entrada *(f)* al ordenador	computer input

entrada *(f)* aleatoria	random access
entrada *(f)* en la depresión (economía)	hard landing (economy)
entrada *(f)* múltiple	multi-access
entradas y salidas: análisis *(m)* de ...	input-output analysis
entradas y salidas: tabla *(f)* de ...	input-output table
entrar (datos)	input (data)
entrega: tiempo *(m)* de ...	delivery time
entrelazada: dirección *(f)* ...	interlocking directorate
entrevista *(f)* a fondo	depth interview
	in-depth interview
enviar un fax	fax (to)
envío *(m)*	forwarding
envío *(m)*: expedición *(f)* ...	dispatching
equilibrio: análisis *(f)* de ...	break-even analysis
equilibrio: punto *(m)* de ...	break-even point
equipo: bienes *(mpl)* de ...	capital goods
equipo *(m)* auxiliar	add-on equipment
equipo *(m)* de dirección	management team
equipo *(m)* de vendedores	sales force
equipo *(m)* "hardware"	hardware
equipo *(m)* periférico	peripheral equipment
equipo: alquiler *(m)* de ...	plant hire
equipo: buen trabajador *(m)* en ...	team player
equipo: líder *(m)* del ...	team leader
equipos: desarrollo *(m)* de ...	team-building
equipos: formación *(f)* de ...	team-building
ergonómica *(f)*	ergonomics
	human engineering
error *(m)*	bug (computer)
escala *(f)* de precios	price range
escala *(f)* móvil	sliding scale
escala: deseconomía *(f)* de ...	diseconomy of scale
escala: economía *(f)* de ...	economy of scale
escalada *(f)* de precios	price escalation
escalado *(m)* de ganancias	earnings differential
escalado *(m)* de precios	price differential
escalado *(m)* de salarios	wage differential
escalonadas: vacaciones *(fpl)* ...	staggered holidays
escalonar	stagger

escasez *(f)* de mano de obra	undermanned
	undermanning
escasez *(f)* de personal	understaffed
	understaffing
escenario *(m)*	scenario
escogidos: lista *(f)* de candidatos ...	shortlist
escrito: acuerdo *(m)* ...	agreement (written ...)
esfuerzo *(m)* para el desarrollo de ventas	sales expansion effort
especial: personal *(m)* para misión ...	task force
especificación *(f)* de personal	personnel specification
especificación *(f)* de un puesto de trabajo	job specification
especulación *(f)* (a la baja)	bear
especulador *(m)* (de acciones)	stag
especulativas: inversiones *(fpl)* ...	hot money
	speculative investments
espera: teoría *(f)* de líneas de ...	queuing theory
espionaje *(m)* industrial	industrial espionage
espíritu *(m)* creativo	creative thinking
espíritu emprendedor: tener ...	go-getter: be a go-getter (to)
espíritu *(m)* empresarial	entrepreneurial spirit
esquema *(m)* de actividades	activity chart
esquema *(m)* de gestión	management chart
esquema *(m)* de sugerencias	suggestion scheme
esquirol *(m)*	blackleg
	scab
establecer prioridades	prioritize (to)
establecimiento *(m)*	establishment
establecimiento *(m)* de la política	policy statement
estadística: verificación *(f)* ...	statistical control
estadístico: muestreo *(m)* ...	statistical sampling
Estado: valor *(m)* del ...	gilt
Estado: valores *(mpl)* garantizados por el ...	gilt-edged security
	gilt-edged stock
estados *(mpl)* financieros consolidados	consolidated accounts

estados *(mpl)* financieros del grupo	group accounts
estancamiento *(m)* con inflación	stagflation
estándar *(m)*	standard
estándar *(m)* de rendimiento	performance standard
	standard performance
estándar: desviación *(f)* ...	standard deviation
estándar: precio *(m)* ...	standard price
estándar: tiempo *(m)* ...	standard time
estándares *(mpl)* de costes	cost standard
estándares *(mpl)* de la producción	production standard
estándares *(mpl)* de presupuesto	budget standard
estándares: costes *(mpl)* ...	standard costs
estándares: método *(m)* de costes ...	standard costing
estandarización *(f)*	standardization
estandarizar	standardize (to)
(estar) en la rueda	rat race
estilo *(m)* de dirección	management style
estilo *(m)* de vida	lifestyle
estilo *(m)* directivo	managerial style
estimular ideas	generate ideas (to)
estímulo *(m)* competitivo	competitive stimulus
estrategia *(f)* comercial	business strategy
	marketing strategy
estrategia *(f)* competitiva	competitive strategy
estrategia *(f)* de beneficios	profit strategy
estrategia *(f)* de crecimiento	growth strategy
estrategia *(f)* de desarrollo	expansion strategy
estrategia *(f)* de diversificación	diversification strategy
estrategia *(f)* de la empresa	company strategy
estrategia *(f)* de la marca	brand strategy
estrategia *(f)* de negociación	negotiation strategy
estrategia *(f)* de negocios	business strategy
estrategia *(f)* de personal	staff strategy
estrategia *(f)* de personal directivo	executive manpower strategy
estrategia *(f)* de precios	pricing strategy
estrategia *(f)* de productos	product strategy
estrategia *(f)* de supervivencia	survival strategy
estrategia *(f)* defensiva	defensive strategy
estrategia *(f)* del consumidor	user strategy

estrategia *(f)* empresarial	corporate strategy
estrategia *(f)* financiera	financial strategy
estrategia *(f)* proactiva	proactive strategy
estrategia *(f)* reactiva	reactive strategy
estrategias: elaboración *(f)* de ...	strategy formulation
estrategias: instrumentación *(f)* de ...	strategy implementation
estrategias: interdependencia *(f)* de ...	strategic interdependence
estratégica: alianza *(f)* ...	strategic alliance
estratégica: planificación *(f)* ...	strategic planning
estratégico: plan *(m)* ...	strategic plan
estratégica: unidad de actividad ...	strategic business unit
estrella: producto *(m)* ...	star product
estrés *(m)* laboral	work stress
estructura *(f)*	structure
estructura *(f)* de autoridad	authority structure
estructura *(f)* de costes	cost structure
estructura *(f)* de la empresa	company structure
estructura *(f)* de la organización	organization structure
estructura *(f)* de precios	price structure
estructura *(f)* de red	grid structure
estructura *(f)* del capital	capital structure
estructura *(f)* del mercado	market structure
estructura *(f)* empresarial	corporate structure
estructura *(f)* jerárquica	line and staff
estructura *(f)* "line-staff"	staff and line
estructura *(f)* salarial	salary structure
	wage structure
estructuración *(f)*	structuring
estructuración *(f)* del trabajo	work structuring
estructurado	structured
estructurado: no ...	unstructured
estructurar	structure (to)
estudio *(m)* de casos	case study
estudio *(m)* de métodos	methods engineering
	methods study
estudio *(m)* de métodos y tiempos	time and methods study
estudio *(m)* de métodos: departamento *(m)* de ...	methods study department
estudio *(m)* de movimientos	motion study
estudio *(m)* de productos	product engineering

estudio *(m)* de proyecto de una planta industrial	plant layout study
estudio *(m)* de proyectos	design engineering
estudio *(m)* de tiempos	time study
estudio *(m)* de tiempos y movimientos	time and motion study
estudio *(m)* de viabilidad	feasibility study
estudio *(m)* del mercado	market study
estudio *(m)* del trabajo	work study
etapas: añadir por ...	phase in (to)
etapas: eliminar por ...	phase out (to)
etapas: formación *(f)* por ...	part-analysis training
eurodólar *(m)*	eurodollar
euromercado *(m)*	euromarket
Europea: Comunidad *(f)* ... (CE)	European Community (EC)
europea: divisa *(f)* ...	eurocurrency
europea: obligación *(f)* ...	eurobond
Europea: Unidad *(f)* Monetaria ... (ECU)	European Currency Unit (ecu)
Europea: Unión *(f)* Monetaria ... (UME)	European Monetary Union (EMU)
Europeo: Sistema *(m)* Monetario ... (SME)	European Monetary System (EMS)
evaluación *(f)*	appraisal
	assessment
evaluación *(f)* de costes	costing
evaluación *(f)* de costes de sistemas	estimating systems costs
evaluación *(f)* de gastos de capital	capex (capital expenditure)
	capital expenditure appraisal
evaluación *(f)* de inversiones	investment appraisal
evaluación *(f)* de la demanda	demand assessment
evaluación *(f)* de operaciones	operations audit
evaluación *(f)* de problemas	problem assessment
evaluación *(f)* de proyectos de capital	capital project evaluation
evaluación *(f)* de puestos de trabajo	job evaluation
evaluación *(f)* de recursos	resource appraisal
evaluación *(f)* del coste de productos	product costing
evaluación *(f)* del mercado	market appraisal

evaluación *(f)* del personal	staff appraisal
evaluación *(f)* del rendimiento	performance appraisal
	performance evaluation
	performance review
evaluación *(f)* dinámica	dynamic evaluation
evaluación y revisión *(f)* de programas: técnica *(f)* de ... (PERT)	PERT (programme evaluation and review technique)
evaluar	appraise (to)
	evaluate (to)
evitacíon de la depresión *(f)* (economía)	soft landing (economy)
evitar rodeando	bypass (to)
examen *(m)* del medio ambiente	environmental scan
excepción: dirección *(f)* por ...	management by exception
excesiva: capacidad *(f)* ...	excess capacity
exceso *(m)* de mano de obra	overmanning
	redundancy
exceso *(m)* de personal	overstaffed
	overstaffing
exclusiva: agente *(m)* en ...	sole agent
exigencias *(fpl)* del puesto	job requirements
existencias: control *(m)* de ...	stock control
existencias: giro *(m)* de ...	inventory turnover
existencias: inventario *(m)* de ...	stocktaking
existencias: rotación *(f)* de ...	stock turnover
existencias: valoración *(f)* de ...	stock valuation
éxito: factor *(m)* clave de ...	key success factor
expectativas *(fpl)* de venta	sales expectations
expectativas *(fpl)* del puesto	job expectations
expedición *(f)*	shipping
	dispatching
experto *(m)* en fallos	troubleshooter
experto *(m)* informático	computer expert
experto: sistema *(m)* ...	expert system
expertos: consultorio *(m)* de ...	brains trust
exploración *(f)*	scanning
explotación *(f)* de contactos profesionales	networking
explotación: potencial *(m)* de ...	development potential
exponencial: aproximación *(f)* ...	exponential smoothing

exponenciales: tendencias *(fpl)* ...	exponential trend
extendida: red *(f)* **de área** ...	wide area network (WAN)
extendido: sobre ...	overextended
exterior: inversión *(f)* **en el** ...	offshore investment
exteriorizar	externalize (to)
externalidades *(fpl)*	externalities
externas de suministro: fuentes *(fpl)* ...	outsourcing
externas: relaciones *(fpl)* ...	external relations
externo	out-house
externo: aprovisionamiento *(m)* ...	outsourcing
externo: trabajo *(m)* ...	outplacement
extraordinarios: gastos *(mpl)* ...	contingencies
extras: horas *(fpl)* ...	overtime
extraterritorial *(f)*	offshore
extrínseco: valor *(m)* ...	goodwill

F

fábrica *(f)* con obreros sindicados exclusivamente	closed shop
F y A (fusiones y adquisiciones)	M & A (mergers and acquisitions)
fábrica: jefe *(m)* de ...	plant manager
	works manager
fábrica: localización *(f)* de la ...	plant location
fábrica: negociación *(f)* a nivel de ...	plant bargaining
fabricación *(f)* asistida por ordenador (CAM)	computer-aided manufacturing (CAM)
fabricación *(f)* en cadena	flow production
fabricación *(f)* en serie	mass production
fabricación *(f)* integrada por ordenador (CIM)	computer-integrated manufacturing (CIM)
fabricación: capacidad *(f)* de ...	manufacturing capacity
fabricación: control *(m)* de ...	manufacturing control
fabricación: gastos *(mpl)* generales de ...	factory overheads
fabricación: tamaño *(f)* del lote económico de ...	economic manufacturing quantity
fabricar o comprar: opción *(f)* de ...	make-or-buy option
fácil de utilizar	user-friendly
fácil: bienes *(mpl)* de consumo de venta ...	fast-moving consumer goods (FMG)
facsimile *(m)*	facsimile
factible	feasible
factor *(m)*	factor
factor *(m)* clave de compra	key buying factor
factor *(m)* clave de éxito	key success factor
factor *(m)* de carga	load factor
factores *(mpl)* de producción	factors of production
factores: descomposición *(f)* en ...	factoring
fallo *(m)*	malfunction
fallo *(m)* en la seguridad	security leak
fallos: experto *(m)* en ...	troubleshooter
fallos: investigación *(f)* de ...	troubleshooting

falsear la situación de la empresa para que no se venda	poison pill
falta *(f)* de caja	cash-poor
falto de caja	cash-strapped
fase *(f)* de ejecución	production run
fax *(m)*	fax
fax (aparato) *(m)*	fax machine
fecha *(f)*: última ...	latest date
fecha *(f)* de caducidad	use-by date
fecha futura: acciones *(fpl)* canjeables con ...	forward swap
fecha futura: tasa *(f)* de cambio en ...	forward exchange rate
fecha *(f)* límite	deadline
	due date
fecha *(f)* límite de venta	sell-by date
fecha *(f)* prevista	expected date
fiabilidad *(f)*	reliability
fiabilidad *(f)* de un producto	product reliability
fijación *(f)* de objetivos	goal-setting
	target-setting
fijación *(f)* de precio de prestigio	prestige pricing
fijación *(f)* de precios	price determination
	price-fixing
fijación *(f)* de precios de penetración	penetration pricing
fijación *(f)* de precios de transferencia	transfer pricing
fijación *(f)* de precios marginales	marginal pricing
fijar el precio	price (to)
fijar objetivos	targeting
fijo: acciones *(fpl)* de dividendo no ...	equity
fijo: activo *(m)* ...	fixed assets
fijos: costes *(mpl)* ...	fixed costs
fijos: gastos *(mpl)* ...	fixed expenses
fijos: sin límites *(mpl)* ...	open-ended
filial *(f)*	subsidiary company
filial: empresa *(f)* ...	affiliate company
filo: límite *(m)* de	cutting edge
filosofía *(f)* de la empresa	company philosophy
filosofía *(f)* global de la empresa	overall company philosophy
filtración: teoría *(f)* de la ...	trickle-down theory

final: hacer la lista ...	shortlist (to)
final: línea *(f)* ...	bottom line
financiación *(f)*	financing
	funding
financiación *(f)* de déficit	deficit financing
financiación *(f)* de la deuda	debt financing
financiar	finance (to)
financiera: administración *(f)* ...	financial administration
financiera: dirección *(f)* ...	financial management
financiera: estrategia *(f)* ...	financial strategy
financiera: gestión *(f)* ...	financial administration
financiera: implicación *(f)* ...	financial involvement
financiera: norma *(f)* ...	financial standard
financiera: planificación *(f)* ...	financial planning
financiera: posición *(f)* ...	financial position
financiera: valoración *(f)* ...	financial appraisal
financiero de la empresa: engranaje *(m)* ...	gearing
financiero: análisis *(m)* ...	financial analysis
	financial review
financiero: control *(m)* ...	financial control
financiero: mercado *(m)* ...	financial market
financiero: ratio *(m)* ...	financial ratio
financieros a largo plazo: créditos *(mpl)* ...	loan stock
financieros consolidados: estados *(mpl)* ...	consolidated accounts
financieros del grupo: estados *(mpl)* ...	group accounts
financieros: disfrazar los resultados ...	massage the figures (to)
financieros: futuros *(mpl)* ...	financial futures
financieros: incentivos *(mpl)* ...	financial incentive
finanzas: jefe *(m)* de ...	financial director
fiscal: año *(m)* ...	fiscal year
fiscal: desgravación *(f)* ...	tax relief
fiscal: ejercicio *(m)* ...	fiscal year
fiscal: incentivo *(m)* ...	tax incentive
fiscal: política *(f)* ...	fiscal policy
fiscal: traba *(f)* ...	fiscal drag
fiscalmente: deducible ...	tax-deductible
física: gestión *(f)* de la distribución ...	physical distribution management

flexible: disco *(m)* ...	floppy disk (floppy)
flexible: empresa *(f)* con horario ...	flexible firm
flexible: horario *(m)* ...	flexitime
flexible: horario *(m)* de trabajo ...	flexible working hours
flexible: presupuesto *(m)* ...	flexible budget
"floppy" *(m)*	floppy disk (floppy)
floreciente: industria *(f)* ...	sunrise industry
flotación *(f)*	flotation
flujo *(m)* de caja negativo	negative cash flow
flujo de datos: diagrama *(m)* de ...	data flow chart
flujo *(m)* de negocios	business stream
flujo *(m)* empresarial	business stream
flujos del proceso: diagrama *(m)* de ...	flow process chart
flujos: diagrama *(m)* de ...	flow chart
	flow diagram
fondo *(m)* de amortización	sinking fund
fondo *(m)* de comercio	brand portfolio
	goodwill
fondo *(m)* de maniobra	working capital
fondo: análisis *(m)* a ...	depth analysis
fondo: entrevista *(f)* a ...	depth interview
	in-depth interview
fondo: tocar ...	bottom out (to)
fondos *(mpl)*	quick assets
fondos: movilización *(f)* de ...	capital raising
fondos: provisión *(f)* de ...	money supply
formación *(f)*	training
formación *(f)* analítica	analytical training
formación *(f)* asistida por ordenador (CBT)	computer-based training (CBT)
formación *(f)* de directivos	management training
formación *(f)* de ejecutivos	executive development
	executive training
formación *(f)* de equipos	team-building
formación *(f)* de la dirección	management development
formación *(m)* dentro de la empresa	in-plant training

formación *(f)* dentro de la industria	training within industry (TWI)
formación *(f)* en grupos	group training
formación *(f)* fuera del trabajo	off-the-job training
formación *(f)* multimedia	multimedia training
formación *(f)* personal	personal growth
formación *(f)* por etapas	part-analysis training
formación *(f)* práctica	hands-on training
formación *(f)* profesional	vocational training
formación *(f)* sobre la práctica	on-the-job training
formación: análisis *(m)* de necesidades de ...	training needs analysis
formación: jefe *(m)* de ...	training officer
formación: necesidades *(fpl)* de ...	training needs
formulación *(f)* de la política	policy formulation
fracaso: profeta *(m)* de ...	doomwatcher
fraccionar	fractionalize (to)
fragmentación *(f)* de mercados	market segmentation
franquicia *(f)*	franchise
	franchising
frecuencia: distribución *(f)* de ...	frequency distribution
freelance	freelance (to go)
freno *(m)*	disincentive
fuegos: apagando ...	fire-fighting
fuente única: aprovisionamiento *(m)* de ...	single sourcing
fuentes *(fpl)* externas de suministro	outsourcing
fuera de línea	off line
fuera del trabajo: formación *(f)* ...	off-the-job training
fuerzas: análisis *(m)* de ..., debilidades, oportunidades y amenazas	strengths, weaknesses, opportunities and threats (SWOT) analysis
función *(f)*	function
función *(f)* clave	function key
función *(f)* directiva	managerial function
función: metodo *(m)* de costes por ...	functional costing

funcional	functional
funcional: análisis *(m)* ...	functional analysis
funcional: disposición *(f)* ...	functional layout
funcional: enfoque *(m)* ...	functional approach
funcional: gestión *(f)* ...	functional management
funcional: organización *(f)* ...	functional organization
funcional: responsabilidad *(f)* ...	functional responsibility
funcionales: relaciones *(fpl)* ...	functional relations
funcionamiento: controlar *(m)* el ...	monitor performance (to)
funciones: desempeño *(m)* de ...	role-playing
fundamental: razón *(f)* ...	rationale
fusión *(f)*	merger
	amalgamation
fusionar	amalgamate (to)
fusionarse	merge (to)
fusiones *(fpl)* **y adquisiciones** *(fpl)*	mergers and acquisitions (M & A)
futura: acciones *(fpl)* **canjeables con fecha** ...	forward swap
futura: tasa *(f)* **de cambio en fecha** ...	forward exchange rate
futuro: mercado *(m)* **a** ...	forward market
futuros *(mpl)*	futures
futuros *(mpl)* **financieros**	financial futures
futuros: mercado *(m)* **de** ...	futures market

G

gabinete: investigación *(m)* de ...	desk research
gama *(f)* de productos	product range
ganancia *(f)* de capital	capital gain
ganancias: escalado *(m)* de ...	earnings differential
garantía *(f)*	quality assurance
garantía *(f)* colateral	collateral security
garantizados por el Estado: valores *(mpl)* ...	gilt-edged security gilt-edged stock
garra *(f)* comercial	sales appeal
gastos *(mpl)* actuales	current expenditure
gastos *(mpl)* corrientes	running expenses
gastos *(mpl)* de administración	administrative expenses
gastos de capital: control *(m)* presupuestario de ...	capital budgeting
gastos de capital: evaluación *(f)* de ...	capex (capital expenditure) capital expenditure appraisal
gastos de capital: presupuesto *(m)* de ...	capital budget
gastos *(mpl)* de constitución	set-up costs
gastos *(mpl)* de instalación	start-up costs
gastos *(mpl)* de operación	operating expenses
gastos *(mpl)* directos	direct expenses
gastos *(mpl)* en capital	capital expenditure
gastos *(mpl)* extraordinarios	contingencies
gastos *(mpl)* fijos	fixed expenses
gastos *(mpl)* generales	on cost overheads
gastos *(mpl)* generales de administración	administrative overheads
gastos *(mpl)* generales de fabricación	factory overheads
gastos generales: recuperación *(f)* de ...	overheads recovery
gastos *(mpl)* indirectos	indirect expenses
gastos *(mpl)* menores	petty expenses
gastos menores: caja *(f)* para ...	petty cash
gastos *(mpl)* variables	variable expenses
gastos: asignación *(f)* de ...	assignment of expenditure
gastos: cuenta *(f)* de ...	expense account

gastos: recuperación *(f)* de ...	recovery of expenses
genealógico: arbol *(m)* ...	family tree
general: dirección *(f)* ...	general management
	management
general: director *(m)* ...	chief executive
	general manager
generales de fabricación: gastos *(mpl)* ...	factory overheads
generales: gastos *(mpl)* ...	on cost
	overheads
generales: recuperación *(f)* de gastos ...	overheads recovery
genérico	generic
gerencia *(f)*	management
gerencia *(f)* automatizada	computerized management
gerencia *(f)* de departamento	departmental management
gerencia: competencia *(f)* de la ...	management competence
gerencial: contabilidad *(f)* ...	management accounting
gerente *(m)*	manager
	staff manager
gerente adjunto: director *(m)* ...	deputy managing director
gerente: director *(m)* ...	managing director (MD)
gerente: presidente *(m)* y director *(m)* ...	chairman and managing director
gestión *(f)* comercial	market management
gestión *(f)* de alta participación de los ejecutivos	management by walking around
gestión *(f)* de cambio	change management (management of change)
gestión *(f)* de cartera (de valores mobiliarios)	portfolio management
gestión *(f)* de créditos	credit management
gestión *(f)* de crisis	crisis management
gestión *(f)* de inversión	investment management
gestión *(f)* de la calidad	quality management
gestión *(f)* de la distribución física	physical distribution management
gestión *(f)* de la seguridad	safety management
gestión *(f)* de negocios	business management
gestión *(f)* de operaciones	operations management
gestión *(f)* de personal: reclutamiento *(m)* y ...	staff resourcing
gestión *(f)* de producto	product management

gestión *(f)* de recursos	resource management
gestión *(f)* de recursos humanos	human resource management (HRM)
gestión *(f)* de riesgos	risk management
	venture management
gestión *(f)* del activo	asset management
gestión *(f)* del activo disponible	cash management
gestión *(f)* del circulante	asset liability management
gestión *(f)* del inventario	inventory management
gestión *(f)* del personal: reclutamiento *(m)* y ...	manpower resourcing
gestión *(f)* del tiempo	time management
gestión *(f)* directiva	management
gestión *(f)* financiera	financial management
gestión *(f)* funcional	functional management
gestión *(f)* integrada	integrated project management (IPM)
gestión *(f)* intuitiva	intuitive management
gestión *(f)* por secciones	divisional management
gestión *(f)* por sistemas	management system
	systems management
gestión *(f)* programada	programmed management
gestión *(f)* supervisora	supervisory management
gestión *(f)* total de calidad	total quality management (TQM)
gestión: esquema *(m)* de ...	management chart
gestión: información *(m)* para la ...	management information
gestión: normas *(fpl)* de ...	management practices
gestión: "ratios" *(m)* de ...	management ratio
gestión: simulación *(f)* de ...	business game
	management game
gestión: sistema *(m)* integrado de ...	integrated management system
gestión: técnicas *(fpl)* de ...	management technique
gestión: valoración *(f)* de ...	management audit
giro *(m)* de existencias	inventory turnover
global de la empresa: filosofía *(f)* ...	overall company philosophy
global: imagen *(f)* ...	global image
global: márketing *(m)* ...	global marketing
global: suma *(f)* ...	lump sum
globales de la empresa: objetivos *(mpl)* ...	overall company objectives
globalizar	globalize (to)

gráfico *(m)* de barras	bar chart
grado *(m)* de saturación	load factor
gráfico *(m)* Z	Z chart
gráfico *(m)* redondo	pie chart
gráficos *(mpl)*	graphics
grupo *(m)*	conglomerate
grupo *(m)* de productos	product group
grupo *(m)* investigador	think-tank
grupo: análisis *(m)* intensivo de ...	brainstorming
grupo: estados *(mpl)* financieros del ...	group accounts
grupos: diagnóstico *(m)* de ...	T-group training
grupos: dinámica *(f)* de ...	group dynamics methectics
grupos: formación *(f)* en ...	group training

H

hacer el seguimiento	follow up (to)
hacer la compra (f) hóstil de acciones de una empresa	raid a company (to)
hacer la lista final	shortlist (to)
hacer la ruta	route (to)
hacer propio (por ejemplo un problema de la empresa)	internalize (to)
halo: efecto (m) de ...	halo effect
hardware	hardware
hecho a la medida	custom-made
herramientas: caja (f) de ...	toolbox
herramientas: cuadro (m) de ...	toolbox
heurística (f)	heuristics
hipótesis (f) pesimista	worst-case scenario pessimistic outlook
histograma (m)	histogram
hoja (f) de cálculo	spreadsheet
hoja (f) de devengos	time sheet
holding	holding company
hombre: adaptación (f) del trabajo al ...	human engineering
hombre en la organización: conducta (f) del ...	organizational behaviour
hombre: adaptación (f) del trabajo al ...	ergonomics
honorarios (mpl) de corretaje	brokerage fees
horario (m) de trabajo	working hours
horario (m) de trabajo flexible	flexible working hours
horario (m) flexible	flexitime
horas (fpl) bajas	down time
horas (fpl) extras	overtime
horas: trabajo (m) por ...	part-time employment
horizontal: integración (f) ...	horizontal integration
huelga (f)	walkout
huelga (f) de brazos caídos	sit-down strike
huelga (f) de celo	work-to-rule
huelga (f) de solidaridad	sympathy strike
huelga (f) de trabajo lento	go-slow work-to-rule
huelga (f) no negociada	wildcat strike

huelga *(f)* **no sindicada**	unofficial strike
huelga *(f)* **oficial**	official strike
humanas: relaciones *(fpl)* ...	human relations
humanos: desarrollo *(m)* **de**	human resource development (HRD)
recursos ...	human resource management (HRM)
humanos: recursos *(mpl)* ...	human resources
hundir (hundir un programa)	crash (to ... a program)

I

ideas: estimular ...	generate ideas (to)
identificación *(f)* de la marca	brand recognition
identificación *(f)* de objetivos	goal-seeking
igualdad *(f)*	equality
igualdad *(f)* de oportunidad	equal opportunity
igualdad *(f)* de oportunidad en el empleo	equal employment opportunity
igualdad *(f)* de salarios	equal pay
iguales: ventajas *(fpl)* ...	level playing-field
imagen *(f)* de la empresa	corporate image
imagen *(m)* de la marca	brand image
imagen *(m)* del producto	product image
imagen *(f)* global	global image
imagen *(f)*: cambiar la ...	re-image (to)
imagen: creación *(f)* de la ...	imaging
impacto *(m)*	impact
impensable: pensar lo ...	think the unthinkable (to)
implementar	implement (to)
implicación *(f)* financiera	financial involvement
importación *(f)* paralela	parallel import
importante: avance *(m)* ...	breakthrough
impresión *(f)* de salida	printout
impresora *(f)* laser	laser printer
imprevistos: reserva *(f)* para ...	contingency reserve
imprimir (informática)	print out (to)
impuesto *(m)* de sociedades	corporation tax
impuesto *(m)* negativo sobre la renta	negative income tax
impuesto *(m)* sobre beneficios	profits tax
impuesto *(m)* sobre el valor agregado	value added tax (VAT)
impuesto *(m)* sobre la renta (IR)	income tax
impuesto sobre la renta: retención *(f)* en origen del ...	pay-as-you-earn (PAYE)
impuestos duplicados: desgravación *(f)* de ...	double taxation relief

impuestos en origen: sistema *(m)* **de retención de ...**	pay-as-you-go
impulsiva: compra *(f)* **...**	impulse buying
impulso: productos *(mpl)* **de consumo por ...**	impulse goods
impulso: venta *(f)* **por ...**	impulse sale
imputar	apportion (to)
inactividad *(f)*	shut-down
inactivo: tiempo *(m)* **...**	down time
incentivo *(m)*	incentive
incentivo *(m)* **(paga de)**	incentive wage
incentivo *(m)* **colectivo**	group incentive
incentivo *(m)* **del puesto**	job challenge
incentivo *(m)* **fiscal**	tax incentive
incentivos *(mpl)* **financieros**	financial incentive
incentivos: sistema *(m)* **de ...**	incentive scheme
incidencia *(f)* **sobre el beneficio**	profit impact
incobrables: créditos *(m)* **...**	bad debts
incobrables: deudas *(f)* **...**	bad-debt losses
incorporación *(f)* **de mano de obra no capacitada**	dilution of labour
incorporado	built-in
incremental	incremental
incrementos de salarios: curva *(f)* **de ...**	salary progression curve
indemnización *(f)* **por despido**	golden handshake
	golden parachute
	severance pay
independiente	stand-alone
independiente: procesador *(m)* **de texto ...**	stand-alone word processor
indicativo *(m)*	answerback code
índice *(m)*	index number
índice *(m)* **administración producción**	administration-production ratio
índice *(m)* **de crecimiento**	growth index
índice *(m)* **de deuda**	gearing ratio
índice *(m)* **de efectivo**	gearing ratio
índice *(m)* **de liquidez**	current ratio
	liquidity ratio
índice *(m)* **de precios**	price index

índice *(m)* de precios al consumidor	retail price index (RPI)
índice *(m)* de precios al consumo (IPC)	consumer price index
indirecta: mano *(f)* de obra ...	indirect labour
indirecto: coste *(m)* ...	indirect costs
indirectos: gastos *(mpl)* ...	indirect expenses
industria *(f)* en declive	sunset industry
industria *(f)* en desarrollo	growth industry
industria *(f)* floreciente	sunrise industry
industria: formación *(f)* dentro de la ...	training within industry (TWI)
industrial: contra-espionaje *(m)* ...	industrial security
industrial: democracia *(f)* ...	industrial democracy
industrial: dinámica *(f)* ...	industrial dynamics
industrial: espionaje *(m)* ...	industrial espionage
industrial: estudio *(m)* de proyecto de una planta ...	plant layout study
industrial: ingeniería *(f)* ...	industrial engineering
industrial: psicología *(f)* ...	industrial psychology
industrial: seguridad *(f)* ...	industrial safety
industriales: bienes *(mpl)* ...	industrial goods
industriales: relaciones *(mpl)* ...	industrial relations
industriales: residuos *(mpl)* ...	industrial waste
industrialización: país *(m)* de reciente ...	newly industrialized country (NIC)
inflación *(f)* de costes	cost-push inflation
inflación *(f)* por la demanda	demand-pull inflation
inflación: estancamiento *(m)* con ...	stagflation
inflacionaria: presión *(f)* ...	inflationary pressure
información: teoría *(f)* de la ...	information theory
información *(f)* comercial	market intelligence
información *(f)* de control	control information
información *(f)* económica	economic intelligence
información para la dirección: sistema *(m)* de la ...	management information system (MIS)
información *(m)* para la gestión	management information
información privilegiada: comercio *(m)* con ...	insider trading

información privilegiada: trato *(m)* **con ...**	insider dealing
información secreta: divulgación *(f)* **de ...**	security leak
información: red *(f)* **de ...**	information network
información: sistema *(m)* **(automatizado) (COINS)**	computerized information system (COINS)
información: sistema *(m)* **de ...**	information system
información: sistema *(m)* **mecanizado de ... (COINS)**	computerized information system (COINS)
información: tecnología *(f)* **de la ...**	information technology
informal: organización *(f)* **...**	informal organization
informar	appraise (to)
informática *(f)*	informatics
	IT (information technology)
informática: con conocimientos *(mpl)* **de ...**	computer-literate
informático: centro *(m)* **...**	computer centre
informático: consultor *(m)* **...**	computer consultant
informático: experto *(m)* **...**	computer expert
informático: programa *(m)* **...**	computer program
informático: programador *(m)* **...**	computer programmer
informático: virus *(m)* **...**	computer virus
informe *(m)*	briefing
informe *(m)* **sobre situación actual**	status report
informe *(m)* **sobre una operación**	debriefing
informes: recabar ...	debrief (to)
infraestructura *(f)*	infrastructure
infrautilización *(f)*	slack
	underutilization
ingeniería *(f)*	engineering
ingeniería *(f)* **industrial**	industrial engineering
ingeniero *(m)* **de programas**	software engineer
ingeniero *(m)* **de sistemas**	systems engineer
ingeniero *(m)* **de ventas**	sales engineer
ingresos *(mpl)* **disponibles**	disposable income
ingresos *(mpl)* **medios**	average revenue
ingresos *(mpl)* **reales**	real income
iniciación *(f)* **de empleados**	induction
inicial: inversión *(f)* **...**	seed money

iniciar	pioneer (to)
iniciativa: tener ...	go-getting
ininterrumpido	ongoing
injusto: despido *(m)* ...	unfair dismissal
inmaterial: activo *(m)* ...	intangible assets
innovador	innovative
innovar	innovate (to)
innovativo	innovative
instalación *(f)* de seguridad	back-up facility
instalación: gastos *(mpl)* de ...	start-up costs
instrumentación *(f)* de estrategias	strategy implementation
insuficiencia *(f)*	shortfall
integración *(f)*	integration
integración *(f)* horizontal	horizontal integration
integración *(f)* vertical	vertical integration
integrada: gestión *(f)*	integrated project management (IPM)
integrada por ordenador: fabricación *(f)* ... (CIM)	computer-integrated manufacturing (CIM)
integrada por ordenador: producción *(f)* ... (CIM)	CIM (computer-integrated manufacturing)
integrado de gestión: sistema *(m)* ...	integrated management system
integrar	amalgamate (to)
	integrate (to)
inteligencia *(f)* artificial	artificial intelligence
inteligente: tarjeta *(f)* ...	smart card
intensiva: producción *(f)* ...	intensive production
intensivo de grupo: análisis *(m)* ...	brainstorming
interactivo	interactive
interdependencia *(f)* de estrategias	strategic interdependence
interés *(m)* en el trabajo	job interest
intereses *(mpl)* creados	vested interest
interface	interface
interfaces: poner	interface (to)
interior bruto: producto *(m)* ... (PIB)	gross domestic product (GDP)
interiorizar	internalize (to)
intermediación *(f)*	deal
intermediador *(m)*	dealer

interna: auditoría *(f)* ...	internal audit
interna: obsolencia *(f)* ...	built-in obsolescence
internacionalizar	internationalize (to)
interno	built-in
	internal
interno (de orden interno)	in-company
	in-house
interno: tasa *(f)* de rendimiento ...	internal rate of return (IRR)
intervalo *(m)*	gap
interventor *(m)*	controller
introducción *(f)* de un producto	product introduction
introducir un producto	roll out (to)
intuitiva: gestión *(f)* ...	intuitive management
inventario *(m)* continuo de mercancías	continuous stocktaking
inventario *(m)* de existencias	stocktaking
inventario *(m)* perpetuo	perpetual inventory
inventario: control *(m)* del ...	inventory control
inventario: gestión *(f)* del ...	inventory management
inversión *(m)* dominante	controlling interest
inversión *(f)* en el exterior	offshore investment
inversión *(f)* inicial	seed money
inversión: bienes *(mpl)* de ...	investment goods
inversión: compromiso *(m)* de ...	capital commitment
inversión: criterios *(mpl)* de ...	investment criteria
inversión: gestión *(f)* de ...	investment management
inversión: período *(m)* de recuperación de la ...	payback period
inversión: programa *(m)* de ...	investment programme
inversiones *(fpl)* especulativas	hot money
	speculative investments
inversiones: análisis *(f)* de ...	investment analysis
inversiones: banco *(m)* de ...	investment bank
inversiones: combinación *(f)* de ...	investment mix
inversiones: evaluación *(f)* de ...	investment appraisal
inversiones: política *(f)* de ...	investment policy

inversiones: presupuesto *(m)* de ...	investment budget
inversiones: rendimiento *(m)* de las ...	return on investment (ROI)
inversiones: rentabilidad *(f)* de las ...	return on investment (ROI)
inversor *(m)* de riesgo	venture capitalist
invertido: capital *(m)* ...	capital employed
invertido: rendimiento *(m)* del capital ...	return on capital employed (ROCE) return on equity (ROE)
investigación *(f)* de base	blue-sky research
investigación *(f)* de consumidores	consumer research
investigación *(f)* de fallos	troubleshooting
investigación *(m)* de gabinete	desk research
investigación *(f)* de la motivación	motivational research
investigación *(f)* de márketing	marketing research
investigación *(f)* de operaciones	operations research (OR)
investigación *(f)* de productos	product research
investigación *(f)* del mercado	market exploration
investigación *(f)* económica	economic research
investigación *(f)* operativa	operational research (OR)
investigación *(f)* publicitaria	advertising research
investigación *(f)* y desarrollo *(m)*	research and development (R& D)
investigación: campo *(m)* de ...	field research
investigación: departamento *(m)* de ...	research department
investigador: grupo *(m)* ...	think-tank
investigadora: comisión *(f)* ...	working party
invisibles: partidas *(fpl)* ...	invisibles
iterativo	iterative
iterativo: proceso *(m)* ...	iterative process

J

jefatura *(f)*	leadership
	management
jefe *(m)*	manager
jefe *(m)* de abastecimiento	procurement manager
jefe *(m)* de alto nivel	first-line manager
jefe *(m)* de compras	chief buyer
	purchasing manager
jefe *(m)* de contabilidad	chief accountant
jefe *(m)* de departamento	departmental head
jefe *(m)* de distribución	distribution manager
jefe *(m)* de fábrica	works manager
jefe *(m)* de finanzas	financial director
jefe *(m)* de formación	training officer
jefe *(m)* de línea	line manager
jefe *(m)* de marca	brand manager
jefe *(m)* de producción	production manager
jefe *(m)* de productos	product manager
jefe *(m)* de publicidad	advertising manager
jefe *(m)* de ventas	sales manager
jerarquía *(f)* de objetivos	hierarchy of goals
jerarquía *(f)* directiva	managerial structure
jerárquica: estructura *(f)* ...	line and staff
jerárquica: organización *(f)* ...	line and staff organization
jerárquica: responsabilidad *(f)* ...	line responsibility
jerárquicas: relaciones *(fpl)* ...	line relations
jubilación *(f)*	retirement
jubilación *(f)* prematura	early retirement
jubilación: amortización *(f)* de puestos de trabajo por ...	natural wastage
jubilarse	retire (to)
juego *(m)* de suma cero	zero-sum game
juego: las reglas *(fpl)* del ...	name of the game
juego *(m)*: otro ...	different ball game
juegos: teoría *(f)* de ...	game theory
justo a tiempo	just in time (JIT)

L

laboral: accidente *(m)* ...	industrial injury
laboral: acción *(f)* ... (huelga)	industrial action
laboral: conflicto *(m)* ...	industrial dispute
	labour dispute
laboral: estrés *(m)* ...	work stress
laboral: movilidad *(f)* ...	labour mobility
laborales: relaciones *(fpl)* ...	labour relations
lanzamiento *(m)* **de nuevos productos**	new-product launching
lanzamiento *(m)* **de un producto**	product launch
largo plazo: créditos *(mpl)* **financieros a ...**	loan stock
largo plazo: planificación *(f)* **a ...**	forward planning
	long-range planning
laser: impresora *(f)* ...	laser printer
lateral: pensamiento *(m)* ...	lateral thinking
lazo *(m)*	closed loop
LBO (compra *(f)* **con apalancamiento)**	LBO (leveraged buyout)
lealtad *(f)* **a la marca**	brand loyalty
leasing	leasing
lecho *(m)* **de pluma**	featherbedding
lectura: memoria *(f)* **de ...**	read-only memory (ROM)
lenguaje *(m)* **común**	common language
lenguaje *(m)* **corporal**	body language
lenguaje *(m)* **de máquina**	machine language
lenguaje *(m)* **de ordenador**	computer language
lento: huelga *(f)* **de trabajo ...**	go-slow
	work-to-rule
liberalización *(f)*	liberalization
libros: valor *(m)* **en ...**	book value
licencia *(f)*	licence
licencia: bajo ...	under licence
licencias: concesión *(f)* **recíproca de ...**	cross-licensing
licitación *(f)* **con apalancamiento**	leveraged bid
licitación *(f)* **preferente**	pre-emptive bid
licitación *(f)* **pública**	competitive tendering

líder de precios: empresa *(f)* ...	market maker
líder *(m)* del equipo	team leader
líder *(m)* del mercado	market leader
limitación *(f)* de daños	damage limitation
limitado: ejecutivo *(m)* con potencial ...	low-flier
límite *(m)* de filo	cutting edge
límite de venta: fecha *(f)* ...	sell-by date
límite: fecha *(f)*	deadline
límite: punto *(m)*	cut-off point
límites *(mpl)* fijos: sin ...	open-ended
line-staff	staff and line
línea blanca: electrodomésticos *(mpl)* de la ...	white goods
línea *(f)* de crédito	borrowing facility
línea *(f)* de guía	guideline
línea *(f)* de mando	line of command
línea *(f)* de montaje	assembly line
línea *(f)* final	bottom line
línea: auxiliar (m/f) de ...	line assistant
línea: directivo *(m)* de ...	line executive
linea: en ...	on line
línea: fuera de ...	off line
línea: jefe *(m)* de ...	line manager
lineal: aumento *(m)* ... de salarios	across-the-board increase
lineal: autoridad *(f)* ...	line authority
lineal: dirección *(f)* ...	line management
lineal: organización *(f)* ...	line organization
lineal: programación *(f)* ...	linear programming
lineal: programación *(f)* no ...	non-linear programming
lineal: responsabilidad *(f)* ...	linear responsibility
líneas de espera: teoría *(f)* de ...	queuing theory
liquidación *(f)*	liquidation
	winding up
liquidación *(f)* de activos	asset-stripping
liquidación: coste *(m)* de ...	closing-down costs
liquidación: valor *(m)* en ...	break-up value
liquidar	liquidate (to)
	sell out (to)
liquidez: índice *(m)* de ...	current ratio
	liquidity ratio
líquido: activo *(m)* ...	liquid assets

lista *(f)* abreviada	shortlist
lista *(f)* de candidatos escogidos	shortlist
lista final: hacer la ...	shortlist (to)
listado *(m)*	listing
llegar a un acuerdo	reach a deal (to)
llegar a una transacción	trade off (to)
local: normas *(fpl)* de contenido ...	local content rules
local: red *(f)* de área ...	local area network (LAN)
localización *(f)*	localization
localización *(f)* de la fábrica	plant location
lock out	lock-out
lógica *(f)*: la ...	rationale
lógicamente: organizar ...	rationalize (to)
logística	logistical
logística *(f)*	logistics
logístico: proceso *(m)* ...	logistic process
logísticos: servicios *(mpl)* ...	extension services
logo *(m)*	logo
logotipo *(m)*	logo
logotipo *(m)* de empresa	company logo
logro *(m)* tecnológico	technological breakthrough
lote económico de fabricación:	economic manufacturing quantity
lote económico: tamaño *(m)* del ...	economic batch quantity
lote: control *(m)* del ...	batch control
lotes: elaboración *(f)* por ...	batch processing
lotes: producción *(f)* por ...	batch production
lugar *(m)* de trabajo	workplace
lugar *(m)* de venta	point of sale (POS)
lugar de venta: material *(m)* de publicidad en el ...	point-of-sale material
lugar de venta: precio *(m)* en el ...	spot price
lugar de venta: publicidad *(f)* en el ... (PLV)	point-of-sale advertising (POS)

M

macro *(m)*	macro
maduro: mercado *(m)* ...	mature market
magnitud *(f)* económica de un pedido	economic order quantity
mailing *(m)*	mailing
malfuncionamiento *(m)*	malfunction
management *(m)*	management
mando: cadena *(f)* de ...	chain of command
mando: don *(m)* de ...	leadership
mando: línea *(f)* de ...	line of command
mando: organización *(f)* del ...	span of control
maniobra: fondo *(m)* de ...	working capital
mano *(f)* de obra	manpower
mano *(f)* de obra cualificada	skilled labour
mano *(f)* de obra directa	direct labour
mano *(f)* de obra indirecta	indirect labour
mano *(f)* de obra no cualificada	unskilled labour
mano *(f)* de obra semicualificada	semi-skilled labour
mano de obra: administración *(f)* de ...	manpower management
mano de obra: con exceso *(m)* de ...	overmanned
mano de obra: coste *(m)* unitario de ...	unit labour costs
mano de obra: escasez *(f)* de ...	undermanned undermanning
mano de obra: exceso *(m)* de ...	overmanning
mano de obra: planificación *(f)* de ...	manpower planning
mano de obra: predominio *(m)* de la ...	labour-intensive
mano de obra: previsión *(f)* de ...	manpower forecast
mano de obra: revisión *(f)* de la ...	manpower audit
mano: (al) alcance de la ...	arm's length
manos *(fpl)* a la obra	hands-on
mantener los márgenes	hold margins (to)

mantenimiento *(m)* de la planta	plant maintenance
mantenimiento *(f)* del precio al detalle	resale price maintenance (RPM)
mantenimiento *(m)* del precio de venta	resale price maintenance (RPM)
mantenimiento *(m)* planificado	planned maintenance
mantenimiento *(m)* preventivo	preventive maintenance
mantenimiento *(m)* productivo	productive maintenance
mantenimiento *(m)* total de los talleres	total plant maintenance
maquillar las cifras	massage the figures (to)
máquina: lenguaje *(m)* de ...	machine language
maquinaciones *(fpl)*	wheeling and dealing
marca *(f)*	brand
marca *(f)* registrada	registered trademark
marca: aceptación *(f)* de ...	brand acceptance
marca: conocimiento *(m)* de la ...	brand awareness
marca: estrategia *(f)* de la ...	brand strategy
marca: identificación *(f)* de la ...	brand recognition
marca: imagen *(m)* de la ...	brand image
marca: jefe *(m)* de ...	brand manager
marca: lealtad *(f)* a la ...	brand loyalty
marca: nombre *(m)* de ...	brand name
marcar objetivos	target (to)
marcas: cartera *(f)* de ...	brand portfolio
marcas: desviación *(f)* de ...	switch selling
marcha: puesta *(f)* en ...	start-up
marco *(m)* de oportunidad	window of opportunity
margen *(m)*	mark-up
margen *(m)* bruto	gross margin (GM)
margen *(m)* de beneficios	profit margin
margen *(m)* de seguridad	margin of safety
margen *(m)* neto	net margin
márgenes: mantener los ...	hold margins (to)
marginal	incremental
marginal: análisis *(m)* ...	incremental analysis marginal analysis
marginal: "cash flow" *(m)* ...	incremental cash flow
marginal: contabilidad *(f)* ...	marginal costing
marginal: mercado *(m)* ...	fringe market
marginales: costes *(mpl)* ...	marginal costs
marginales: fijación *(f)* de precios ...	marginal pricing

marginales: método *(m)* **de costes ...**	marginal costing
marginalizar	marginalize (to)
marginar	marginalize (to)
márketing *(m)*	marketing
márketing *(m)* **creativo**	creative marketing
márketing *(m)* **directo**	direct marketing
márketing *(m)* **global**	global marketing
márketing: asignación *(f)* **para ...**	marketing appropriation
márketing: combinación *(f)* **de medios de ...**	marketing mix
márketing: departamento *(m)* **de ...**	marketing department
márketing: director *(m)* **de ...**	marketing manager
márketing: investigación *(f)* **de ...**	marketing research
márketing: presupuesto *(m)* **de ...**	marketing budget
más abajo	downstream
más barato: vender ...	undercut (to)
masa *(f)* **crítica**	critical mass
matemática: programación *(f)* **...**	mathematical programming
material *(m)* **de publicidad en el lugar de venta**	point-of-sale material
material: activo *(m)* **...**	tangible assets
materiales: movimientos *(mpl)* **de ...**	materials handling
matricial: organización *(f)* **...**	matrix organization
matriz: empresa *(f)* **...**	parent company
matriz: organización *(f)* **en ...**	matrix management
maximización *(f)* **de beneficios**	profit maximization
maximizar *(f)*	maximize (to)
máximo discrecional: tiempo *(m)* **...**	time span of discretion
mayoritaria: participación *(f)* **...**	majority interest
mecanismo *(m)* **de tasas de cambio**	Exchange Rate Mechanism (ERM)
mecanizado de información: sistema *(m)* **(COINS)**	computerized information system (COINS)
media *(f)* **ponderada**	weighted average
mediación *(f)*	mediation
mediana *(f)*	median
mediar	mediate (to)

medición *(f)* de productividad	productivity measurement
medición *(f)* del rendimiento	performance measurement
medición *(f)* del trabajo	work measurement
medición *(f)* del trabajo administrativo	clerical work measurement (CWM)
medidas *(fpl)* del trabajo	ergonometrics
medio *(m)*	mean
medio ambiente: análisis *(m)* del ...	environmental analysis
medio ambiente: examen *(m)* del ...	environmental scan
medio ambiente: temas *(mpl)* del ...	green issues
medio: coste *(m)* ...	average cost
medio: punto *(m)* ...	median
medio: rendimiento *(m)* ...	average yield
medio: término *(m)* ...	average
medioambiente: previsión *(f)* sobre el ...	environmental forecasting
medios *(mpl)* de comunicación	media
medios de comunicación: análisis *(f)* de los ...	media analysis
medios de comunicación: seleccion *(f)* de ...	media selection
medios de márketing: combinación (f) de ...	marketing mix
medios de producción: arrendamiento *(m)* de ...	equipment leasing
medios de promoción: combinación *(f)* de ...	promotional mix
medios *(mpl)* de publicidad	advertising media
medios de venta: combinación *(f)* de ...	sales mix
medios: cuadros *(mpl)* ...	middle management
medios: ingresos *(mpl)* ...	average revenue
mejor de los casos: en el ...	best-case scenario
mejora *(f)*	upturn
mejora *(f)* de la rentabilidad	profit improvement
mejora *(f)* del producto	product improvement
mejora *(f)* del trabajo	job improvement
memoria *(f)*	memory
memoria *(f)* de lectura	read-only memory (ROM)
memoria *(f)* de ordenador	computer memory

memoria *(f)* **ROM (memoria de lectura)**	read-only memory (ROM)
menores: caja *(f)* **para gastos ...**	petty cash
menores: gastos *(mpl)* **...**	petty expenses
menos desarrollado: país *(m)* **...**	less-developed country (LDC)
mercado *(m)* **a futuro**	forward market
mercado *(m)* **abajo**	down-market
mercado *(m)* **alcista**	bull market
mercado *(m)* **bursátil a la baja**	bear market
Mercado *(m)* **Común**	Common Market
mercado *(m)* **de acciones**	equity market
mercado *(m)* **de demanda**	sellers' market
mercado *(m)* **de futuros**	futures market
mercado *(m)* **de oferta**	buyers' market
mercado *(m)* **de productos básicos**	commodity market
mercado *(m)* **financiero**	financial market
mercado *(m)* **maduro**	mature market
mercado *(m)* **marginal**	fringe market
mercado *(m)* **minoritario**	bear market
mercado *(m)* **objetivo**	target market
mercado *(m)* **paralelo**	grey market
mercado *(m)* **único**	single market
mercado *(m)* **único (de la CE)**	Single Market (of the EC)
mercado: acaparar el ...	corner the market (to)
mercado: creador *(m)* **de ...**	market leader
mercado: dinámica *(f)* **del ...**	market dynamics
mercado: encuesta *(f)* **sobre el ...**	market survey
mercado: estructura *(f)* **del ...**	market structure
mercado: estudio *(m)* **del ...**	market study
mercado: evaluación *(f)* **del ...**	market appraisal
mercado: investigación *(f)* **del ...**	market exploration
mercado: líder *(m)* **del ...**	market leader
mercado: parte *(f)* **del ...**	market share
mercado: penetración *(f)* **del ...**	market penetration
mercado: percepción *(f)* **del ...**	market awareness
mercado: perfil *(m)* **del ...**	market profile
mercado: potencial *(f)* **del ...**	market potential
mercado: precio *(m)* **de ...**	market price
mercado: previsión *(f)* **del ...**	market forecast
mercado: prueba *(f)* **del ...**	test marketing
mercado: prueba *(f)* **en el ...**	market test
mercado: saturación *(f)* **del ...**	market saturation

mercado: segmento *(m)* de ...	market segment
mercado: sensible al ...	market-sensitive
mercado: tendencia *(f)* del ...	market trend
mercado: tendencias *(fpl)* del ...	market forces
mercado: tipo *(m)* de ...	market rating
mercado: valor *(m)* de ...	market value
mercados: análisis *(m)* de ...	market research
mercados: fragmentación *(f)* de ...	market segmentation
mercados: planificación *(f)* de ...	market planning
mercancía *(f)*	commodity
mercancías: inventario *(m)* continuo de ...	continuous stocktaking
mercancías: técnica *(f)* de ...	merchandising
mercantíl: banco *(m)* ...	merchant bank
méritos: clasificación *(f)* por ...	merit rating
método *(m)* PERT (técnica *(f)* de evaluación y revisión de programas)	programme evaluation and review technique (PERT)
método *(m)* de calificación por puntos	points-rating method
método *(m)* de costes completos	full-cost method
método *(m)* de costes directos	direct costing
método *(m)* de costes estándares	standard costing
método *(m)* de costes marginales	marginal costing
metodo *(m)* de costes por función	functional costing
método *(m)* de observación aleatoria	random observation method
método *(m)* de trabajo	procedure
método *(m)* del camino crítico	critical path method (CPM)
método *(m)* del valor actual	present value method
método *(m)* simplex	simplex method
métodos y tiempos: estudio *(m)* de ...	time and methods study
métodos: departamento *(m)* de estudio de ...	methods study department
métodos: estudio *(m)* de ...	methods study methods engineering
métodos *(mpl)*: organización *(f)* y ... (O and M)	organization and methods (O & M)
micro *(m)*	micro
microchip *(m)*	microchip

minimizar los riesgos	minimize risks (to)
mínimo: coste *(m)* ...	least-cost
mínimo: salario *(m)* ...	minimum wage
minoritaria: participación *(f)* ...	minority interest
minoritario: mercado *(m)* ...	bear market
minusvalía *(f)*	capital loss
misión *(f)* de la empresa	corporate mission
misión *(f)* económica	economic mission
misión especial: personal *(m)* para ...	task force
misión: declaración *(f)* de la ...	mission statement
moda: palabra *(f)* de ...	buzz-word
modelo *(m)*	model
modelo *(m)* de contabilidad	accounting model
modelo *(m)* de decisiones	decision model
modelo *(m)* de la empresa	company model
	corporate model
modelo *(m)* dinámico de administración	dynamic management model
módem *(m)*	modem
modo *(m)*	mode
modular: producción *(f)* ...	modular production
modularidad *(f)*	modularity
moneda *(f)* paralela	parallel currency
moneda *(f)* única	single currency
Monetaria Europea: Unidad *(f)* ... (ECU)	European Currency Unit (ecu)
Monetaria Europea: Unión *(f)* ... (UME)	European Monetary Union (EMU)
monetaria: política *(f)* ...	monetary policy
Monetario Europeo: Sistema *(m)* ... (SME)	European Monetary System (EMS)
monetarismo *(m)*	monetarism
monopolio *(m)*	monopoly
monopolizar	corner the market (to)
	monopolize (to)
montaje: línea *(f)* de ...	assembly line
morfológico: análisis *(m)* ...	morphological analysis
morosos: deudores *(mpl)* ...	bad debts
	bad debtors
motivación *(f)*	motivation
motivación *(f)* por el beneficio	profit motive

motivación: investigación *(f)* de la ...	motivational research
motivador	motivational
motivador *(m)*	motivator
motivar	motivate (to)
motor *(m)* de compra	purchasing motivator
móvil: escala *(f)* ...	sliding scale
movilidad *(f)* de personal	staff mobility
movilidad *(f)* laboral	labour mobility
movilización *(f)* de fondos	capital raising
movimiento *(m)* de capital	funds flow
movimientos *(mpl)* de materiales	materials handling
movimientos predeterminados: sistema *(f)* de ... (PMTS)	predetermined motion time system (PMTS)
movimientos: economía *(f)* de ...	motion economy
movimientos: estudio *(m)* de ...	motion study
movimientos: estudio *(m)* de tiempos y ...	time and motion study
muestreo *(m)* al azar	random sampling
muestreo *(m)* de actividades	activity sampling
muestreo *(m)* estadístico	statistical sampling
multi-funcional: tarjeta *(f)* ...	smart card
multimedia: formación *(f)* ...	multimedia training
múltiple: análisis *(m)* de regresión ...	MRA (multiple regression analysis) multiple regression analysis (MRA)
múltiple: dirección *(f)* ...	multiple management
múltiple: empresa *(f)* de representación sindical ...	open shop
múltiple: entrada *(f)* ...	multi-access
mundialmente reconocida: clase *(f)* ...	world-class
mutuo: reconocimiento *(m)* ...	mutual recognition

N

necesidad: bien *(m)* de primera ...	primary commodity
necesidad: producto *(m)* de primera ...	primary commodity
necesidades *(fpl)* de formación	training needs
necesidades de formación: análisis *(m)* de ...	training needs analysis
necesidades: análisis *(m)* de ...	needs analysis
negativo sobre la renta: impuesto *(m)* ...	negative income tax
negativo: "cash flow" *(m)* ...	negative cash flow
negativo: flujo *(m)* de caja ...	negative cash flow
negociable: opción *(f)* ...	traded option
negociación *(f)* a nivel de fábrica	plant bargaining
negociación *(f)* colectiva	collective bargaining
negociación *(f)* conjunta	joint negotiation
negociación *(f)* de productividad	productivity bargaining
negociación: estrategia *(f)* de ...	negotiation strategy
negociaciones *(fpl)* sobre salarios	pay talks
negociada: huelga *(f)* no ...	wildcat strike
negociado: convenio *(m)* colectivo ...	collective bargaining agreement
negociar	negotiate (to)
negocio: vender parte del ...	hive off (to)
negocios: cartera *(f)* de ...	business portfolio
negocios: cifra *(f)* de ...	turnover
negocios: estrategia *(f)* de ...	business strategy
negocios: flujo *(m)* de ...	business stream
negocios: propuesta *(f)* de ...	business proposition
negra: caja *(f)* ...	slush fund
neto actualizado: valor *(m)* ...	net present value (NPV)
neto: activo *(m)* ...	net assets
neto: activo *(m)* circulante ...	net current assets
neto: beneficio *(m)* ...	net profit
neto: margen *(m)* ...	net margin
neto: salario *(m)* ...	take-home pay
	net salary

neto: valor *(m)* ...	net worth
neto: valor *(m)* ... actualizado	net present value (NPV)
nicho *(m)*	niche
nivel de fábrica: negociación *(f)* a ...	plant bargaining
nivel *(m)* de percepción	awareness level
nivel *(m)* de producción	flow line
nivel *(m)* de referencia	benchmark
nivel *(m)* de vida	standard of living
nivel *(m)* salarial	salary grade
	wage level
nivel: jefe *(m)* de alto ...	first-line manager
no admitidos a cotización: valores *(mpl)* ...	unlisted security
no cotizada en Bolsa: empresa *(f)* ...	unlisted company
no cualificada: mano *(f)* de obra ...	unskilled labour
no distribuidos: beneficios *(mpl)* ...	undistributed profit
no estructurado	unstructured
no negociada: huelga *(f)* ...	wildcat strike
no rentable	non-profit-making
no sindicada: acción *(f)* ...	unofficial action
no sindicada: huelga *(f)* ...	unofficial strike
noche: turno *(m)* de ...	night shift
nombre *(m)* comercial	trade name
nombre *(m)* de marca	brand name
nombre *(m)* del puesto	job title
nómina *(f)*	payroll
norma *(f)*	yardstick
norma *(f)* financiera	financial standard
normas *(fpl)* de contenido local	local content rules
normas *(fpl)* de gestión	management practices
nuevos productos: desarrollo *(m)* de ...	new-product development
nuevos productos: lanzamiento *(m)* de ...	new-product launching
numérico: control *(m)* ...	numerical control
número de empleados: disminución *(f)* del ...	demanning

O

objetivo *(m)*	objective
	target
objetivo *(m)* confidencial	hidden agenda
objetivo *(m)* de beneficio	profit goal
	profit target
objetivo *(m)* de la empresa	company goal
	corporate goal
	corporate objective
objetivo *(m)* de producción	production target
objetivo *(m)* de ventas	sales goal
	sales target
objetivo *(m)* del trabajo	job design
objetivo: mercado *(m)* ...	target market
objetivos *(mpl)* globales de la empresa	overall company objectives
objetivos: definición *(f)* de ...	objective-setting
objetivos: dirección *(f)* por ...	management by objectives (MBO)
objetivos: fijación *(f)* de ...	goal-setting
	target-setting
objetivos: fijar ...	targeting
objetivos: identificación *(f)* de ...	goal-seeking
objetivos: jerarquía *(f)* de ...	hierarchy of goals
objetivos: marcar ...	target (to)
obligación *(f)* desvalorizada	junk bond
obligación *(f)* europea	eurobond
obligaciones *(fpl)*	debenture
	liabilities
obra: administración *(f)* de mano de ...	manpower management
obra: coste *(m)* unitario de mano de ...	unit labour costs
obra: escasez *(f)* de mano de ...	undermanned
	undermanning
obra: exceso *(m)* de mano de ...	redundancy
obra: mano *(f)* de ...	manpower
obra: manos *(fpl)* a la ...	hands-on
obra: planificación *(f)* de mano de ...	manpower planning

obra: predominio *(m)* de la mano de ...	labour-intensive
obra: previsión *(f)* de mano de ...	manpower forecasting
obra: revisión *(f)* de la mano de ...	manpower audit
obrera: participación *(f)* ...	worker participation
obrera: representación *(f)* ...	worker representation
obrero: personal *(m)* ...	shop-floor
obreros: consejo *(m)* de ...	works council
obreros: despedir *(m)* ...	lay off (to)
observación aleatoria: método *(m)* de ...	random observation method
obsolencia *(f)*	obsolescence
obsolencia *(f)* interna	built-in obsolescence
obsolencia *(f)* planificada	planned obsolescence
obtención *(f)*	procurement
ociosa: capacidad *(f)* ...	spare capacity
ocultos: bienes *(mpl)* ...	hidden assets
ocupacional: riesgo *(m)* ...	occupational hazard
oferta *(f)*	tender
oferta *(f)* combinada	package deal
oferta *(f)* pública de compra (OPA)	takeover bid (TOB)
oferta: mercado de ...	buyers' market
oficial: huelga *(f)* ...	official strike
oficina *(f)* electrónica	electronic office
oficina *(f)* principal	head office
oficina: planificación *(f)* de la ...	office planning
oficinista *(m/f)*	white-collar (worker) clerical worker
ofimática *(f)*	office automation
opción *(f)* de compra de acciones	stock option
opción *(f)* de fabricar o comprar	make-or-buy decision
opción *(f)* negociable	traded option
opcional de acciones: plan *(m)* de compra ...	stock option plan
operación: analisis *(m)* de ...	analysis operations operations analysis
operación: gastos *(mpl)* de ...	operating expenses

operación: informe *(m)* sobre una ...	debriefing
operacional: dirección *(f)* ...	operating management
operacional: división *(f)* ...	operating division
operacional: planificación *(f)* ...	operational planning
operaciones *(fpl)*	operations
operaciones: desglose *(m)* de ...	operations breakdown
operaciones: director *(m)* de ...	operations manager
operaciones: evaluación *(f)* de ...	operations audit
operaciones: gestión *(f)* de ...	operations management
operaciones: investigación *(f)* de ...	operations research (OR)
operaciones: planificación *(f)* de ...	operations planning
operativa: investigación *(f)* ...	operational research (OR)
operativo	operational
opiniones: encuesta *(f)* de ...	attitude survey
	opinion survey
oportunidad *(f)* comercial	market opportunity
oportunidad en el empleo: igualdad *(f)* de ...	equal employment opportunity
oportunidad: coste *(m)* de ...	opportunity costs
oportunidad: igualdad *(f)* de ...	equal opportunity
oportunidad: marco *(m)* de ...	window of opportunity
optimización *(f)* de beneficios	profit optimization
optimizar	optimize (to)
ordenador *(m)*	computer
ordenador *(m)* analógico	analog computer
ordenador *(m)* central	mainframe
ordenador *(m)* digital	digital computer
ordenador *(m)* personal	PC (personal computer)
ordenador *(m)* portátil	desktop computer
	laptop computer
ordenador: almacenamiento *(m)* del ...	computer storage
ordenador: aprendizaje *(m)* asistido por ... (CAL)	computer-aided learning (CAL)
ordenador: banco *(m)* de datos del ...	computer bank

ordenador: enseñanza *(f)* asistida por ... (CAT)	computer-aided teaching (CAT)
ordenador: entrada *(f)* al ...	computer input
ordenador: fabricación *(f)* asistida por ... (CAM)	computer-aided manufacturing (CAM)
ordenador: fabricación *(f)* integrada por ... (CIM)	computer-integrated manufacturing (CIM)
ordenador: formación *(f)* asistida por ... (CBT)	computer-based training (CBT)
ordenador: lenguaje *(m)* de ...	computer language
ordenador: memoria *(f)* de ...	computer memory
ordenador: producción *(f)* integrada por ... (CIM)	computer-integrated manufacturing (CIM)
ordenador: producto *(m)* del ...	computer output
ordenador: salida *(f)* del ...	computer output
ordenador: simulación *(f)* por ...	computer simulation
ordenador: terminal *(f)* del ...	computer terminal
órdenes: reunión *(f)* para dar ...	briefing
orgánico: crecimiento *(m)* ...	organic growth
organización *(f)*	management
organización *(f)* científica del trabajo	management science scientific management
organización *(f)* del mando	span of control
organización *(f)* en matriz	matrix management
organización *(f)* funcional	functional organization
organización *(f)* informal	informal organization
organización *(f)* jerárquica	line and staff organization
organización *(f)* lineal	line organization
organización *(f)* matricial	matrix organization
organización *(f)* por secciones	departmentalization
organización *(f)* "staff"	staff organization
organización *(f)* y métodos *(mpl)* (O and M)	organization and methods (O & M)
organización: conducta *(f)* del hombre en la ...	organizational behaviour
organización: desarrollo *(m)* de la ...	organizational development
organización: eficacia *(f)* de la ...	organizational effectiveness
organización: estructura *(f)* de la ...	organization structure
organización: planificación *(f)* de la ...	organization planning

organización: transformación *(f)* **de la ...**	organizational change
organizar	deploy (to)
organizar lógicamente	rationalize (to)
organizativa: teoría *(f)* **...**	organization theory
organógrama *(m)*	organization chart
	organogram
orientación *(f)* **al consumidor**	consumer orientation
orientación *(f)* **del consumidor**	customer orientation
orientación *(f)* **profesional**	vocational guidance
orientativa: cifra *(f)* **...**	ballpark figure
origen del impuesto sobre la renta: retención *(f)* **en ...**	pay-as-you-earn (PAYE)
origen *(m)* **y aplicación de recursos**	source and disposition of funds
origen: país *(m)* **de ...**	home country
origen: sistema *(m)* **de retención de impuestos en ...**	pay-as-you-go
oro: salario *(m)* **de ...**	golden handcuffs
	golden salary

P

paga *(f)* voluntaria	ex gratia payment
pago *(m)* de beneficios	profit-related pay
país *(m)* anfitrión	host country
país *(m)* de origen	home country
país *(m)* de reciente industrialización	newly industrialized country (NIC)
país *(m)* menos desarrollado	less-developed country (LDC)
palabra *(f)* de moda	buzz-word
"pallets": utilización *(f)* de ...	palletization
panel	consumers' panel
pantalla: datos *(mpl)* de ...	viewdata
paquete *(m)* accional	stake
paquete *(m)* de sistemas	programme package
paquete *(m)* de software	software package
par *(f)*	par
paralela: importación *(f)* ...	parallel import
paralela: moneda *(f)* ...	parallel currency
paralelo: crédito *(m)* ...	parallel loan
paralelo: mercado *(m)* ...	grey market
paramétrica: programación *(f)* ...	parametric programming
parámetro *(m)*	parameter
parcial: empleado *(m)* a tiempo ...	part-timer
paridad *(f)* de poder adquisitivo	purchasing power parity
parque *(m)* de producción	production complex
parte del consumidor: aceptación *(m)* por ...	consumer acceptance
parte *(f)* del mercado	market share
parte del negocio: vender ...	hive off (to)
parte *(f)*: tercera ...	third party
participación *(f)*	participation
	stake
participación conjunta: sociedad *(f)* en ...	joint-venture company
participación *(f)* de control	controlling interest
participación de los ejecutivos: gestión *(f)* de alta ...	management by walking around

participación en la producción: plan *(m)* de ...	share of production plan
participación *(f)* en los beneficios	profit-sharing
participación *(f)* mayoritaria	majority interest
participación *(f)* minoritaria	minority interest
participación *(f)* obrera	worker participation
participativa: dirección *(f)* ...	participative management
partidas *(fpl)* invisibles	invisibles
pasivo *(m)*	liabilities
pasivo *(m)* circulante	current liabilities
pasivo *(m)* real	current liabilities
patente *(f)*	patent
patentes: comercio *(m)* de ...	patent trading
patrocinio *(m)*	sponsorship
patrones: cierre *(m)* por los ...	lock-out
pauta *(f)*	guideline
pauta *(f)* de precio	price leader
pauta *(f)* de rendimiento	performance indicator
payback	payback
pedido *(m)* por correo	mail order
pedido: magnitud *(f)* económica de un ...	economic order quantity
peligrosidad: productos *(mpl)* químicos de alta ...	hazchem (hazardous chemicals)
penetración *(f)* del mercado	market penetration
penetración: fijación *(f)* de precios de ...	penetration pricing
pensamiento *(m)* lateral	lateral thinking
pensar lo impensable	think the unthinkable (to)
PER	price-earnings ratio (P/E)
percepción *(f)* del mercado	market awareness
percepción: nivel *(m)* de ...	awareness level
pérdida *(f)* de capital	capital loss
pérdidas propias: disminuir las ...	cut one's losses (to)
perecederos: bienes *(mpl)* de consumo no ...	consumer durables
perecederos: productos *(mpl)* ...	non-durable goods
perfil *(m)* de adquisición	acquisition profile
perfil *(m)* de la empresa	company profile
perfil *(m)* de riesgos	risk profile
perfil *(m)* del consumidor	customer profile

perfil *(m)* del mercado	market profile
perfil *(m)* del producto	product profile
perfil *(m)* del puesto	job profile
pericia *(f)*	know-how
pericias: análisis *(m)* de ...	skills analysis
periférico: equipo *(m)* ..	peripheral equipment
periféricos *(mpl)*	peripherals
período *(m)* de contabilidad	accounting period
período *(m)* de recuperación de la inversión	payback period
permanencia: prima *(f)* de ...	golden handcuffs
perpetuo: inventario *(m)* ...	perpetual inventory
personal *(m)* directivo	management staff
personal directivo: estrategia *(f)* de ...	executive manpower strategy
personal *(m)* obrero	shop-floor
personal *(m)* para misión especial	task force
personal: administración *(f)* de ...	personnel management
personal: auditoría *(f)* de ...	staff audit
personal: clasificación *(f)* de ...	personnel rating
personal: compromiso *(m)* del ...	staff commitment
personal: departamento *(m)* del ...	personnel department
personal: dirección *(f)* del ...	personnel management staff management
personal: director *(m)* de ...	personnel manager
personal: escasez *(f)* de ...	understaffed understaffing
personal: especificación *(f)* de ...	personnel specification
personal: estrategia *(f)* de ...	staff strategy
personal: evaluación *(f)* del ...	staff appraisal
personal: exceso *(m)* de ...	overstaffed overstaffing
personal: formación *(f)* ...	personal growth
personal: movilidad *(f)* de ...	staff mobility
personal: planificación *(f)* de ...	staff planning
personal: política *(f)* de ...	personnel policy
personal: previsión *(f)* de ...	staff forecasting
personal: reclutamiento *(m)* y gestión *(f)* de ...	staff resourcing

personal: reducción *(f)* del ...	staff cut-back
personal: relaciones *(fpl)* con el ...	employee relations
personal: rotación *(f)* de ...	labour turnover
	staff turnover
personal: traslados *(mpl)* del ...	staff transfer
personalizar	personalize (to)
perspectiva *(f)* empresarial	business outlook
perspectivas *(fpl)* comerciales	market prospects
perspectivas *(fpl)* de beneficio	profit outlook
PERT técnica *(f)* de evaluación	programme evaluation and review technique (PERT)
pertinencia: árbol *(m)* de ...	pertinence tree
pesimista: hipótesis *(f)* ...	worst-case scenario
PIB (producto interior bruto)	GDP (gross domestic product)
pila *(f)* de trabajo atrasado	backlog
piloto: producción *(f)* ...	pilot production
piloto: serie *(f)* ...	pilot run
	test run
pionero: producto *(m)* ...	pioneer product
piquete *(m)* (de huelga)	picket
pirata *(m)* (informática)	hacker
pirateado *(m)* (informática)	hacking
piratería *(f)*	piracy
plan *(m)*	plan
plan *(m)* abierto	open-plan
plan *(m)* comercial	market plan
plan *(m)* de acción	action plan
plan *(m)* de compra opcional de acciones	stock option plan
plan *(m)* de participación en la producción	share of production plan
plan *(m)* de trabajo	schedule
	work schedule
plan *(m)* departamental	departmental plan
plan *(m)* estratégico	strategic plan
plan *(m)* táctico	tactical plan
planificación *(f)*	planning
planificación *(f)* a corto plazo	short-range planning
	short-term planning

planificación *(f)* **a largo plazo**	forward planning
	long-range planning
	long-term planning
planificación *(f)* **de beneficios**	profit planning
planificación *(f)* **de distribución**	distribution planning
planificación *(f)* **de la oficina**	office planning
planificación *(f)* **de la organización**	organization planning
planificación *(f)* **de la producción**	production planning
planificación *(f)* **de mano de obra**	manpower planning
planificación *(f)* **de mercados**	market planning
planificación *(f)* **de operaciones**	operations planning
planificación *(f)* **de personal**	staff planning
planificación *(f)* **de presupuestos: sistema** *(m)* **de programación y ...**	planning, programming, budgeting system (PPBS)
planificación *(f)* **de recursos humanos**	human resource planning (HRP)
planificación *(f)* **de sistemas**	systems planning
planificación *(f)* **de sucesión de directivos**	management succession planning
planificación *(f)* **de ventas**	sales planning
planificación *(f)* **del desarrollo profesional**	career planning
planificación *(f)* **del producto**	product planning
planificación *(f)* **empresarial**	company planning
	corporate planning
planificación *(f)* **estratégica**	strategic planning
planificación *(f)* **financiera**	financial planning
planificación *(f)* **operacional**	operational planning
planificación *(f)* **táctica**	tactical planning
planificación *(f)* **y control** *(m)* **de la producción**	production planning and control
planificación: departamento *(m)* **de ...**	planning department
planificada: obsolencia *(f)* **...**	planned obsolescence
planificado: mantenimiento *(m)* **...**	planned maintenance
planta industrial: estudio *(m)* **de proyecto de una ...**	plant layout study
planta: capacidad *(f)* **de ...**	plant capacity

planta: mantenimiento *(m)* **de la ...**	plant maintenance
plantilla *(f)*	manning
	staff
plantilla *(f)* **de dirección**	managerial grid
plazo *(m)* **de ejecución**	turnaround time
plazo *(m)* **de tiempo**	time frame
plazo: activo *(m)* **disponible a corto ...**	quick assets
plazo: cambio *(m)* **a ...**	forward rate
plazo: créditos *(mpl)* **financieros a largo ...**	loan stock
plazo: planificación *(f)* **a corto ...**	short-range planning
	short-term planning
plazo: planificación *(f)* **a largo ...**	forward planning
	long-range planning
plena capacidad	full capacity
pleno empleo *(m)*	full-time employment
pluma: lecho *(m)* **de ...**	featherbedding
pluriempleo *(m)*	moonlighting
plusvalía *(f)*	capital gain
PNB (producto *(m)* **nacional bruto)**	GNP (gross national product)
poder *(m)* **adquisitivo**	purchasing power
poder adquisitivo: paridad *(f)* **de ...**	purchasing power parity
poderes: delegación *(f)* **de ...**	delegation
política *(f)* **comercial**	business policy
política *(f)* **de distribución**	distribution policy
política *(f)* **de dividendos**	dividend policy
política *(f)* **de inversiones**	investment policy
política *(f)* **de la empresa**	company policy
	corporate policy
política *(f)* **de personal**	personnel policy
política *(f)* **de precios**	pricing policy
política *(f)* **de promoción**	promotional policy
política *(f)* **de remesas**	remittance policy
política *(f)* **de ventas**	sales policy
	selling policy
política directiva: ciencia *(f)* **de ...**	management science
política directiva: teoría *(f)* **de ...**	management theory
política *(f)* **fiscal**	fiscal policy

política *(f)* monetaria	monetary policy
política *(f)* salarial	wage policy
política: ejecución *(f)* de la ...	policy execution
política: establecimiento *(m)* de la ...	policy statement
política: formulación *(f)* de la ...	policy formulation
ponderación *(f)*	weighting
ponderada: media *(f)* ...	weighted average
poner a prueba un proyecto	chunk a project (to)
poner al día	update (to)
poner interfaces	interface (to)
por debajo de la capacidad	undercapacity
portátil: ordenador *(m)* ...	desktop computer
	laptop computer
portátil: teléfono *(m)* ...	cellphone
	mobile phone
posesión: toma *(f)* de ...	takeover
posición *(f)* financiera	financial position
posicionamiento *(m)*	positioning
positiva: discriminación *(f)* ...	positive discrimination
postventa: servicio *(m)* ...	after-sales service
potencia: cliente *(m)* ...	prospective customer
potencial *(m)* de crecimiento	growth potential
potencial *(m)* de directivos	management potential
potencial *(m)* de explotación	development potential
potencial *(m)* de ventas	sales potential
potencial *(f)* del mercado	market potential
potencial limitado: ejecutivo *(m)* con ...	low-flier
potencial: comprador *(m)* ...	potential buyer
potencial: ejecutivo *(m)* de alto ...	high-flier
práctica: formación *(f)* ...	hands-on training
práctica: formación *(f)* sobre la ...	on-the-job training
prácticas *(fpl)* restrictivas	restrictive practices (industrial)
	restrictive practices (legal)
precio al detalle: mantenimiento *(m)* del ...	resale price maintenance (RPM)
precio *(m)* competitivo	competitive price
precio *(m)* de mercado	market price

precio de prestigio: fijación *(f)* de ...	prestige pricing
precio de venta: mantenimiento *(m)* del ...	resale price maintenance (RPM)
precio *(m)* en el lugar de venta	spot price
precio *(m)* estándar	standard price
precio: aumento *(m)* de ...	price increase
precio: fijar el ...	price (to)
precio: pauta *(f)* de ...	price leader
precios al consumidor: índice *(m)* de ...	retail price index (RPI)
precios al consumo: índice *(m)* de ... (IPC)	consumer price index retail price index (RPI)
precios de acciones: rendimiento *(m)* de ...	share price performance
precios de penetración: fijación *(f)* de ...	penetration pricing
precios de transferencia: fijación *(f)* de ...	transfer pricing
precios marginales: fijación *(f)* de ...	marginal pricing
precios: abaratamiento *(m)* de ...	price-cutting
precios: abaratar *(mpl)* ...	cut prices (to)
precios: diferencia *(f)* de ...	differential price
precios: discriminación *(f)* de ...	price discrimination
precios: empresa *(f)* líder de ...	market maker
precios: escala *(f)* de ...	price range
precios: escalada *(f)* de ...	price escalation
precios: escalado *(m)* de ...	price differential
precios: estrategia *(f)* de ...	pricing strategy
precios: estructura *(f)* de ...	price structure
precios: fijación *(f)* de ...	price determination price-fixing
precios: índice *(m)* de ...	price index
precios: política *(f)* de ...	pricing policy
precios: rebaja *(f)* desleal de ...	dumping
precios: tirar los ...	underprice (to)
predador *(m)*	predator
predador *(m)* de acciones de empresas	corporate raider
predeterminados: sistema *(m)* de movimientos ... (PMTS)	predetermined motion time system (PMTS)

predominio *(m)* de la mano de obra	labour-intensive
preferencial: acción *(f)* ...	golden share
preferente de suscripción: derecho *(m)* ...	rights issue
preferente: empresa *(f)* ... (en una adquisición)	white knight
preferente: licitación *(f)* ...	pre-emptive bid
prematura: jubilación *(f)* ...	early retirement
presentación *(m)*	launching
presidente *(m)*	president
	chairman
presidente *(m)* y director *(m)* gerente	chairman and managing director
presión *(f)*	pressure
presión *(f)* inflacionaria	inflationary pressure
presionar	hustle (to)
prestación *(f)* de servicios	contracting out
préstamo *(m)* para arrendamiento	lease-lend
prestigio: fijación *(f)* de precio de ...	prestige pricing
prestigio de una empresa: valor *(m)* de ...	goodwill
presupuestar	budget (to)
presupuestaria: contabilidad *(f)* ...	budgeting
presupuestaria: dotación *(f)* ...	budget allotment
presupuestaria: previsión *(f)* ...	budget forecast
	budget forecasting
presupuestaria: varianza *(f)* ...	budgetary variance
presupuestario: control *(m)* ...	budgetary control
presupuestario: control *(m)* ... de gastos de capital	capital budgeting
presupuestario de caja: control *(m)* ...	cash budgeting
presupuesto *(m)*	budget
presupuesto *(m)* de base cero	zero-base budget
presupuesto *(m)* de caja	cash budget
presupuesto *(m)* de gastos de capital	capital budget
presupuesto *(m)* de inversiones	investment budget
presupuesto *(m)* de márketing	marketing budget

presupuesto *(m)* de publicidad	advertising budget
presupuesto *(m)* de ventas	sales budget
presupuesto *(m)* flexible	flexible budget
presupuesto: asignación *(f)* del ...	budget appropriation
presupuesto: estándares *(mpl)* de ...	budget standard
presupuesto: restricción *(f)* del ...	budget constraint
presupuestos: sistema *(m)* de programación y planificación de ...	PPBS (planning, programming, budgeting system)
presupuestos programados: sistema *(m)* de ...	programme budgeting
preventivo: mantenimiento *(m)* ...	preventive maintenance
previsión *(f)*	forecast forecasting
previsión *(f)* comercial	business forecasting
previsión *(f)* de caja	cash forecasting
previsión *(f)* de la demanda	demand forecasting
previsión *(f)* de mano de obra	manpower forecast
previsión *(f)* de personal	staff forecasting
prevision *(f)* de ventas	sales estimate sales forecast
previsión *(f)* de vida de un producto	product life expectancy
previsión *(f)* del mercado	market forecast
previsión *(f)* presupuestaria	budget forecast budget forecasting
previsión *(f)* sobre el medioambiente	environmental forecasting
previsión *(f)* tecnólogica	technological forecasting
prevista: fecha *(f)* ...	expected date
prima *(f)*	bonus golden share premium
prima *(f)* colectiva	group bonus
prima *(f)* de enganche	golden hello
prima *(f)* de permanencia	golden handcuffs
prima *(f)* por rendimiento	premium bonus
primas: sistema *(m)* de ...	bonus scheme
primera clase: acción *(f)* de ...	blue-chip stock

primera clase: valor *(m)* de ...	blue-chip stock
primera necesidad: bien *(m)* de ...	commodity
primera necesidad: producto *(m)* de ...	primary commodity
principal: oficina *(f)* ...	head office
prioridades: establecer ...	prioritize (to)
privada: empresa *(f)* ...	private enterprise
privatización *(f)*	privatization
privatizar	privatize (to)
privilegiada: comercio *(m)* con información ...	insider trading
privilegiada: trato *(m)* con información ...	insider dealing
pro rata	pro rata
proactiva: estrategia *(f)* ...	proactive strategy
proactivo	proactive
probabilidad: teoría *(f)* de la ...	probability theory
problema: análisis *(m)* del ...	problem analysis
problemas: evaluación *(f)* de ...	problem assessment
problemas: resolución *(f)* de ...	problem solving
problemática: zona *(f)* ...	problem area
procedimental	procedural
procedimiento *(m)*	procedure
procedimientos *(mpl)* administrativos	systems and procedures
procedimientos *(mpl)* de decisión	decision process
procesable	actionable
procesador *(m)* de textos	word processor (WP)
procesador de textos: diccionario *(m)* en ...	spellcheck
procesamiento *(m)* de textos	word processing
procesar (informática)	process (to)
proceso *(m)* automático de datos (ADP)	automatic data processing (ADP)
proceso central: unidad *(f)* de ... (CPU)	central processing unit (CPU)
proceso *(m)* de control administrativo	administrative control procedure
proceso *(m)* de datos	data processing
	information processing
proceso de datos: departamento *(f)* de ...	computer services department

proceso *(m)* **de producción**	production process
proceso *(m)* **de tomar decisiones**	decision-making process
proceso *(m)* **electrónico**	electronic processing
proceso *(m)* **electrónico de datos (EDP)**	electronic data processing (EDP)
proceso *(m)* **iterativo**	iterative process
proceso *(m)* **logístico**	logistic process
proceso: control *(m)* **del ...**	process control
proceso: diagrama *(m)* **de flujos del ...**	flow process chart
producción *(f)*	output production
producción *(f)* **contínua**	continuous-flow production
producción *(f)* **en cadena**	chain production line production production line
producción *(f)* **integrada por ordenador (CIM)**	computer-integrated manufacturing (CIM)
producción *(f)* **intensiva**	intensive production
producción *(f)* **modular**	modular production
producción *(f)* **piloto**	pilot production
producción *(f)* **por lotes**	batch production
producción *(f)* **total**	throughput
producción: administración *(f)* **de ...**	production management
producción: arrendamiento *(m)* **de medios de ...**	equipment leasing
producción: cadena *(f)* **de ...**	chain of production
producción: contabilidad *(f)* **de ...**	process costing
producción: control *(m)* **de ...**	output budgeting production control
producción: costes *(mpl)* **de ...**	production costs
producción: director *(m)* **de ...**	production director
producción: estándares *(mpl)* **de la ...**	production standard
producción: factores *(mpl)* **de ...**	factors of production
producción: índice *(m)* **administración ...**	administration-production ratio
producción: jefe *(m)* **de ...**	production manager
producción: nivel *(m)* **de ...**	flow line

producción: objetivo *(m)* de ...	production target
producción: parque *(m)* de ...	production complex
producción: plan *(m)* de participación en la ...	share of production plan
producción: planificación *(f)* de la ...	production planning
producción: planificación *(f)* y control *(m)* de la ...	production planning and control
producción: proceso *(m)* de ...	production process
producción: programa *(m)* de ...	production schedule
producción: programación *(f)* de la ...	production scheduling
producción: técnica *(f)* de ...	production technique
producción: técnicas *(fpl)* de ...	production engineering
productividad *(f)*	productivity
productividad: campaña *(f)* de ...	productivity campaign productivity drive
productividad: convenio *(m)* de ...	productivity agreement
productividad: medición *(f)* de ...	productivity measurement
productividad: negociación *(f)* de ...	productivity bargaining
productivo: mantenimiento *(m)* ...	productive maintenance
productivo: tiempo *(m)* ...	uptime
producto *(m)* clave	core product
producto *(m)* de primera necesidad	primary commodity basic product
producto *(m)* del ordenador	computer output
producto *(m)* estrella	star product
producto *(m)* interior bruto (PIB)	gross domestic product (GDP)
producto *(m)* no rentable	loss-maker
producto *(m)* pionero	pioneer product
producto: abandono *(m)* del ...	product abandonment
producto: análisis *(m)* del ...	product analysis
producto: ciclo *(m)* de la vida de un ...	product life product life cycle
producto: comercialización *(f)* del ...	marketing merchandising
producto: diseño *(m)* del ...	product design
producto: fiabilidad *(f)* de un ...	product reliability

producto: gestión *(f)* de ...	product management
producto: imagen *(m)* del ...	product image
producto: introducción *(f)* de un ...	product introduction
producto: introducir un ...	roll out (to)
producto: lanzamiento *(m)* de un ...	product launch
producto: mejora *(f)* del ...	product improvement
producto: perfil *(m)* del ...	product profile
producto: planificación *(f)* del ...	product planning
producto: previsión *(f)* de vida de un ...	product life expectancy
producto: rendimiento *(m)* del ...	product performance
producto: rentabilidad *(f)* del ...	product profitability
productos básicos: mercado *(m)* de ...	commodity market
productos *(mpl)* de consumo por impulso	impulse goods
productos *(mpl)* de venta por impulso	impulse goods
productos *(mpl)* duraderos	durables
productos *(mpl)* perecederos	non-durable goods
productos *(mpl)* químicos de alta peligrosidad	hazchem (hazardous chemicals)
productos: cartera *(f)* de ...	product portfolio
productos: combinación *(f)* de ...	product mix
productos: concepción *(f)* de ...	product conception
productos: creación *(f)* de ...	product generation
productos: desarrollo *(m)* de ...	product development
productos: desarrollo *(m)* de nuevos ...	new-product development
productos: diferenciación *(f)* entre ...	product differentiation
productos: diferenciar ...	product differentiate (to)
productos: dinámica *(f)* de ...	product dynamics
productos: diversificación *(f)* de ...	product diversification
productos: estrategia *(f)* de ...	product strategy
productos: estudio *(m)* de ...	product engineering
productos: evaluación *(f)* del coste de ...	product costing
productos: gama *(f)* de ...	product range
productos: grupo *(m)* de ...	product group

productos: investigación *(f)* **de ...**	product research
productos: jefe *(m)* **de ...**	product manager
productos: lanzamiento *(m)* **de nuevos ...**	new-product launching
productos: prueba *(f)* **de ...**	product test
productos: publicidad *(f)* **de ...**	product advertising
productos: sector *(m)* **de ...**	product area
productos: serie *(f)* **de ...**	product line
productos: "test" *(m)* **de ...**	product testing
profesional que hace selección de directivos	head-hunter
profesional: formación *(f)* **...**	vocational training
profesional: orientación *(f)* **...**	vocational guidance
profesional: planificación *(f)* **del desarrollo ...**	career planning
profesional: readaptación *(f)* **...**	booster training
profesional: reeducación *(f)* **...**	booster training retraining
profesional: secreto *(m)* **...**	Chinese wall professional secret
profesionales: explotación *(f)* **de contactos ...**	networking
profesionalización *(f)*	professionalization
profeta *(m)* **de fracaso**	doomwatcher
programa *(m)*	programme schedule
programa *(m)* **comercial**	trading programme
programa *(m)* **de desarrollo**	development programme
programa *(m)* **de inversión**	investment programme
programa *(m)* **de producción**	production schedule
programa *(m)* **informático**	computer program
programación *(f)*	computer programming scheduling
programación *(f)* **científica**	scientific programming
programación *(f)* **de la producción**	production scheduling
programación *(f)* **dinámica**	dynamic programming
programación *(f)* **lineal**	linear programming
programación *(f)* **matemática**	mathematical programming
programación *(f)* **no linear**	non-linear programming
programación *(f)* **paramétrica**	parametric programming
programación y planificación de presupuestos: sistema de ...	planning, programming, budgeting system (PPBS)

programación: sistema *(m)* **de ...**	programme package
programada: enseñanza *(f)* **...**	programmed instruction
	programmed learning
programada: gestión *(f)* **...**	programmed management
programador *(m)* **informático**	computer programmer
programados: sistema *(m)* **de presupuestos ...**	programme budgeting
programar	program(me) (to)
	schedule (to)
programas *(mpl)*	software
programas: ingeniero *(m)* **de ...**	software engineer
programas: método *(m)* **PERT (técnica** *(f)* **de evaluación y revisión de ...)**	programme evaluation and review technique (PERT)
programas: técnica *(f)* **de evaluación y revisión de ... (PERT)**	programme evaluation and review technique (PERT)
progreso: trabajo *(m)* **en ...**	work in progress
promedio *(m)*	average
	mean
promoción *(f)* **(del personal)**	promotion (personnel)
promoción *(f)* **de ventas**	sales promotion
promoción: combinación *(f)* **de medios de ...**	promotional mix
promoción: política *(f)* **de ...**	promotional policy
promocional	promotional
pronóstico *(m)* **comercial**	business forecasting
propias: disminuir las pérdidas ...	cut one's losses (to)
propietario: director *(m)* **...**	owner-manager
propia: trabajar por cuenta ...	freelance (to go)
propio: hacer (por ejemplo un problema de la empresa)	internalize (to)
proporción *(f)* **de cobertura**	cover ratio
proporción *(f)* **de valores disponibles**	cash ratio
propuesta *(f)* **de negocios**	business proposition
propuesta *(f)* **de valorización**	value proposal
protección *(f)* **al consumidor**	consumer protection
protección *(f)* **de datos**	data protection
protección *(f)* **del territorio**	turf protection
proveerse del exterior	buy in (to)
provisión *(f)* **de dinero**	money supply

provisión (f) de fondos	money supply
proyección (f)	projection
proyección (f) del beneficio	profit projection
proyecto de una planta industrial: estudio (m) de ...	plant layout study
proyecto: director (m) de ...	project manager
proyectos de capital: evaluación (f) de ...	capital project evaluation
proyectos: departamento (m) técnico y de ...	engineering and design department
proyectos: estudio (m) de ...	design engineering project analysis
proyectos: evaluación (f) de ...	project assessment
proyectos: gestión (f) de ...	project management
proyectos: planificación (f) de ...	project planning
prueba (f) de aptitud	aptitude test
prueba (f) de ventas	sales test
prueba (f) del mercado	test marketing
prueba (f) en el mercado	market test
prueba (f) psicométrica	psychometric testing
prueba: campo (m) de ...	field testing
psicología (f) industrial	industrial psychology
psicométrica: prueba (f) ...	psychometric testing
pública de compra: oferta (f) ... (OPA)	takeover bid (TOB)
pública: empresa (f) ...	public enterprise
pública: empresa (f) de utilidad ...	public utility
pública: licitación (f) ...	competitive tendering
públicas: relaciones (fpl) ...	public relations (PR)
publicidad (f) de productos	product advertising
publicidad (f) directa	mailing
publicidad (f) empresarial	corporate advertising
publicidad (f) en el lugar de venta (PLV)	point-of-sale advertising (POS)
publicidad en el lugar de venta: material (m) de ...	point-of-sale material
publicidad (f) subliminal	subliminal advertising
publicidad: agente (m) de ...	advertising agent
publicidad: asignación (f) para ...	advertising appropriation
publicidad: campaña (f) de ...	advertising campaign

publicidad: eficacia *(f)* **de ...**	advertising effectiveness
publicidad: jefe *(m)* **de ...**	advertising manager
publicidad: medios *(mpl)* **de ...**	advertising media
publicidad: presupuesto *(m)* **de ...**	advertising budget
publicitaria: investigación *(f)* **...**	advertising research
publicitario: empuje *(m)* **...**	advertising drive
publicitario: tema *(m)* **...**	advertising message advertising theme
puerta *(f)*	gateway
puesta *(f)* **en marcha**	start-up
puesto *(m)* **de trabajo**	work station
puesto de trabajo: especificación *(f)* **de un ...**	job specification
puesto: características *(fpl)* **del ...**	job characteristics
puesto: contenido *(m)* **del ...**	job content
puesto: exigencias *(fpl)* **del ...**	job requirements
puesto: expectativas *(fpl)* **del ...**	job expectations
puesto: incentivo *(m)* **del ...**	job challenge
puesto: nombre *(m)* **del ...**	job title
puesto: perfil *(m)* **del ...**	job profile
puesto: responsabilidades *(fpl)* **del ...**	job breakdown
puesto: simplificación *(f)* **del ...**	job simplification
puesto: valoración *(f)* **del ...**	job enrichment
puestos de trabajo: análisis *(m)* **de ...**	job analysis
puestos de trabajo: clasificación *(f)* **de ...**	job classification
puestos de trabajo: evaluación *(f)* **de ...**	job evaluation
puestos de trabajo por jubilación: amortización *(f)* **de ...**	natural wastage
punta: tecnología *(f)* **...**	high-tech leading edge technology
punto *(m)* **de equilibrio**	break-even point
punto de equilibrio: alcanzar el ...	break-even (to)
punto de equilibrio: cantidad *(f)* **necesaria para alcanzar el ...**	break-even quantity

punto *(m)* de venta	POS (point of sale)
punto *(m)* de venta: transferencia electronica de fondos al ...	electronic funds transfer at point of sale (EFTPOS)
punto *(m)* límite	cut-off point
punto *(m)* medio	median
puntos: método *(m)* de calificación por ...	points-rating method

Q

queja *(f)*	grievance
quejas: tramitación *(f)* de ...	grievance procedure
quiebra *(f)*	failure (of firm)
	crash
químicos de alta peligrosidad: productos *(mpl)* ...	hazchem (hazardous chemicals)

R

racionalización *(f)*	rationalization
racionalizar	streamline (to)
racionamiento *(f)* de capital	capital rationing
RAM (memoria *(f)* RAM)	RAM (random-access memory)
ranura *(f)*	slot
rápido: arreglo *(m)* ...	quick fix
"ratio" *(m)*	ratio
ratio *(m)* de endeudamiento	debt ratio
ratio *(m)* de gestión	management ratio
ratio *(m)* deuda-activo	debt-equity ratio
ratio *(m)* financiero	financial ratio
ratio *(m)* rendimiento/capital	capital-output ratio
ratón *(m)*	mouse
razón *(f)* fundamental	rationale
re-estructuración *(f)*	restructuring
reacción consumista: de ...	consumer-responsive
reactivo *(m)*	reactive
readaptación *(f)* profesional	booster training
real: pasivo *(m)* ...	current liabilities
real: tiempo *(m)* ...	real time
reales: ingresos *(mpl)* ...	real income
realizable: activo *(m)* ...	current assets
rebaja *(f)* desleal de precios	dumping
recabar informes	debrief (to)
recentrar	recentring
reciclaje *(m)*	recycling
reciclar	recycle (to)
reciente industrialización: país *(m)* de ...	newly industrialized country (NIC)
recíproca de licencias: concesión *(f)* ...	cross-licensing
reclamo: venta *(f)* ...(con pérdida)	loss-leader
reclamos: comercialización *(f)* con líder venta *(f)* de objetos ...	leader merchandising
reclutamiento *(m)*	recruitment
reclutamiento *(m)* de directivos	executive search
reclutamiento *(m)* y gestión *(f)* de personal	staff resourcing manpower resourcing
reclutar	recruit (to)

recogida (f) de datos	data gathering
recompensa (f) de directivos	executive compensation
reconfiguración (f)	reconfiguration
reconocida: clase (f) mundialmente ...	world-class
reconocimiento (m) mutuo	mutual recognition
reconstitución (f) de la empresa	company reconstruction
recopilar	brief (to)
recuperación (f) de datos	data retrieval
	information retrieval
recuperación (f) de gastos	recovery of expenses
recuperación (f) de gastos generales	overheads recovery
recuperación de la inversión: período (m) de ...	payback period
recuperación: valor (m) de ...	break-up value
recursos (mpl) humanos	human resources
recursos humanos: desarrollo (m) de ...	human resource development (HRD)
recursos humanos: planificación (m) de ...	human resource management (HRM)
	human resource planning (HRP)
recursos: asignación (f) de ...	resource allocation
recursos: evaluación (f) de ...	resource appraisal
recursos: gestión (f) de ...	resource management
recursos: origen (m) y aplicación de ...	source and disposition of funds
red (f) de área extendida	wide area network (WAN)
red (f) de área local	local area network (LAN)
red (f) de comunicaciones	communications network
red (f) de distribución	distribution network
red (f) de información	information network
red: análisis (m) de la ...	network analysis
red: estructura (f) de ...	grid structure
rédito (m)	earnings yield
redondear	round off (to)
redondo: gráfico (m) ...	pie chart
reducción (f) de costes	cost reduction
reducción (f) de la variedad	variety reduction
reducción (f) del activo	divestment
reducción (f) del personal	staff cut-back
reducir	wind down (to)
reducir tamaño	chunk down (to)

reeducación *(f)* **profesional**	booster training
	retraining
reembolsar	to pay back
reembolso *(m)*	payback
reenfocado *(m)*	refocusing
reestructurar *(m)*	restructure (to)
referencia: nivel *(m)* **de ...**	benchmark
reforzar (la inversión)	top up (to)
registrada: marca *(f)* **...**	registered trademark
registro *(m)* **de antecedentes** *(mpl)*	track record
reglamento *(m)*	regulation
reglas *(fpl)* **del juego, las**	name of the game
regresión: análisis *(m)* **de ...**	regression analysis
regresión múltiple: análisis *(m)* **de ...**	multiple regression analysis (MRA)
regulación *(f)*	regulation
regulador: stock *(m)* **...**	buffer stock
regular	regulate (to)
reinventar la rueda	reinvent the wheel (to)
reinvertidos: beneficios *(mpl)* **...**	ploughback
relación con el coste: eficaz en ...	cost-effective
relación con el coste: eficiente *(m)* **en ...**	cost-efficient
relación *(f)* **resultados/ objetivos**	performance against objectives
relacionarse	network (to)
relaciones *(fpl)* **comerciales**	business relations
relaciones *(fpl)* **con el personal**	employee relations
relaciones *(fpl)* **externas**	external relations
relaciones *(fpl)* **funcionales**	functional relations
relaciones *(fpl)* **humanas**	human relations
relaciones *(mpl)* **industriales**	industrial relations
relaciones *(fpl)* **jerárquicas**	line relations
relaciones *(fpl)* **laborales**	labour relations
relaciones *(fpl)* **públicas**	public relations (PR)
remesas: política *(f)* **de ...**	remittance policy
remuneración *(f)*	remuneration
remuneración *(f)* **de directivos**	executive remuneration
rendimiento *(m)*	efficiency
	profit performance
	return
	yield

rendimiento capital: "ratio" *(m)* ...	capital-output ratio
rendimiento *(m)* **de las acciones**	return on equity (ROE)
rendimiento *(m)* **de las inversiones**	return on investment (ROI)
rendimiento *(m)* **de precios de acciones**	share price performance
rendimiento *(m)* **del activo**	earnings on assets
	return on assets
rendimiento *(m)* **del capital**	return on capital
rendimiento *(m)* **del capital invertido**	return on capital employed (ROCE)
	return on equity (ROE)
rendimiento *(m)* **del producto**	product performance
rendimiento *(m)* **del trabajo**	job performance
rendimiento interno: tasa *(f)* **de** ...	internal rate of return (IRR)
rendimiento *(m)* **justo**	fair return
rendimiento *(m)* **medio**	average yield
rendimiento: bajar el ...	underperform (to)
rendimiento: control *(m)* **de** ...	performance budgeting
	efficiency audit
	performance monitoring
rendimiento: estándar *(m)* **de** ...	performance standard
	standard performance
rendimiento: evaluación *(f)* **del** ...	performance appraisal
	performance evaluation
	performance review
rendimiento: medición *(f)* **del** ...	performance measurement
rendimiento: pauta *(f)* **de** ...	performance indicator
rendimiento: prima *(f)* **por** ...	premium bonus
rendimiento: tasa *(f)* **de** ...	rate of return
rendimiento: valoración *(f)* **del** ...	performance rating
rendir	perform (to)
renta *(f)* **del capital**	return on capital
renta: impuesto *(m)* **negativo sobre la** ...	negative income tax
renta: impuesto *(m)* **sobre la ... (IR)**	income tax
renta: retención *(f)* **en origen del impuesto** sobre la ...	pay-as-you-earn (PAYE)

rentabilidad (f)	earnings performance
	earnings performance
	pay-off
	profitability
rentabilidad (f) de las inversiones	return on investment (ROI)
	ROI (return on investment)
rentabilidad (f) de ventas	return on sales
rentabilidad (f) del producto	product profitability
rentabilidad: análisis (m) de ...	profitability analysis
rentabilidad: mejora (f) de la ...	profit improvement
rentabilidad: umbral de ...	break-even point
rentable: no ...	non-profit-making
rentable: producto (m) no ...	loss-maker
reorganización (f)	reorganization
repartidos: beneficios (mpl) ...	distributed profit
repartir	apportion (to)
reparto (f) del trabajo	job-sharing
repercusión (f) sobre el beneficio	profit implication
repetir la ejecución	rerun (to)
representación (f) analógica	analog(ue) representation
representación (f) conjunta	joint representation
representación (f) obrera	worker representation
representación sindical múltiple: empresa (f) de ...	open shop
representación: unidad (f) de ...	display unit
representación visual: unidad (f) de ...	visual display unit (VDU)
representante (m/f) del sindicato	trade union representative
reserva (f) para amortización	depreciation allowance
reserva (f) para imprevistos	contingency reserve
residuos (mpl) industriales	industrial waste
resistencia (f) del consumidor	consumer resistance
resolución (f) de problemas	problem solving
responsabilidad (f)	accountability
responsabilidad (f) contable	responsibility accounting
responsabilidad (f) funcional	functional responsibility
responsabilidad (f) jerárquica	line responsibility
responsabilidad (f) lineal	linear responsibility
responsabilidad: centro (m) de ...	responsibility centre
responsabilidad: zona (f) de ...	jurisdiction

responsabilidades *(fpl)* del puesto	job breakdown
responsabilidades: asignación *(f)* de ...	allocation of responsibilities
respuesta *(f)*	feedback
respuesta *(f)* anticipada	anticipatory response
respuesta *(f)* retrasada	lag response
restricción *(f)* comercial	trade restriction
restricción *(f)* crediticia	credit squeeze
restricción *(f)* del presupuesto	budget constraint
restrictivas: prácticas *(fpl)* ...	restrictive practices (industrial)
	restrictive practices (legal)
resultado *(m)*	pay-off
resultados financieros: disfrazar los ...	massage the figures (to)
resultados/objetivos: relación *(f)* ...	performance against objectives
resumir	brief (to)
retención de impuestos en origen: sistema *(m)* de ...	pay-as-you-go
retención *(f)* en origen del impuesto sobre la renta	pay-as-you-earn (PAYE)
retenidos: beneficios *(mpl)* ...	retained profits
retiro *(m)*	retirement
retrasada: respuesta *(f)* ...	lag response
retraso *(m)*	time-lag
reunión *(f)* del consejo de administración	board meeting
reunión *(f)* para dar órdenes	briefing
revalorización *(f)* del activo	re-evaluation of assets
	revaluation of assets
revalorizar	appreciate (to)
revisar	review (to)
	check (to)
revisar cuentas *(fpl)*	audit (to)
revisión *(f)* de la mano de obra	manpower audit
revisión *(f)* de programas: técnica *(f)* de evaluación y ... (PERT)	PERT (programme evaluation and review technique)
revisión *(f)* salarial	salary review
revisor *(m)*	supervisor
rico de caja	cash-rich
riesgo *(m)* ocupacional	occupational hazard

riesgo: capital *(m)* de ...	risk capital
riesgo: inversor *(m)* de ...	venture capitalist
riesgos: análisis *(m)* de ...	risk analysis
riesgos: apreciación *(f)* de ...	risk assessment
riesgos: gestión *(f)* de ...	risk management
	venture management
riesgos: minimizar los ...	minimize risks (to)
riesgos: perfil *(m)* de ...	risk profile
río *(m)* arriba	upstream
robot *(m)*	robot
robótica *(f)*	robotics
robotizar	robotize (to)
rodeando: evitar ...	bypass (to)
rodear	bypass (to)
ROM: memoria *(f)* ... (memoria de lectura)	ROM (read-only memory)
rotación *(f)* de aprendices	trainee turnover
rotación *(f)* de existencias	stock turnover
rotación *(f)* de personal	labour turnover
	staff turnover
rotación *(f)* de trabajos	job rotation
rotación *(f)* del activo	asset turnover
rueda: (estar) en la ...	rat race
rueda: reinventar la ...	reinvent the wheel (to)
rumor: comunicación *(f)* por ...	grapevine
ruta: hacer la ...	route (to)
rutina *(f)*	routine
rutina *(f)* del diagnóstico	diagnostic routine

S

sala *(f)* de consejos	boardroom
salarial: congelación *(f)* ...	wage freeze
salarial: desviación *(f)* ...	wage drift
salarial: estructura *(f)* ...	salary structure
	wage structure
salarial: nivel *(m)* ...	salary grade
	wage level
salarial: política *(f)* ...	wage policy
salarial: revisión *(f)* ...	salary review
salarial: sistema *(m)* ...	wage system
salarial: techo *(m)* ...	wage ceiling
salario *(m)* de oro	golden handcuffs
salario *(m)* mínimo	minimum wage
salario *(m)* neto	take-home pay
salarios: congelación *(f)* de ...	pay pause
salarios: curva *(f)* de incrementos de ...	salary progression curve
salarios: escalado *(m)* de ...	wage differential
salarios: igualdad *(f)* de ...	equal pay
salarios: negociaciones *(fpl)* sobre ...	pay talks
saldar	liquidate (to)
salida de datos *(f)*	output
salida *(f)* del ordenador	computer output
salida: impresión *(f)* de ...	printout
salidas: análisis *(m)* de entradas y ...	input-output analysis
salidas: tabla *(f)* de entradas y ...	input-output table
saltar por encima de	leap-frog (to)
satisfacción *(f)* del consumidor	consumer satisfaction
satisfacción *(f)* en el empleo	job satisfaction
saturación *(f)* del mercado	market saturation
saturación: grado *(m)* de ...	load factor
secciones: gestión *(f)* por ...	divisional management
secciones: organización *(f)* por ...	departmentalization
secreta: divulgación *(f)* de información ...	leak: security
	security leak
secreto *(m)* profesional	Chinese wall
sector *(m)* de crecimiento	growth area

sector *(m)* de productos	product area
secuencial: análisis *(m)* ...	sequential analysis
secundarios: efectos *(mpl)* ...	spill-over effects
	spin-off effects
segmentación *(f)*	segmentation
segmentar	segment (to)
segmento *(m)* de mercado	market segment
seguimiento: hacer el ...	follow up (to)
según balance: valor *(m)* ...	book value
seguridad *(f)* en el empleo	job security
seguridad en el empleo: acuerdo *(m)* sobre ...	job security agreement
seguridad *(f)* industrial	industrial safety
seguridad: fallo *(m)* en la ...	security leak
seguridad: gestión *(f)* de la ...	safety management
seguridad: instalación *(f)* de ...	back-up facility
seguridad: margen *(m)* de ...	margin of safety
seguridad: "stock" *(m)* de ...	safety stock
selección *(f)* de cartera	portfolio selection
selección *(f)* de medios de comunicación	media selection
seleccionar	screen (to)
seleccionar candidatos	shortlist (to)
	select candidates (to)
seleccionar directivos	head-hunt (to)
	select managers (to)
sello *(m)* de la empresa	house style
semi-variables: costes *(mpl)* ...	semi-variable costs
semiconductor *(m)*	semiconductor
semicualificada: mano *(f)* de obra ...	semi-skilled labour
sensibilidad: análisis *(m)* de ...	sensitivity analysis
sensibilidad: enseñanza *(f)* para la ...	sensitivity training
sensibilizar	sensitize (to)
sensible a los costes	cost-sensitive
sensible al mercado	market-sensitive
separación *(f)* comercial	demerger
separación *(f)* de aranceles	separation of tariffs
serie *(f)* de productos	product line
serie *(f)* piloto	pilot run
	test run
serie: fabricación *(f)* en ...	mass production

series *(fpl)* de tiempos	time series
servicio *(m)* al cliente	customer service
servicio de ventas: alcance *(m)* del ...	sales coverage
servicio *(m)* postventa	after-sales service
servicios *(mpl)* auxiliares	ancillary operations
servicios *(mpl)* de dirección	management services
servicios *(mpl)* del ordenador	computer services
servicios *(mpl)* informáticos	computer services
servicios *(mpl)* logísticos	extension services
servicios: prestación *(f)* de ...	contracting out
sexual: acoso *(m)* ...	sexual harassment
significante	significant
significativo	meaningful
simplex: método *(m)* ...	simplex method
simplificación *(f)* del puesto	job simplification
simplificación *(f)* del trabajo	work simplification
simplificar	rationalize (to)
simulación *(f)*	simulation
simulación *(f)* de gestión	business game
	management game
simulación *(f)* por ordenador	computer simulation
simular	simulate (to)
sin defectos	zero defects
sin límites *(mpl)* fijos	open-ended
sin valor *(m)* contable	write-off
sindicada: acción *(f)* no ...	unofficial action
sindicada: huelga *(f)* no ...	unofficial strike
sindical múltiple: empresa *(f)* de representación ...	open shop
sindicato *(m)*	syndicate
	trade union
sindicato: representante *(m/f)* del ...	trade union representative
sinergía *(f)*	synergy
sinergismo *(m)*	synergism
sistema *(m)*	system
sistema *(m)* (automatizado) de información (COINS)	COINS (computerized information system)
Sistema *(m)* Monetario Europeo (SME)	European Monetary System (EMS)

sistema *(m)* de incentivos	incentive scheme
sistema *(m)* de información	information system
sistema *(m)* de información para la dirección	management information system (MIS)
sistema *(m)* de movimientos predeterminados	predetermined motion time system (PMTS)
sistema *(m)* de presupuestos programados	programme budgeting
sistema *(m)* de primas	bonus scheme
sistema *(m)* de programación	programme package
sistema de programación y planificación de presupuestos	planning, programming, budgeting system (PPBS)
sistema *(m)* de retención de impuestos en origen	pay-as-you-go
sistema *(m)* electrónico de contabilidad	electronic accounting system
sistema *(m)* empresarial	business system
sistema *(m)* experto	expert system
sistema *(m)* integrado de gestión	integrated management system
sistema *(m)* mecanizado de información (COINS)	computerized information system (COINS)
sistema *(m)* salarial	wage system
sistemas: análisis *(m)* de ...	systems analysis
sistemas: comprobar ... (de ordenador)	debug (to)
sistemas: elaboración *(f)* de ...	systems design
sistemas: elaboración *(f)* de ...	systems engineering
sistemas: enfoque *(m)* según la teoría de ...	systems approach
sistemas: evaluación *(f)* de costes de ...	estimating systems costs
sistemas: gestión *(f)* por ...	systems management
sistemas: ingeniero *(m)* de ...	systems engineer
sistemas: paquete *(m)* de ...	programme package
sistemas: planificación *(f)* de ...	systems planning
sistemas: teoría *(f)* de ...	systems theory
sistemático: enfoque *(m)* ...	systems approach
sistematización *(f)* de datos	information processing
sistematizada: dirección *(f)* ...	management system systems management
sistematizada: empresa *(f)* dirigida de forma ...	system-managed company
sistematizar	systematize (to)

situación actual: informe *(m)* sobre ...	status report
situación *(f)* competitiva	competitive position
situación: balance *(m)* de ...	balance sheet
sobre capacidad *(f)*	overcapacity
sobre carga *(f)*	mark-up
sobre extendido	overextended
sobre par/por encima del valor nominal	above par
sobrecapitalizado	overcapitalized
sobrepreciar	overprice (to)
social autorizado: capital *(m)* ...	authorized capital
social: análisis *(m)* ...	social analysis
sociedad *(f)*	partnership
sociedad *(f)* anónima	business corporation
sociedad *(f)* en participación conjunta	joint-venture company
sociedad *(f)* "holding"	holding company
sociedades: impuesto *(m)* de ...	corporation tax
socio *(m)*	partner
socio-cultural	socio-cultural
socioeconómico	socio-economic
sociométrico	sociometric
software *(m)*	software
software: aplicaciones *(fpl)* de ...	software applications
software: empresa *(f)* de ...	software company
software: paquete *(m)* de ...	software package
solicitar	canvass (to)
solidaridad: huelga *(f)* de ...	sympathy strike
sólido	robust
solvencia: clasificación *(f)* de ...	credit rating
"staff": organización *(f)* ...	staff organization
"stock" *(m)* de seguridad	safety stock
"stock" *(m)* regulador	buffer stock
suave: venta *(f)* ...	soft sell
sub-optimización *(f)*	sub-optimization
subcontratación *(f)*	subcontracting
subcontratar	contract out (to) subcontract (to)
subdirector *(m)*	deputy manager
subliminal: publicidad *(f)* ...	subliminal advertising
subordinados *(mpl)*	down the line subordinates

subproducto *(m)*	by-product
subsidiaridad *(f)*	subsidiarity
sucesión de directivos: planificación *(f)* de ...	management succession planning
sucursal *(f)*	branch office
	subsidiary company
sugerencias: esquema *(m)* de ...	suggestion scheme
suma cero: juego *(m)* de ...	zero-sum game
suma *(f)* global	lump sum
sumária: despedida *(f)* ...	summary dismissal
suministración *(f)* de dos fuentes	dual sourcing
suministro *(m)*	supply
suministro: fuentes *(fpl)* externas de ...	outsourcing
supervisar	supervise (to)
supervisión *(f)*	supervision
supervisor *(m)*	supervisor
supervisor: consejo *(m)* ...	supervisory board
supervisora: gestión *(f)* ...	supervisory management
supervivencia: estrategia *(f)* de ...	survival strategy
suplente: director *(m)* ...	outside director
supletorias: ventajas *(fpl)* ...	fringe benefits
suscripción: derecho *(m)* preferente de ...	rights issue
sustitución *(f)*	trade-off
sustitución: coste *(m)* de ...	replacement costs

T

tabla *(f)* de entradas y salidas	input-output table
tablón *(m)* de anuncios	bulletin board
táctica: planificación *(f)* ...	tactical planning
tácticas *(fpl)* competitivas	competitive tactics
táctico: plan *(m)* ...	tactical plan
taller *(m)*	shop-floor
talleres: mantenimiento *(m)* total de los ...	total plant maintenance
tamaño *(m)* del lote económico	economic batch quantity
tamaño *(f)* del lote económico de fabricación	economic manufacturing quantity
tamaño: reducir ...	chunk down (to)
tamizar	screen (to)
tanto *(m)* alzado	lump sum
tareas: ampliación *(f)* de las ...	job enlargement
tareas: asignación *(f)* de ...	job assignment
tareas: clasificación *(f)* de ...	job evaluation
tareas: descomposición *(f)* de las ...	breakdown of operations
tarjeta *(f)* inteligente	smart card
tarjeta *(f)* multi-funcional	smart card
tasa *(f)* base	base rate
tasa *(f)* cero: exento de impuestos de ...	zero-rating
tasa *(f)* de beneficio sobre ventas	profit-volume ratio (P/V)
tasa *(f)* de cambio	exchange rate
tasa *(f)* de cambio en fecha futura	forward exchange rate
tasa *(f)* de capitalización de beneficios (TCB)	price-earnings ratio (P/E)
tasa *(f)* de rendimiento	rate of return
tasa *(f)* de rendimiento interno	internal rate of return (IRR)
tasa *(f)* en vigor	going rate
tasación: centro *(m)* de ...	assessment centre
tasar	appraise (to)
	assess (to)
tasas de cambio: mecanismo *(m)* de ...	Exchange Rate Mechanism (ERM)
techo *(m)* salarial	wage ceiling

técnica (f) de evaluación y revisión de programas (PERT)	programme evaluation and review technique (PERT)
técnica (f) de mercancías	merchandising
técnica (f) de producción	production technique
técnicas (fpl) de gestión	management technique
técnicas (fpl) de producción	production engineering
técnico y de proyectos: departamento (m) ...	engineering and design department
técnico: director (m) ...	technical manager
tecnología (f) baja	low-tech
tecnología (f) de la información	information technology
tecnología (f) punta	high-tech
	leading edge
tecnológica: previsión (f) ...	technological forecasting
tecnología: transferencia (f) de ...	technology transfer
tecnológico: logro (m) ...	breakthrough
teleconferencia (f)	teleconference
telefónico: contestador ...	answerphone
teléfono (m) de coche	car phone
teléfono (m) portátil	cellphone
	mobile phone
teléfono: ventas (fpl) por ...	telesales
telemárketing (m)	telemarketing
telemática (f)	telematics
teletexto (m)	teletext
televentas (fpl)	telesales
tema (m) publicitario	advertising message
	advertising theme
temas (mpl) del medio ambiente	green issues
tendencia (f)	trend
tendencia (f) del mercado	market forces
	market trend
tendencia (f) económica	economic trend
tendencias (fpl) exponenciales	exponential trend
tenencia (f) de acciones	shareholding
tener espíritu emprendedor	go-getter: be a go-getter (to)
tener iniciativa	go-getting
teoría (f) de colas	queuing theory
teoría (f) de comunicación	communications theory
teoría (f) de decisiones	decision theory
teoría (f) de juegos	game theory
teoría (f) de la administración	administrative theory

teoría *(f)* de la filtración	trickle-down theory
teoría *(f)* de la información	information theory
teoría *(f)* de la probabilidad	probability theory
teoría *(f)* de las contingencias	contingency theory
teoría *(f)* de líneas de espera	queuing theory
teoría *(f)* de política directiva	management theory
teoría *(f)* de sistemas	systems theory
teoría de sistemas: enfoque *(m)* según la ...	systems approach
teoría *(f)* organizativa	organization theory
tercera parte *(f)*	third party
terminal *(f)*	terminal
terminal *(f)* del ordenador	computer terminal
terminar	wind up (to)
término *(m)* medio	average
términos *(mpl)* (de un contrato)	conditions (of a contract)
terreno: empleados *(mpl)* del ...	front-line employees
territorio *(m)* de ventas	sales territory
territorio: protección *(f)* del ...	turf protection
test	product testing
texto independiente: procesador *(m)* de ...	stand-alone word processor
textos: diccionario *(m)* en procesador de ...	spellcheck
textos: procesador *(m)* de ...	word processor (WP) WP (word processor)
textos: procesamiento *(m)* de ...	word processing
tiempo *(m)* de ejecución	lead time
tiempo *(m)* de entrega	delivery time
tiempo *(m)* estándar	standard time
tiempo *(m)* inactivo	down time
tiempo *(m)* máximo discrecional	time span of discretion
tiempo parcial: empleado *(m)* a ...	part-timer
tiempo *(m)* productivo	uptime
tiempo *(m)* real	real time
tiempo total: empleado *(m)* a ...	full-timer
tiempo: compartición *(f)* de ...	time-sharing
tiempo: gestión *(f)* del ...	time management
tiempo: justo a ...	just in time (JIT)
tiempo: plazo *(m)* de ...	time frame
tiempos: estudio *(m)* de ...	time study

tiempos: estudio *(m)* de métodos y ...	time and methods study
tiempos: series *(fpl)* de ...	time series
tiempos y movimientos: estudio *(m)* de ...	time and motion study
tipo *(m)* bancario	bank rate
tipo *(m)* base	base rate
tipo *(m)* de mercado	market rating
tirar los precios	underprice (to)
titularización *(f)*	securitization
titularizar	securitize (to)
tocar fondo	bottom out (to)
toma *(f)* de posesión	takeover
tomar decisiones: proceso *(m)* de ...	decision-making
total: producción *(f)* ...	throughput
total de calidad: gestión *(f)* ...	total quality management (TQM)
total de los talleres: mantenimiento *(m)* ...	total plant maintenance
totales: ventas *(fpl)* ...	sales turnover
traba *(f)* fiscal	fiscal drag
trabajador *(m)* en equipo: buen ...	team player
trabajadores: compra *(f)* por los ...	worker buyout
trabajar por cuenta propia	freelance (to go)
trabajo *(m)* a desatajo	piecework
trabajo administrativo: medición *(f)* de ...	clerical work measurement (CWM)
trabajo al hombre: adaptación *(f)* del ...	human engineering ergonomics
trabajo atrasado: pila *(f)* de ...	backlog
trabajo *(m)* bajo	franchising
trabajo *(m)* en progreso	work in progress
trabajo *(m)* externo	outplacement
trabajo flexible: horario *(m)* de ...	flexible working hours
trabajo lento: huelga *(f)* de ...	go-slow work-to-rule
trabajo *(m)* por contrato	work by contract
trabajo *(m)* por horas	part-time employment

trabajo por jubilación: amortización *(f)* de puestos de ...	natural wastage
trabajo *(m)* por turnos	shiftwork
trabajo: análisis *(m)* de puestos de ...	job analysis
trabajo: aptitud *(f)* en el ...	job competence
trabajo: cantidad *(f)* de ...	workload
trabajo: ciclo *(m)* de ...	work cycle
trabajo: clasificación *(f)* de puestos de ...	job classification
trabajo: contenido *(m)* del ...	work content
trabajo: descripción *(f)* del ...	job description
trabajo: despido *(m)* del ...	lay-off
trabajo: ejecución *(f)* del ...	job performance
trabajo: especificación *(f)* de un puesto de ...	job specification
trabajo: estructuración *(f)* del ...	work structuring
trabajo: estudio *(m)* del ...	work study
trabajo: formación *(f)* fuera del ...	off-the-job training
trabajo: horario *(m)* de ...	working hours
trabajo: interés *(m)* en el ...	job interest
trabajo: lugar *(m)* de ...	workplace
trabajo: medición *(f)* del ...	work measurement
trabajo: medidas *(fpl)* del ...	ergonometrics
trabajo: mejora *(f)* del ...	job improvement
trabajo: método *(m)* de ...	procedure
trabajo: objetivo *(m)* del ...	job design
trabajo: organización *(f)* científica del ...	management science scientific management
trabajo: plan *(m)* de ...	work schedule
trabajo: puesto *(m)* de ...	work station
trabajo: rendimiento *(m)* del ...	job performance
trabajo: reparto *(f)* del ...	job-sharing
trabajo: simplificación *(f)* del ...	work simplification
trabajos: rotación *(f)* de ...	job rotation
tramitación *(f)* de quejas	grievance procedure
transacción: llegar a una ...	trade off (to)
transaccional	transactional
transaccional: análisis *(m)* ...	transactional analysis (TA)
transferencia *(f)* de tecnología	technology transfer
transferencia *(f)* electrónica de fondos al punto de venta	electronic funds transfer at point of sale (EFTPOS)

transferencia: fijación (f) de precios de ...	transfer pricing
transformación (f) de la organización	organizational change
transitorio	transitional
transporte (m)	transportation
traslados (mpl) del personal	staff transfer
tratada: cantidad (f) ...	throughput
trato (m) con información privilegiada	insider dealing
trucada: contabilidad (f) ...	window-dressing
trueque: comercio (m) de ...	barter trade
turno (m) de día	day shift
turno (m) de noche	night shift
turnos: trabajo (m) por ...	shiftwork

U

última fecha *(f)*	latest date
umbral de rentabilidad	break-even point
única: aprovisionamiento *(m)* de fuente ...	single sourcing
única: moneda *(f)* ...	single currency
único: argumento *(m)* ... de venta	unique selling point/proposition (USP)
único: mercado *(m)* ...	single market
único: mercado (m) ... *(de la CE)*	Single Market of the EC
Unidad *(f)* Monetaria Europea (ECU)	European Currency Unit (ecu)
unidad *(f)* central	mainframe
unidad *(f)* de discos	disk drive
unidad *(f)* de proceso central (UPC)	central processing unit (CPU)
unidad *(f)* de representación	display unit
unidad *(f)* de representación visual	visual display unit (VDU)
unión *(f)*	amalgamation
Unión *(f)* Monetaria Europea (UME)	European Monetary Union (EMU)
unitario de mano de obra: coste *(m)* ...	unit labour costs
urbanizador *(m)*	developer
usos *(m)* y costumbres *(f)*	custom and practice
usuarios: actitud de los ...	user attitude
utilidad pública: empresa *(f)* de ...	public utility
utilización *(f)* de "pallets"	palletization
utilización *(f)* de contenedores	containerization
utilización *(f)* de datos	information handling
utilización *(f)* de la capacidad	capacity utilization
utilizada: capacidad *(f)* no ...	idle capacity
utilizar: difícil de ...	user-unfriendly
utilizar: fácil de ...	user-friendly

V

vacaciones *(fpl)* escalonadas	staggered holidays
valor actual: método *(m)* del ...	present value method
valor agregado: impuesto *(m)* sobre el ...	value added tax (VAT)
valor *(m)* contable	asset value
valor *(m)* de mercado	market value
valor *(m)* de prestigio de una empresa	goodwill
valor *(m)* de primera clase	blue-chip stock
valor *(m)* del Estado	gilt
valor *(m)* del activo	asset value
valor *(m)* en libros	book value
valor *(m)* en liquidación	break-up value
valor *(m)* extrínseco	goodwill
valor *(m)* neto	net worth
valor *(m)* neto actualizado	net present value (NPV)
valor *(m)* según balance	book value
valor: cadena *(f)* de ...	value chain
valor: concepto *(m)* del ...	value concept
valoración *(f)* de existencias	stock valuation
valoración *(f)* de gestión	management audit
valoración *(f)* de la calidad	quality assessment
valoración *(f)* del puesto	job enrichment
valoración *(f)* del rendimiento	performance rating
valoración *(f)* diferencial	differential pricing
valoración *(f)* financiera	financial appraisal
valorar	appraise (to)
	assess (to)
	evaluate (to)
valores *(m)*	securities
valores disponibles: proporción *(f)* de ...	cash ratio
valores *(mpl)* garantizados por el Estado	gilt-edged security
	gilt-edged stock
valores *(mpl)* no admitidos a cotización	unlisted security
valores: análisis *(m)* de ...	value engineering

valores: cartera *(f)* **de ...**	stock portfolio
vanguardia: de ...	state of the art
variables: costes *(mpl)* **...**	variable costs
variables: gastos *(mpl)* **...**	variable expenses
variables: propuesta *(f)* **de valorización ...**	value proposal
varianza *(f)*	gap
	variance
varianza *(f)* **de costes**	cost variance
varianza *(f)* **presupuestaria**	budgetary variance
varianza: análisis *(m)* **de ...**	variance analysis
varianzas: análisis *(m)* **de las ...**	gap study
variedad: reducción *(f)* **de la ...**	variety reduction
vendedores: equipo *(m)* **de ...**	sales force
vender más barato	undercut (to)
vender parte del negocio	hive off (to)
venta *(f)* **difícil**	hard sell
venta *(f)* **directa**	direct selling
venta *(f)* **dura**	hard sell
venta *(f)* **suave**	soft sell
venta fácil: bienes *(mpl)* **de consumo de ...**	fast-moving consumer goods (FMCG)
	FMG (fast-moving consumer goods)
venta *(f)* **por impulso**	impulse sale
venta por impulso: productos *(mpl)* **de ...**	goods: impulse
venta *(f)* **reclamo (con pérdida)**	loss-leader
venta: argumentos *(mpl)* **de ...**	sales talk
venta: combinación *(f)* **de medios de ...**	sales mix
venta: expectativas *(fpl)* **de ...**	sales expectations
venta: fecha *(f)* **límite de ...**	sell-by date
venta: lugar *(m)* **de ...**	point of sale (POS)
venta: mantenimiento *(m)* **del precio de ...**	resale price maintenance (RPM)
venta: material *(m)* **de publicidad en el lugar de ...**	point-of-sale material
venta: precio *(m)* **en el lugar de ...**	spot price
venta: publicidad *(f)* **en el lugar de ... (PLV)**	point-of-sale advertising (POS)

venta: punto *(m)* de ...	point of sale (POS)
ventaja *(f)* competitiva	competitive advantage
ventaja *(f)* sobre la competencia	competitive edge
ventajas *(fpl)* iguales	level playing-field
ventajas *(fpl)* supletorias	fringe benefits
ventana *(f)*	window
ventas *(fpl)* al contado	countertrade
	cash sales
ventas *(fpl)* por teléfono	telesales
ventas *(fpl)* totales	sales turnover
ventas: alcance *(m)* del servicio de ...	sales coverage
ventas: análisis *(m)* de ...	sales analysis
ventas: bajón *(m)* de ...	sales slump
ventas: cifra *(f)* de ...	sales turnover
ventas: cupo *(m)* de ...	sales quota
ventas: departamento *(m)* de ...	sales department
ventas: dirección *(f)* de ...	sales management
ventas: empuje *(m)* de ...	sales drive
ventas: esfuerzo *(m)* para el desarrollo de ...	sales expansion effort
ventas: ingeniero *(m)* de ...	sales engineer
ventas: jefe *(m)* de ...	sales manager
ventas: objetivo *(m)* de ...	sales goal
	sales target
ventas: planificación *(f)* de ...	sales planning
ventas: política *(f)* de ...	sales policy
	selling policy
ventas: potencial *(m)* de ...	sales potential
ventas: presupuesto *(m)* de ...	sales budget
ventas: previsión *(f)* de ...	sales estimate
	sales forecast
ventas: promoción *(f)* de ...	sales promotion
ventas: prueba *(f)* de ...	sales test
ventas: rentabilidad *(f)* de ...	return on sales
ventas: tasa *(f)* de beneficio sobre ...	P/V (profit-volume ratio)
	profit-volume ratio (P/V)
ventas: territorio *(m)* de ...	sales territory
ventas: volumen *(m)* de ...	sales volume
ventas: zona *(f)* de ...	sales area
verbal: comunicación *(f)* ...	verbal communication
verbal: comunicación *(f)* no ...	non-verbal communication
verificación *(f)*	control

verificación *(f)* **del balance**	balance sheet auditing
verificación *(f)* **estadística**	statistical control
verificador *(m)* **de cuentas**	comptroller
verificar	verify (to)
verificar cuentas *(fpl)*	audit (to)
vertiginoso: ascenso *(m)* ...	fast-track
viabilidad *(f)*	viability
viabilidad: estudio *(m)* **de ...**	feasibility study
viable	viable
vicepresidente *(m)*	deputy chairman
	vice-chairman
	vice-president
vida: ciclo *(m)* **de ... (de un producto)**	life cycle (of a product)
vida de un producto: ciclo *(m)* **de ...**	product life
	product life cycle
vida de un producto: previsión *(f)* **de ...**	product life expectancy
vida *(f)* **económica**	economic life
vida: coste *(m)* **de la ...**	cost of living
vida: duración *(f)* **de ...**	shelf-life
vida: estilo *(m)* **de ...**	lifestyle
vida: nivel *(m)* **de ...**	standard of living
video *(m)*	video
vigor: tasa *(f)* **en ...**	going rate
viraje *(m)* **abajo**	downswing
virus *(m)* **informático**	computer virus
visión *(f)*	vision
visión: declaración *(f)* **de ...**	vision statement
visual: unidad *(f)* **de representación ...**	visual display unit (VDU)
vocal *(m)*	non-executive director
volumen *(m)*	volume
volumen *(m)* **de ventas**	sales volume
volumen y beneficio: análisis *(m)* **de coste ...**	cost-volume-profit analysis
voluntaria: paga *(f)* ...	ex gratia payment

W

winchester: disco *(m)* ...   Winchester disk

Z

Z: gráfico *(m)* ...   Z chart
zona *(f)* **comercial**   trading area
zona *(f)* **de competencia**   jurisdiction
zona *(f)* **de responsabilidad**   jurisdiction
zona *(f)* **de ventas**   sales area
zona *(f)* **problemática**   problem area